ENGENDERING ORIGINS

SUNY SERIES, FEMINIST PHILOSOPHY
JEFFNER ALLEN, EDITOR

ENGENDERING ORIGINS

CRITICAL FEMINIST READINGS IN PLATO AND ARISTOTLE

EDITED BY

Bat-Ami Bar On

STATE UNIVERSITY OF NEW YORK PRESS

Published by
State University of New York Press, Albany

For information, address State University of New York
Press, State University Plaza, Albany, N.Y., 12246

Production by Diane Ganeles
Marketing by Fran Keneston

Library of Congress Cataloging-in-Publication Data

Engendering origins : critical feminist readings in Plato and
    Aristotle / edited by Bat-Ami Bar On.
        p.   cm. — (SUNY series, feminist philosophy)
    Includes bibliographical references and index.
    ISBN 0-7914-1643-7 (alk. paper). — ISBN 0-7914-1644-5 (pbk. :
alk. paper)
    1. Plato. 2. Aristotle. 3. Feminist theory. I. Bar On, Bat
—Ami, 1948–   II. Series.
B395.E64   1994
184′.082—dc20   92-36046
                                                                  CIP

10   9   8   7   6   5   4   3   2   1

*This book is dedicated to my students
and to my teachers.*

Contents

Preface

The idea for an anthology of feminist critical readings in Plato and Aristotle was inspired by my teaching and by my students, especially by Cathy Martin. Following some work Cathy did with me in a course about the history of ancient Greek philosophy at the end of the 1988 spring semester, she told me how upset she was about the history of philosophy curriculum since it was not relevant enough to her life as a woman, let alone a black woman. Cathy did not object to studying the canonical philosophers, but what she wanted most was to (1) examine their views about women; and (2) look at other views and analyze them in relation to views about women.

While Cathy inspired the idea for the anthology, Jeffner Allen coached the development of this idea into a proposal to the press, and an incredible network of women philosophers encouraged me to implement the idea and helped me do so by suggesting possible contributors to the anthology or by contributing to the anthology themselves. The contributors—Eve Browning Cole, Cynthia A. Freeland, Judith Genova, Cynthia Hampton, Susan Hawthorne, Deborah K. W. Modrak, Christine Pierce, Christine M. Senack, Elizabeth V. Spelman, and Nancy Tuana—are the ones who actualized the idea, and I would like to thank each one for their work, for indulging my editorial requests, even the quirky ones, and doing so with a sense of humor, and for the generosity of their spirits.

Introduction

Bat-Ami Bar On

Whether we like it or not, we are within philosophy, surrounded by masculine-feminine divisions that philosophy has helped to articulate and refine. The problem is whether we want to remain there and be dominated by them, or whether we can take up a critical position in relation to them, a position which will necessarily involve the deciphering of the basic philosophical assumptions latent in discussions about women.

Michéle Le Doeuff[1]

I

This anthology introduces several feminist voices into the study of Platonic and Aristotelian texts that modern Western philosophy has treated as foundational to the discipline of philosophy. What they are primarily concerned with is the extent to which Platonic and Aristotelian texts are (un)redeemably sexist, masculinist, or phallocentric.

The feminist voices in this anthology contribute to a Western feminist project that is constituted by a multiplicity of feminist critiques of various aspects and elements of Western culture. The project aims at exposing the hegemonic, though flexible and changing, system of interrelated gender differences and their valuations. It includes critiques of literature, art, and even music, of medical and scientific texts, as well as of approaches to criticism. The feminist critiques do not have a theoretical unity. Such unity as they do have is a function of a shared yet vague and contested methodological assumption according to which a critical understanding of a culture in which gender is significant requires letting gender play a role in the way one approaches the examination of the culture in question. This vague and contested methodological assumption is shared by the essays in this anthology.

The assumption about the analytical importance of gender does not lead to a uniformed reading of the Platonic and Aristotelian texts. The chapters in this book come into conflict with each other, leaving behind a tension-filled interpretation of Plato's and Aristotle's views. Thus, for example, Judith Genova's "Feminist Dialectics: Plato and Dualism" and Cynthia Hampton's "Overcoming Dualism: The Importance of the Intermediate in Plato's *Philebus*" suggest together that Plato's metaphysics and epistemology are dualistic and hierarchical and inferiorize the feminine and that, nonetheless, Plato valorized certain feminine qualities and used them to develop ways to overcome dualism and hierarchy. And in Aristotle's case, Cynthia A. Freeland's "Nourishing Speculation: A Feminist Reading of Aristotelian Science" suggests both that Aristotle's biological texts seem to provide an example of a science that could measure up to feminist criticisms and that, nonetheless, they are engendering texts that inferiorize woman and the feminine.

The chapters also bring the views of Plato and Aristotle into conflict with each other, suggesting that ancient Greek philosophy is not a seamless cloth. So, for example, according to Christine Pierce's "Eros and Epistemology", Plato does not epistemically privilege man but only the men who choose homoerotic love. Plato's arguments could be used to show that women who choose lesbian love should also be construed as epistemically privileged. On the other hand, in "Aristotle: Women, Deliberation, and Nature" and in "Aristotle on the Woman's Soul" Deborah K. W. Modrak and Christine M. Senack respectively, argue that Aristotle believed that all women, without any exceptions, were morally defective, and this defect was a function of a weakness of women's deliberative faculty.

The essays' portrayal of Plato's and Aristotle's philosophies as ambiguous and rich with contradictions could, but should not, be taken to imply that there is no hegemonic tendency of engendering in ancient Greek philosophy. As Susan Bordo, following Foucault,[2] claims in response to Jean Grimshaw's *Philosophy and Feminist Thinking*,[3] where Grimshaw argues that canonical inconsistencies indicate that there is no hegemonic view:

> [I]ntellectual dominance does not take the form of univocal, majesterial decree, but exercises itself through perpetual "local battle" organized around "innumerable points of confrontation [and] focuses of instability." Dominance emerges *through,* not in the absence of contestation.[4]

The importance of Bordo's answer to Grimshaw in the case of Platonic and Aristotelian texts is a function of their location in the Western philosophical canon, a location that assigns to them a power that shaped the rest of the canon. If the feminist suggestion that despite contradictions, there is a hegemonic tendency is true, then Platonic and Aristotelian texts form the origin of a philosophical canon that is thoroughly infused with gender. On the other hand, if Grimshaw is right, then even Platonic and Aristotelian thinking cannot be described as engendered.

One of the things that is tempting about Grimshaw's suggestion is that it seems to make it a little easier to consider the redeemability of those points in the Platonic and Aristotelian texts that seem to not devalue women or femininity and point out ways to overcome the dualisms that feminists have argued are part of phallocentric reasoning. Under her view, contradictions suggest discontinuities and therefore the separability of elements of the text. And what her view implies is that according to feminists a sexist text is so in a saturated way.

There are feminists that believe this.[5] But, as the title of the anthology indicates, I suspect Platonic and Aristotelian texts as primary contributors to the origins of the engendered philosophical tradition that builds on their works, and would like to present the anthology as a whole as suggesting that a position can be hegemonic and yet not determine every possible aspect and element of a text. I believe, therefore, that texts, specifically the Platonic and Aristotelian texts that are the subject of this anthology, are programmatically raidable for what one needs conceptually for a current project such as the feminist project. I would not, however, encourage raiding without a careful critique and a healthy dose of ambivalence toward the Western tradition in general and Plato and Aristotle in particular.

II

I first situated the voices in this anthology in relation to a Western feminist project of cultural criticism. But the voices in this anthology also contribute very specifically to Western feminist philosophical projects and are influenced by recent feminist philosophical work in ethics, social and political philosophy, epistemology, philosophy of mind, and philosophy of science.[6] This work raises questions about the philosophical construction of reality through a value-laden binary oppositional prism. It questions the adequacy of moral theories that construe normative evaluations as a kind of a straightforward correct application of principles. It also questions the idea of moral autonomy and agency, as well as scientific autonomy and agency, insofar as they are understood exclusively in terms of a general and unsituated reason.

This work does not only question but also argues for alternatives. Thus, it argues for alternatives to the normative dualism of canonical Western philosophy, seeking them not in unifying methodologies that obliterate difference but in methodologies that emphasize plurality and heterogeneity. It argues for alternative approaches to normative evaluations, emphasizing the importance of human relations and relatedness, therefore, of care for and responsibility toward particular groups and individuals in normative evaluations. It also argues for alternative conceptions of autonomy and agency, emphasizing their historicity, sensibility, and embodiment.

Because they are motivated by the issues of feminist philosophy, the essays in this anthology raise certain kinds of questions and search the texts that they are about for certain kinds of traces. Thus, for example, in "Hairy Cobblers and Philosopher-Queens" and "Who is Who in the Polis?" Elizabeth V. Spelman criticizes Plato and Aristotle respectively, arguing that while they admitted the possibility of excellence for women, they were suspicious of the body, especially the female body, seeing it as a source of possible epistemic and social disorder and rupture. Susan Hawthorne finds a different kind of feminine body in Plato's *Symposium*. In "Diotima Speaks through the Body," she attends to the significance of the various aspects of the feminine body as the central metaphor of Diotima's teachings, believing that the metaphor is used in an attempt to articulate an epistemology that overcomes the subject-object epistemological dualism by not objectifying and alienating what knowledge is about from the knower.

Some of the issues that motivate the essays or aspects of the essays in this anthology show more clearly than others the double sources of the foci of feminist philosophy, i.e., feminism as a movement and canonical Western philosophy. This is particularly clear in the two Spelman chapters which, in addition to exposing Plato's and Aristotle's fear of and inferiorization of the feminine body, concern themselves with the class structure of the ideal societies of Plato's *Republic* and Aristotle's *Politics* and with the division of gender that results from the interaction of class and gender.

The influence of feminist philosophy on the essays in this anthology goes beyond focusing them on certain issues. Some of the essays, for example, Hampton's, Hawthorne's and Freeland's, attempt to trace the feminine in the texts they read, and this kind of tracing is a response to the influence of feminist philosophy and its response to post-structuralism. Not too long ago, at least in the U.S., were one to pursue a feminist criticism of a canonical Western philosopher, one would emphasize the tracing of the masculine, which one would do by pointing out the sexism embedded in the text and its phallocentrism. Feminists influenced by post-structuralism have criticized this approach as tending to presuppose the total unifying power of hegemony and have argued that texts can have something about them that resists the hegemonic pressures. Insofar as these pressures are toward masculinization, what one can expect to find, were one to search for traces of resistance, are feminine traces.

Another way in which feminist philosophy influences the essays methodologically, due to the influences of post-structuralism, is by urging a modified cultural genealogy or something that resembles what Rorty calls intellectual history because it "consists of descriptions of what intellectuals were up to at a given time, and of their interactions with the rest of society".[7] One example of this is Eve Browning Cole's "Women, Slaves, and 'Love of Toil' in Aristotle's Moral Philosophy" which situates Aristotle's assignment of women to the margins of the moral community in relations with other Greek intellectual discussions of gender and in relation to the sociopolitical institutions of the time. Another example is Nancy Tuana's "Aristotle and the Politics of Reproduction", which argues that Aristotle's ascription of lack to women is a descendent of a gradual cultural process in Greece, while his ascription of generative capacities to men arises out of the metaphysical framework of his time.

III

Though influenced by post-structuralist feminism, the essays in this anthology are silent about the way they have problematized gender for feminism.[8] While, even if in different ways, they take gender seriously and make it matter interpretively, taken very literally, they only imply that what Plato and Aristotle have to say about gender and how they use it is culturally and theoretically important. In a way, this is also all that the anthology as a whole implies.

But, the essays, and maybe more so the anthology, are caught in a problematic situation. Their stance is that of the feminist critic of culture, and the danger that the feminist critic of culture faces is that of perpetuating just what she or he criticizes. The feminist critic of culture is motivated ethically and politically to take gender seriously and makes it matter interpretively. The criticism is part of a struggle whose end, however, is, ironically, the elimination of gender as a significant category.

One could argue that the feminist critic of culture deploys gender strategically and one can show that this deployment has been very fruitful.[9] Still, as Joan Cocks points out, the feminist critic of culture's situation is rather odd. She says:

> How odd to remain faithful to the terms of Masculine/Feminine just at this point! How odd to obey a rule when one is looking to show the rule's political tyranny rather than categorical truth— and more, when one is looking to show that tyranny's less than total triumph over life.[10]

The odd problematic bind of this anthology is that it may perpetuate not only gender as a significant category but also the existing canon of Western philosophy and its Eurocentric underpinnings. By engaging in a critique of canonical Western philosophers that is motivated by current concerns, the essays make what these philosophers had to say come to life and matter. Since they are collected into an anthology that is focused on the canon and is not struggling with its revisions and expansions, while offering a very different reading of the canon, and thus violating the interpretive rules that bind it, they also preserve the canon. Yet, since it contains essays about ethics and politics, as well as aesthetics, epistemology, and the philosophy of science, the anthology does not perpetuate the story of canonical Western philosophy as the story of battles among and developments of positions about the certainty of knowledge, its origin, and its objectivity.

Still, due to its positioning of essays and the kinds of essays it includes, what the anthology seems to do is to preserve the mostly eighteenth-century European pretense that philosophy is a natural kind, a distinct form of thought, as well as the eighteenth-century's construal of the European seventeenth century as the century in which philosophy became modern.[11] In addition, because the anthology situates Plato and Aristotle in the canonically acceptable way vis-à-vis European philosophers proper, it perpetuates the Eu-

rocentric view of philosophy.[12] It may also p
tric view of philosophy by being part of the W
   The bind of this anthology is a function
complex reality that is configured by a mult
and resistance to dominance. In such a reali
and how they are executed just cannot dic
they wholly powerless. And in light of this, the critical feminist
readings of Plato and Aristotle that are in this anthology are important because they do several things and do them well: They challenge the general philosophical claim to abstract neutrality that
Plato and Aristotle attempted to protect among other ways by ex-
cluding women, showing that Platonic and Aristotelian texts are indeed gendered and in multiple ways. At the same time, they
identify elements of Platonic and Aristotelian views that might be
useful for the current feminist project. And, they show that reading
ancient Greek philosophy through the multiple lenses of current
feminist philosophical concerns is interpretively productive.

Notes

1. Le Doeuff, Michéle. "Women and Philosophy" in Moil, Toril (ed.), *French Feminist Thought: A Reader*. Oxford: Basil Blackwell, 1987, p. 182.

2. Foucault, Michel. *Discipline and Punish*. (French, 1975). NY: Vintage, 1977.

3. Grimshaw, Jean. *Philosophy and Feminist Thinking*. Minneapolis: University of Minnesota, 1986.

4. Bordo, Susan. "Feminist Skepticism and the 'Maleness' of Philosophy". Paper read at the 1988 American Philosophical Meeting in Washington, D.C., p. 8. A shorter version of this paper is published in *The Journal of Philosophy*.

5. See discussion in Braidotii, Rosi. *Patterns of Dissonance: A Study of Women in Contemporary Philosophy*. NY: Routledge, 1991.

6. Some recent anthologies provide excellent examples of current feminist philosophical work. See: Benhabib, Seyla and Cornell, Drucilla (eds.). *Feminism as Critique: On the Politics of Gender*. Minneapolis: University of Minnesota, 1987; Code, Lorraine, Mullett, Sheila, and Overall, Christine (eds.). *Feminist Perspectives: Philosophical Essays on Method and Morals*. University of Toronto, 1988; Griffiths, Morwenna and Whitford, Margaret (eds.). *Feminist Perspectives in Philosophy*. Bloomington: Indiana University Press, 1988; Kittay, Eva Fedder and Meyers, Diana T. (eds.). *Women

oral Theory. Totowa, NJ: Rowman and Littlefield, 1987. An anthology brings together a number of essays from different philosophical fields Garry, Ann and Pearsall, Marilyn (eds.). *Women, Knowledge and Reality: Explorations in Feminist Philosophy.* Boston: Unwin Hyman, 1989. Other sources for such examples are *Hypatia* and the newsletter of *Feminism and Philosophy.*

7. Rorty, Richard. "The Historiography of Philosophy: Four Genres" in Rorty, Richard, Schneewind, J. B. and Skinner, Quentin (eds.). *Philosophy in History.* Boston: Cambridge University, 1984, p. 69.

8. See, for example: Butler, Judith. *Gender Trouble: Feminism and the Subversion of Identity.* NY: Routledge, 1990; Fuss, Diana. *Essentially Speaking: Feminism, Nature and Difference.* NY: Routledge, 1989; Riley, Denise. *"Am I That Name?": Feminism and the Category of "Women" in History.* Minneapolis: University of Minnesota, 1988.

9. See, for example, Scott, Joan Wallace. Gender and the Politics of History. NY: Columbia University. 1988, especially the first part "Toward A Feminist History."

10. Cocks, Joan. *The Oppositional Imagination: Feminism, Critique and Political Theory.* London: Routledge, 1989, p. 195.

11. I am relying in my formulations on Jonathan Ree's "Philosophy and the History of Philosophy" in Ree, Jonathan, Ayers, Michael and Westoby, Adam. *Philosophy and Its Past.* Atlantic Highland, NJ: Humanities, 1978, pp. 3–39.

12. This point is made by Amin Samir in *Eurocentrism.* NY: Monthly Review, 1989. See, in particular the first chapter, "The Formation of Tributary Ideology in the Mediterranean Region", pp. 13–59.

PART ONE

PLATO

Hairy Cobblers and Philosopher-Queens

Elizabeth V. Spelman

and what pure happiness to know all our high-toned questions breed in a lively animal.

Adrienne Rich

In book 5 of Plato's *Republic,* Socrates proposes that women are potentially just as good guardians or philosopher-rulers of the state as men. The notion of the equality of men and women must have been startling to Plato's contemporaries, since it went so much against the grain of Athenian society and its history.[1] But it should also be startling to modern readers of Plato who know how deeply undemocratic and antiegalitarian his views in general are.

In this chapter, I will describe what made it possible for Plato to imagine women in roles quite other than those defined by their society, and I also hope to make clear how he must have perceived their equality to men in light of his otherwise inegalitarian politics. Plato's notion of the equality of the sexes is carefully sculpted so as not to be inconsistent with his thinking of one class of people as the superiors of other classes.[2] If we can understand why it is not inconsistent, then perhaps we can gain some insight into troubling features of contemporary feminist thought: that is, perhaps we can see how one can argue against sexism in a way that leaves other forms of oppression intact; how one can argue for views that support, or at least leave unexamined, the domination of some women over others. We will see the sad irony in the description of Plato as the first feminist philosopher.[3]

I

Let us turn to the *Republic* for Plato's views about women. This central dialogue of the Platonic corpus is an examination of the nature of justice, and it becomes perforce a prescription for the best society: we can come to understand what justice in the individual is, Socrates urges, if we look at justice "writ large" in the state. What is justice in a state or society? Plato assumes the following as general principles of construction of that society in which we can find justice: (1) different kinds of people have different natures, and (2) both individuals and the state are best served if people perform the functions for which their natures, complemented by the appropriate education, best suit them.[4] The ideal state is based on the recognition of the mutuality of need among people who do different things. People stand in need of each other because not everybody does everything well; indeed, no one does everything well; in fact, everyone does only one thing well. People will lead the best and most flourishing lives of which they are capable, and the state will be the best and the happiest possible state, if each person fulfills his or her "natural" role. Justice consists in the harmony that prevails under these conditions. Individuals will enjoy the harmony that is justice if their reason, aided by the spirited part of their souls, rules their appetites; the state will enjoy the harmony that is justice if those individuals in whom the power of reasoning is strongest rule, with the aid of high-spirited soldiers, over the multitudes. That is, justice will prevail to the extent that a guardian class of philosophers, aided by the class of "auxiliaries" whom they command, rules over the class of artisans or producers. (Plato appears to assume that in addition to these three classes there will be the underclass of slaves.)[5]

It follows from Plato's argument that if women and men have different natures, they ought not to have the same pursuits, they ought not to perform the same functions in the state. Indeed, given Plato's definition of justice, it would be unjust for them to be delegated the same functions and responsibilities.

In book 5 of the *Republic* Socrates insists that there is no reason women ought not to be included among the philosopher-rulers. He manages to do so without giving up the principle that we ought to assign "different pursuits to different natures and the same to the same" (454b) and without giving up entirely the notion that men and women have different natures. He points out to Glaucon that if one is careful enough to "apply the proper divisions and distinctions to the subject under consideration" (454a) one will think not simply about whether two natures are different or the same but whether they are different or the same *with respect to a particular pursuit*. In this connection, Socrates insists that just as whether a person is bald or long-haired is irrelevant to whether he has the kind of nature that makes him a good cobbler, so whether a person is male or female is irrelevant to whether he or she is suited to a task—indeed, a male and a female physician are more alike than a male physician and a male carpenter (454d–e). The two cases suggest that a difference in bodily features is not necessarily a sign of a difference in nature; what is crucial is whether two people have the same mind or soul: "A man and a woman who have a physician's mind[6] have the same nature" (454d). Yes, male and female differ in that "the female bears and the male begets," but this does nothing to show that "the woman differs from the man for our purposes" (454e). While the body can be a hindrance to performing a task well (455c)—that is, in cases in which "bodily faculties" do not adequately serve the mind—whether the body is or is not a hindrance doesn't depend on whether it is male or female.

So not all men will do the same things because they are men; not all women will do the same things because they are women. Some men will be suited to being carpenters, others suited to being guardians; similarly, "one woman has the qualities of a guardian and another not. . . . The women and the men, then, have the same nature in respect to the guardianship of the state, save in so far as the one is weaker, the other stronger" (456a).

In short, Socrates says, people ought to engage in different pursuits only when their differences are relevant to the capacity to carry out the task. He does not challenge the idea that men and women are different in some respects—specifically, in terms of their role in reproduction—but says that there are other respects in which they are or might be the same. Similarly, he does not challenge the idea that two men may be alike in some respect, or that two women may be the same in some respect, but argues that there may be other respects in which they are different. What is visible about you does not tell the whole story, or maybe any of the story, of who you are. Plato wants us to see that it takes the skill of a real philosopher to see which differences and similarities are relevant to which pursuits. Part of what enables Socrates to imagine women engaged in the same pursuits as men is this capacity.

The importance of being able to know what differences make a difference appears in another dialogue in which the significance of apparent differences between men and women is discussed. When Socrates asks young Meno, in the dialogue of that name, if he knows what virtue is, he replies by telling Socrates about the virtue of men and the virtue of women:

> The virtue of a man consists in managing the city's affairs capably . . . a woman's virtue . . . is easily described. She must be a good housewife, careful with her stores and obedient to her husband. (71e)

Socrates responds by getting Meno to acknowledge that bees don't differ from one another as bees, even though they differ in size and beauty; he then leads Meno into considering by analogy whether "even if [virtues] are many and various, . . . they all have some common character which makes them virtues" (72c). He wants Meno to see that virtue will not "differ, in its character as virtue, whether it be in a child or an old man, a woman or a man" (73a).

Thus a man's having virtue doesn't mean the virtue he has is manly—that it belongs to him by virtue of his being male—and a woman's having virtue doesn't mean that her virtue is womanly. Just as a bee *qua* bee is neither big nor small, beautiful nor ugly, so virtue *qua* virtue is neither manly nor womanly—it is just virtue. Virtue itself cannot be various, even though there may be a variety of virtues. Again, it is Socrates' capacity to note similarities and to know their significance that is presented as crucial to his ability to see beyond the physical differences that exist between people or things.

Finally, Socrates is able to argue that sexual identity is irrelevant to the capacities required for the philosopher-ruler because he thought of those capacities as being of the soul and distinct from the qualities of the body. Whether or not you have the capacity to rule is determined by your soul and not your body; no inferences can be drawn from the fact that someone has a particular kind of body about what kind of soul they have.

Someone might well agree with Socrates that we can't simply note physical differences between people and conclude that they must have different natures. As Socrates makes us see, it would be absurd to think that because the excellent cobbler one knows has a full head of hair, no bald man could be a good cobbler; the presence or absence of hair is irrelevant to whether or not one might be a cobbler "by nature." But how, Socrates' critic might ask, could sexual identity *not* make a difference to one's ability? Young Meno easily grants Socrates the point about bees all being essentially the same, and about health being the same, as health, in men and women; but about whether virtue can be the same in men and women he expresses some reservations: "I somehow feel that this is not on the same level as the other cases" (73a).

There are at least two ways Plato could silence such doubts. He could argue that *no* facts about a person's body entail facts about that person's nature, or soul.[7] Or he could maintain that while some bodily facts entail something about people's natures, their sexual identities aren't among such facts. There is much in Plato's treatment of the soul/body distinction that suggests that his holding the former view enabled him to "see beyond" a person's sex. But we need to remind ourselves of the way, or ways, in which Plato described the soul and the body and the relation between them.

II

Plato took soul and body to be distinctly different kinds of things. The distinction hums continuously throughout the dialogues. According to Plato, souls are invisible, not observable by the senses; they are subject neither to generation or decay. Bodies, to the contrary, are quite visible, apprehendable by the senses, and they are entirely subject to generation and decay. In the *Phaedo,* Socrates summarizes a discussion with Cebes about the distinction between soul and body:

> [The soul is] most like that which is divine, immortal, intelligible, uniform, indissoluble, and ever self-consistent and invariable, whereas [the] body is most like that which is human, mortal, multiform, unintelligible, dissoluble, and never self-consistent. (80b)

Precisely because the soul is not visible and is unchanging, it can "see" the invisible and unchanging things the senses never can (*Republic* 510e, 527e, 532a). Soul and body each have a kind of beauty, health, pleasure, and good and evil distinct from the qualities of the other (*Phaedo* 114e; *Gorgias* 464a, 477b–c, 501b; *Philebus* 33c). There are concerns peculiar to the soul and those specific to the body (*Republic* 535b; *Laws* 673a, 795d).

The soul not only is different in kind from the body; it can exist without it. At death, the invisible, indissoluble soul separates from the visible decaying body (*Phaedo* 64c, 67d; *Gorgias* 524b; *Laws* 828e, 927a). The soul thus *is* the person; immortality is the continued existence of the person, the soul, after the death of the body.[8] The connection to the body is so contingent as to allow the soul to inhabit an entirely different body: for example, a soul that was in a man's body in one lifetime might inhabit a woman's body in another (*Timaeus* 42b–c, 76e, 91a; *Laws* 944e; *Republic* 614–21).

Finally, those who really care about the state of their souls (i.e., those who are or aspire to being philosophers) will do everything they can to keep the body from interfering with the proper work of the soul. In the *Apology,* this is portrayed as the central concern of Socrates' life:

> [I have spent] all my time going about trying to persuade you, young and old, to make your first and chief concern not for your bodies nor for your possessions, but for the highest welfare of your souls. (30a–b)

It is only through the soul that a person can come to have any real knowledge, for it is only through the soul that one can "see" what is real—the invisible, eternal, unchanging Forms. The body, with its deceptive senses, keeps us from real knowledge, insofar as it rivets us in a world of material things far removed from the world of reality. We are mistaken if we think that what we can touch or see or otherwise sense are real: the beautiful things we can hold in our hands are not Beauty itself, which is

> an everlasting loveliness which neither comes nor goes, which neither flowers nor fades, for such beauty is the same on every hand, the same then as now, here as there, this way as that way, the same to every worshipper as it is to every other (*Symposium* 221a)

Only the soul can know the Forms, those eternal and unchanging denizens of reality; our changing, decaying bodies can put us in touch only with changing, decaying pieces of the material world. The philosophers who will rule the ideal state

> are those who are capable of apprehending that which is eternal and unchanging, while those who are incapable of this, but lose themselves and wander amid the multiplicities of multifarious things, are not philosophers. (*Republic* 484b)

Our bodies (or sometimes, the lower parts of the soul) also are the source of temptations that must be resisted if we are to lead lives of virtue. "Enjoyment of flesh by flesh" is "wanton shame," while desire of soul for soul is at the heart of a relationship that "reverences, aye, and worships, chastity and manhood, greatness and wisdom" (*Laws* 837c–d). At a less anxious moment in the dialogues, Plato isn't so worried about the enjoyment of flesh by flesh as long as the enjoyment doesn't get in the way of the spiritual development of both lovers.[9]

The body is not without use, however: for example, appreciation of the physical beauty of another can lead to an understanding of Beauty itself. One can begin to learn about Beauty in the contemplation of those who are beautiful, which leads to the realization that Beauty is something beyond any particular beautiful body or thing.[10] We also learn from the dialogues that one shouldn't neglect the body: an ill-tuned body can prevent the proper functioning of the soul; and one ought to understand as well that the well-tuned body can serve certain epistemological ends, albeit severely limited ones.

But in general the dialogues tell us that one has no hope of understanding Knowledge, Reality, Goodness, Love, or Beauty unless one recognizes the distinction between soul and body; and one has no hope of attaining or comprehending any of these essential Forms unless one works hard on freeing the soul from the lazy, vulgar, beguiling body. The person is not only distinct from the body but is much better off finally without it.

These lessons from the dialogues about the relation of soul and body enable us to see, then, why Plato could see beyond someone's sex: What difference can having a male or female body make to whether one can be a philosopher-ruler, if it is the state of one's soul that determines whether or not one is a philosopher, and if the soul not only is distinct from the body but can exist without it? What kind of inference about someone's soul could possibly be based on whether their body is male or female, if the same soul could be in either a male or female body, or in no body at all? While one's body can be an obstacle to the proper functioning of the soul of a philosopher, a woman who is a philosopher will by her nature avoid the ensnarements of her body; and her education, which is the same as that of her male equals, will strengthen her natural resolve. Thus whatever differences there are between men and women are irrelevant in terms of their eligibility for guardianship of the state.

III

This was for the most part a startling political position: not even the democrats of Athens were proposing that women ought to share in the governance of the polis. But the arguments Plato relied on were not so clearly political as they were logical and metaphysical: he was trying to get his companions to see that it is irrational to differentiate between people on the basis of sex if sex is irrelevant to the point at hand.

What is particularly important here is that he does not appeal to existing arguments or institutions about equality—for example, he didn't turn to the democrats and try to convince them that on their own grounds women ought to have the chance to shape the policies of the state.[11] Paradoxically, his case rests on a metaphysical argument that establishes *inequality* in two ways: (1) People have different natures and in light of that ought to be educated differently to play different roles in the polis (as opposed to being given the opportunity to do anything they want.) (2) It takes a special skill to see which differences and similarities are relevant to which pursuits; only people with this skill should be leaders. That is, the very same arguments meant to establish the equality of some women to some men are also meant to establish or reflect the inequality of some groups of women and men to other groups of women and men.

Now we must look more closely at the relation between the equality Plato appears to posit between men and women who are philosopher-rulers and the inequality he posits between the class of philosopher-rulers and all the other members of the state.

Plato's inegalitarianism—his view that some people are by nature meant to rule, others to assist them, and still others to be ruled—requires that there are different natures, rooted in different kinds of souls. His egalitarianism—his view that some women are as fit to rule as some men are—requires that whatever else might differentiate souls, being male or female does not. His inegalitarianism and egalitarianism thus seem to go neatly together: while the natures of men and women as philosophers do not differ, the natures of philosophers and cobblers do. In other words, the claim that souls are distinct from bodies—which is crucial to the idea that it doesn't matter whether you have a male or female body—does not mean that there cannot be different kinds of souls. All it means is that we can't tell from the kind of body a person has, what kind of soul she or he has. Some souls are of the kind to rule, some are of the kind to be ruled—but the body does not reveal, simply on the basis of whether it is male or female, what kind of soul is inside it.

Now as we've just seen, Plato seems to say not only that being male or female is irrelevant to the kind of soul you have, but that no aspect of the physical self can tell us anything about the kind of soul someone has. If that is the case, then given that souls are not visible, how are we to decide where the ruling and where the ruled souls reside?

When we ask this question, we end up wondering whether Plato can after all sustain the grounds for both his arguments. For it begins to look as if those he uses to establish a kind of equality of men and women among the rulers will finally undermine his description of the inequality among philosopher-rulers, auxiliaries, and the "multitude." Any argument strong enough to show that sexual identity is irrelevant must undermine attempts to make crucial distinctions between any people or groups of people.

The dialogues provide us with at least two ways to get around the dilemma. First of all, among the special skills of the philosopher-kings and -queens is the ability to tell what kind of nature a person has. Their nature and their training enable them to "distinguish the baseborn from the trueborn" (*Republic* 536a), and the well-being of the state depends on this ability:

> For when the knowledge necessary to make such discriminations is lacking in individual or state, they unawares employ at random for any of these purposes the crippled and baseborn natures, as their friends or rulers. (*Republic* 536a)

The rulers' responsibility for "assign[ing] to each the status due to his nature" is described as one they must address with the greatest care.[12] In fact they must be prepared to "thrust [their own sons] out among the artisans or the farmers" in the unlikely but possible case that they do not inherit their parent's nature (*Republic* 415b–c).

Second, we find in the dialogues that while Plato is at pains to argue that we can't tell, simply from the fact of someone's having a female body, what kind of soul she has, he is very concerned about how one behaves, since what happens in or to the body has profound effects on what happens in and to the soul, and vice versa. Thus although one's nature is not revealed through the kind of body one has, it is revealed through the activities one engages in. Plato is concerned about how philosophers comport themselves and what kind of activities they engage in. He thinks it crucial that those with philosophers' souls behave in certain ways rather than others—this is why education is so important in the *Republic*. The living conditions of philosopher-rulers resembles what in our time Erving Goffmann has called a "total institution": every aspect of their lives is controlled, for every action, every gesture, Plato thinks, has an effect on the state of their souls.[13] For example, since philosophers ought not to give in to grief when afflicted in their own lives, they should not give in to it in the theater either (*Republic* 604a–b): there are no occasions on which what we do does not seriously affect the quality of our souls. Philosophers-in-training thus have to be tested again and again to see if their souls are up to par—for example, to see if rather than being overcome by fear or by pleasure they remain "immune to such witchcraft and preserve [their] composure throughout," thereby showing themselves to be "good guardian[s] of [themselves] and the culture [they have] received" (*Republic* 13e). All children will receive the same initial education (there is no sure way of telling at birth what kind of nature a person has, so all should be educated up to the point at which differences among them emerge), but only those who pass such tests can be established as philosopher-rulers (*Republic* 414a, 503a).

Although the life of philosopher-rulers requires a kind of constant vigilance, it also requires a particular leisure. As Socrates said to his judges in the *Apology* (36d), anyone whose appointed task is to care for people's souls must be free of the need to earn a living. Wage-earning is suitable only for those

> servitors who in the things of the mind are not altogether worthy of our fellowship, but whose strength of body is sufficient for toil; so they, selling the use of this strength and calling the price wages, are designated, I believe, "wage earners," are they not? (*Republic* 371e)

Indeed, some commentators have insisted that "the whole of Plato's political philosophy is grounded in the conviction that to earn a livelihood, and especially by means of manual labour, corrupts the soul and disqualifies a man for politics, making it not only justifiable but necessary for him to subject himself to the command of others."[14]

We see now why Plato's example of the carpenter (*Republic* 454d–e; see p. 21 above) is so telling: Socrates is trying to get Glaucon to understand that if we think carefully about who is fit to be a ruler of the state, what matters is not whether you are male or female but what kinds of pursuits you are suited for, what kinds of activities you can do well, and how you respond to challenges to self-control. What matters is not what kind of body you have, but what you do with it, and how well you can control it. If you have the kind of soul that a carpenter does, you don't have the kind of soul a ruler does; both rulers and ruled might be male or female. We can only tell that some women have the souls of philosopher-rulers if they do what philosopher-rulers do and not what carpenters, say, or male or female slaves do.[15]

IV

Our rendering of Plato's account of the significance of being male or female becomes more complicated if we move beyond the fifth book of the *Republic,* the *Meno,* and aspects of the *Laws.* For the dialogues are very liberally peppered with misogynistic remarks of the most casual and off-hand kind. We realize that Plato's proposals in book 5 of the *Republic* are surprising not only in light of the sexism of fifth-century Athens, and his inegalitarianism, but especially in light of the sexism otherwise rampant in his own work. So even if Plato's account of the potential equality of men and women is one we could heartily embrace (a point to which we shall return), we nevertheless must admit that his vision of equality is hardly the whole story about women to be found in the dialogues.

Plato routinely tosses off what might appear to be gratuitous remarks about the foibles of womanhood. But these comments almost always function to clarify or make vivid an important philosophical point. As we saw earlier, for the most part he wants to convince us that the soul is much more important than the body: it is to our peril that we let ourselves be beckoned by the rumblings of the body at the expense of the soul. Plato sets out to convince us of this by holding up for our inspection the silly and sordid lives of those who pay too much attention to their bodies and do not care enough for their souls; he wants to remind us of how unruly, how without direction, are the lives of those in whom the lower part of the soul holds sway over the higher part.

Because he can't point to an adulterated soul—they are invisible—he points instead to those embodied beings whose lives are in such disarray that we can be sure their souls are corrupted. And whose lives exemplify the proper soul/body relationship gone haywire? Well, says Plato, look at the lives of women.[16] It is women who get hysterical at the thought of death; obviously, their emotions have overpowered their reason, and they can't control themselves (*Phaedo* 60a, 112d; *Apology* 356). "A woman, young or old or wrangling with her husband, defying heaven, loudly boasting, fortunate in her own conceit, or involved in misfortune or possessed by grief and lamentation" is a dreadful model for a young man—still worse is "a woman that is sick, in love, or in labor" (*Republic* 395d–e).

When in our own lives some affliction comes to us you are aware that we plume ourselves ... on our ability to remain calm and endure, in the belief that this is the conduct of a man, and [giving in to grief] that of a woman. (*Republic* 605c–d)

To have more concern for your body than your soul is to act just like a woman; hence, the most proper penalty for a soldier who surrenders to save his body, when he should be willing to die out of the courage of his soul, is for him to be turned into a woman (*Laws* 944c).[17] Plato sometimes expresses the belief that souls can go through many different embodied lifetimes. There will be certain indications, in one's life, of the kind of life one is leading; and unless a man lives righteously, he will as his next incarnation "pass into a woman," and if he doesn't live rightly then, he'll become a brute (*Timaeus* 42b–c, 76e, 91a).[18]

The message is that in matters of knowledge, reality, and beauty, don't follow the example of women. They can only be mistaken about those things. In matters of love, women's lives serve as negative examples also. Those men who are drawn by "vulgar" love, that is, love of body for body, "turn to women as the object of their love, and raise a family" (*Symposium* 208e); those men drawn by a more "heavenly" kind of love, that is, love of soul for soul, turn to other men. But there are strong sanctions against physical love between men: physical unions, especially between older and younger men, are "unmanly." The older man isn't strong enough to resist his lust (as in women, the irrational part of the soul has overtaken the rational part), and the younger man, "the impersonator of the female," is reproached for this "likeness to the model" (*Laws* 836e). The problem with physical love between men, then, is that men are acting like women.[19]

It is true that Socrates apparently held at least one woman in very high regard: Diotima.[20] In the *Symposium,* Socrates describes her as being "deeply versed in this [love] and many other fields of knowledge" (201d). But this praise occurs in the context of a discussion from which women have been excluded in order to keep matters on a serious note, in the inquiry in the *Symposium* in which the love of men for women has been referred to—by Diotima among others—without challenge as vulgar and unmanly.

Socrates' reference to Diotima is perhaps of a piece with what he says in book 5 of the *Republic* about women who would be philosopher-rulers; it stands in stark contrast to the generous scattering of misogynistic remarks throughout the dialogues. Misogyny has always been compatible with having high regard for "exceptional" (and surely for imaginary) women.

(and "manly")

V

It is clear that the contradictory sides of Plato's views about women are in part tied to the distinction he makes between soul and body and the somatophobic lessons he hopes to teach his readers about their relative value. When preaching about the overwhelming importance of the soul, he can't but regard the kind of body one has as of no final significance, so there is no way for him to assess differentially the lives of women and men. But when making gloomy pronouncements about the worth of the body, he points an accusing finger at a class of people with a certain kind of body—a female body—because he regards them as embodying the very traits he wishes no one to have. In this way, women constitute a deviant class in Plato's philosophy. They live the kinds of lives that no one, especially philosophers, ought to live. It is true that Plato chastises certain kinds of men: sophists, tyrants, and cowards, for example. But he frequently puts them in their place by comparing them to women. We've already seen some examples of this, such as the ridicule of homosexuals for their likeness to women. There is a highly polished moral gloss to the soul/body distinction in Plato. A device that brings this moral gloss to a high luster is his holding up, for our contempt and ridicule, the lives of women in order to demonstrate that it makes no small difference whether you lead a soul-directed or a body-directed life.

If one explanation of Plato's apparently contradictory remarks about women is linked to the sharp distinction he makes between soul and body and the ranks he assigns them, a second explanation, paradoxically, is connected to the fact that sometimes the distinction is not so sharp.

Earlier we focused on Plato's insistence that we can't infer anything about a person's soul from the kind of body she or he has. This insistence has to be qualified when we notice that Plato elsewhere treats the soul as having a much closer, indeed an essential, relation to the body, inasmuch as certain states of the soul can only be expressed, or can best be expressed, in particular kinds of bodies. For example, Plato sometimes speaks as if he thought it easily imaginable for a soul of a man to come to inhabit the body of a woman. However, this kind of transformation is regarded as the appropriate turn of events only for the coward or for the man who has not led a righteous life.[21]

Plato seems to be saying—at least in these comments about reincarnation—that there is a fittingness of one kind of soul to one kind of body: the kind of soul you have shows in the kind of body you have, and can't be shown in another kind of body.[22] Or perhaps he is saying that the kind of soul you have *ought* to show in the kind of body you have—souls in the bodies of male soldiers ought to be brave souls—and if there isn't a good fit in this life there will be in the next. What we must notice here is that being stuck in a woman's body can be described as appropriate for a cowardly soul only if Plato believes that courage cannot be expressed in a body of the female form. The bodily medium is crucial to the message about the soul.[23]

I think we are observing here the conjunction of the two criteria said to reveal one's nature, that is, the kind of body one has and the kind of behavior one displays. Plato is implying that if a body is male, we expect certain kinds of behavior from it, for example, brave behavior. Given his general view, this means that if the body is male we expect the soul connected to it to be able to control it in a particular way. If the behavior of a male body is not what we'd expect from a male body, then the soul is not appropriate to that body; it ought really to live in a female body. So while we can't simply deduce from the presence of a male body what kind of soul it has, we can deduce what kind of soul it ought to have, that is, how the body ought to be conducted. This means that at least in these passages from the *Laws* and *Timaeus*, even if not always so clearly elsewhere, Plato is treating souls as if they are gendered—that is, he argues that some kinds of souls are manly, some are womanly; manly souls belong in males, womanly ones in females.

In the *Republic*, Plato makes sure that the expression of courage in women will not be different from the expression of courage in men: he insists that men and women have to *behave* in the same way to show that they are relevantly the same. Every act you perform counts. Your bodily activity is not simply correlated with activity and states of your soul; your bodily activity is the necessary expression of the state of your soul.[24] Doing what a cobbler does cannot be the expression of a soul contemplating the eternal Forms; thus the soul of a philosopher cannot be expressed in the life of a male cobbler. And though it can be expressed in the life of a woman, this is only so long as she acts in particular ways and engages in particular pursuits.

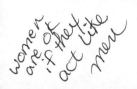
women are ok if they act like men

VI

We have been trying to account for Plato's apparently contradictory remarks about women—that they can be counted among the philosopher-rulers; that they lead just the kinds of lives the philosopher-rulers ought to avoid. But there is an alternative hypothesis to the idea that Plato contradicts himself: he uses "woman" ambiguously.

Plato's thinking of people as made up of body and soul allows for at least three different configurations of "woman." The female philosopher-ruler has a female body, but she doesn't have a typically feminine soul—that is, the kind of soul found in the typical Athenian female, a soul unable to resist the temptations of the body, a soul that doesn't know and doesn't care about the difference between appearance and reality. The female philosopher-ruler has a manly soul: the kind of soul that true philosophers have. Similarly, cowardly male soldiers have feminine souls: that is why in their next life they will come back in female bodies. In the examples below, the soul/body configurations described in b, c, and d all represent "woman" in some sense:

a. manly soul/male body: brave soldier; male philosopher-ruler
b. manly soul/female body: female philosopher-ruler
c. womanly soul/male body: cowardly male soldier
d. womanly soul/female body: typical Athenian woman

We might be tempted to use configuration b to represent the reincarnation of the cowardly soldier: for isn't such a person someone who used to be a man but now is in a woman's body? But d is really the better way to represent the reembodied cowardly soldier: if the soul always really belonged in a female body, it is a feminine or womanly soul. Example c represents a bad fit. We might have hoped that since there was a male body there would be a manly soul, as in a; but if someone with a male body behaves in a cowardly way, this shows that "he" really has a womanly soul. The configuration in b should be reserved for the philosopher-queens, who have a manly soul in a female body.

Part of what is confusing in the idea that there has to be the right "fit" between soul and body is this: if we can tell that there is not a fit between body and soul, then presumably there doesn't have to be a fit in order for us to know what kind of soul a person has. If we can tell that the soldier has a woman's cowardly soul without his having a female body, why is a "fit" necessary? For Plato, we see that the right fit in these cases represents the appropriate punishment for the soldier's cowardice. But we are still left in an epistemological and metaphysical quandary: Despite the demand for a right "fit," there doesn't have to be a male body in order for a manly soul to be recognized, nor does there have to be a female body for a womanly soul to be recognized.

example: ↘

This quandary appears in modern dress in Jan Morris's description of the complicated phenomenon of transsexualism. In *Conundrum* (New York: Signet, 1974), Morris insists that "she" had always had a woman's soul housed in a man's body. That she could think about herself in this way suggests that she thought her bodily identity to be neither indicative of nor necessary for her having a particular kind of soul: she "knew," even though she had a male body, that she had a womanly soul. On the other hand, she felt compelled to change her body in order to reveal the gender of her soul.

Morris seems to be saying that while gender identity is more important than sexual identity, a person's sex is the clue others take to his or her gender. Gender systems teach us to expect certain kinds of behavior from persons who have male bodies and other kinds from persons who have female bodies. If our expectations are met, the fit is supposed to be right; if they are not met, the fit is wrong. Though Morris can't be said to be a whole lot like Plato, her example may help us understand what makes Plato's ambiguous use of "woman" possible by reminding us that the existence of gender identities represents the likelihood that not all males will be masculine nor all females feminine.

Plato is indeed revolutionary in his imagining and his valuing the possibility that there are women who are not typically feminine. In contrast, his contempt for the feminine in both its male and female embodiments indicates the extent to which he accepted the sexist stereotypes of the time. The problem with the mass of women, according to Plato, is that they can't become the people male philosopher-rulers are; the problem with the mass of men is that they are too much like most women.

In criticizing men for being feminine, Plato opens up the logical space to think of women as masculine and to praise them for it. However, it is not clear that people must be either masculine or feminine. We have heard nothing about the third class of people in Plato's world, the artisans, farmers, and other producers, who may not be masculine in the way philosopher-rulers are but are not feminine in the way typical Athenian women or cowardly guardians are. (We shall return to the question of whether "masculine" and "feminine" exhaust the terrain of gender in the next chapter.)

What, then, can we conclude from this about what Plato might have meant when talking about "woman"? What he means by "woman" in the fifth book of the *Republic* is quite different from what he means by "woman" elsewhere. Though both kinds of women are females, one kind is a female with a manly soul, the other kind a female with a womanly soul. That is, the one is what could become of a female person if she has a certain nature and is trained in the way of the philosophers; the other is what happens to a female person who hasn't such a nature and does not receive such training.

VII

Plato's claim to being a feminist surely has to do with his holding (1) that a woman's biology ought not to settle the question of her destiny, and (2) that women's intelligence and reason ought to be called upon in the running of the state. He refuses to assume that since women have different bodies than men they must have capacities significantly different from, and inferior to, those of men. According to Plato, not all women are inferior to all men; some women are equal to the best of men, and in fact superior to other men. In the best and most wisely governed state, we can expect to find women as well as men among the ruling class.

As has often been pointed out, Plato is not here relying upon or defending the notion of women's "rights." While the positions to which women will have access along with men are ones that involve great power and authority, every aspect of their lives is shaped to enable them to see and carry out their duties. They are not "free" in a sense very common to modern ears—free to do what they want, free not to have their lives interfered with by the needs and demands of others. As Ernest Barker puts it: "Plato is not a teacher of woman's rights so much as of woman's duties."[25] Or as Julia Annas has remarked: Plato "sees women merely as a huge untapped pool of resources: here are half the citiznes sitting at home wasting effort doing identical trivial jobs! . . . Benefit to the state is the sole, frequently repeated ground" for the proposals about women's role in the ideal state.[26] Guardians have a single function: to run the state. From infancy they are to be trained to make sure that they develop the self-control and knowledge necessary for such heavy responsibility. If they are educated as Plato imagines, then in a sense they will be free to do what they want, but only because their desires will be constructed in such a way that they'll want to do exactly what they are supposed to do.

Moreover, part of the shaping of desire among the guardians and auxiliaries is their not wanting to have or own something by themselves: they will have no private property, which means among other things that men will not have their own wives or their own children (*Republic* 464a–b). However, this does not mean that women—even guardian women—cease to be property, or are to be in a position to decide whether or not they wish to with men or to have children.[27] Women are now common property. Indeed, "more frequent intercourse with the women" will be the honor and prize for young men "who excel in war and other pursuits" (*Republic* 460b). Nevertheless, Plato's claims are useful for feminists to turn back to, especially when what is claimed to be the wisdom of the ages is thrown against feminist proposals for creating a world in which it would not be assumed that women are the political, social, moral, and intellectual inferiors of men. But we must keep in mind that Plato's argument for the equality of some women to some men was inextricably intertwined with an argument for the superiority of that group of men and women to all other people. He may have refused to assume that biology is destiny, but that does not mean that all ways of ranking people disappear. The equality Plato talks about is only between men and women who would be guardians and philosopher-rulers. He is not talking about equality between slave men and philosopher women, or between slave women and philosopher women. Surely, then, we ought to ask: what kind of feminism is it that would gladly argue for a kind of equality between men and women of a certain class and at the same time for radical inequality between some women and some men, some women and some other women, some men and some other men?

When we emphasize that according to Plato bodily features don't provide grounds for distinguishing between people, we may thereby obscure the fact that he hardly thought that all people were the same "underneath"—indeed, that he didn't think all women were the same "underneath." Plato arrogates to philosopher-rulers the capacity and authority to decide what differences between people matter and why. Anybody can know whether a person is male or female; only philosopher-kings and -queens can tell what a person's soul is really like. This is very important authority to have—as we saw, some take the exercise of it to be the most crucial task of philosopher-rulers.

Is the kind of power and authority Plato ascribes to philosopher-rulers a kind of power and authority that feminists ought to embrace? Should feminists support the notion that some women ought to be in the business of deciding what kinds of "natures" different kinds of people have and therefore what their best interests are? In order to find out the extent to which some versions of feminism may have more of Plato in them than they might ever have imagined, we need to ask still more questions: Is the authority about the significance of differences among people something that feminists have assumed in analyses of differences among women? How do we know which differences among us are significant and which aren't? Are some women in a better position than others to answer this? If so, how does that authority come to inhere in them? Through some kind of special metaphysical insight such as Plato thought philosopher-rulers had? Through the political contests waged and adjudicated in all the usual places, including academic conferences, publishing houses, and the pages of book reviews?

We shall return to these questions in later chapters. For now, let us see what Aristotle thought to be important differences among women and what he took those differences to mean.

Notes

1. There is evidence that Pythagoras treated women as the equals of men, but as Sarah Pomeroy argues, "this phenomenon was unique in the Greek world of the sixth and fifth centuries B.C." (*Women in Hellenistic Egypt* [New York: Schocken, 1984], 65). There is considerable debate about the meaning of the portrayal of women in classical literature. See, for example, Sarah B. Pomeroy, *Goddesses, Whores, Wives, and Slaves: Women in Classical Antiquity* (New York: Schocken, 1975); Eva Cantarella, *Pandora's Daughters: The Role and Status of Women in Greek and Roman Antiquity* (Baltimore: Johns Hopkins University Press, 1987); M. R. Lefkowitz, *The Lives of the Greek Poets* (Baltimore: Johns Hopkins University Press, 1981); Martha C. Nussbaum, *The Fragility of Goodness: Luck and Ethics in Greek Tragedy and Philosophy* (Cambridge: Cambridge University Press, 1986).

2. Plato thus inverts what appears to us as a paradoxical situation in the Athenian society of his time: Democratic reforms in Athens in some ways lowered the status of many women (on this, see Pomeroy, *Goddesses, Whores, Wives, and Slaves*, 57–58, and Ellen M. Wood and Neal Wood, *Class Ideology and Ancient Political Theory: Socrates, Plato, and Aristotle in Social Context* [New York: Oxford University Press, 1978], 49–50), but

Plato in effect raises the status of some women in the process of constructing a very undemocratic society.

3. Plato has most recently been described as a feminist by Nussbaum in *The Fragility of Goodness,* 4n.

4. For a useful summary of the meaning of "nature" or *phusis,* see Okin, *Women in Western Political Thought,* 51ff.

5. See G. Vlastos, "Does Slavery Exist in Plato's *Republic?*" *Classical Philology* 63 (1968): 291–95.

6. Plato uses *psuchē* here, which usually is translated as "soul."

7. Soul (*psuchē*) and nature (*phusis*) are different concepts, but as we saw earlier, in the context of the inquiry into whether men and women have different natures, having the same soul settles for Plato the question of whether people have the same nature. See *Republic* 454d.

8. Plato does sometimes speak of a mortal part of the soul; see, for example, *Timaeus* 61d.

9. See G. Vlastos, "The Individual as an Object of Love in Plato," in his *Platonic Studies,* 2d ed. (Princeton: Princeton University Press, 1981), 40: "Body-to-body and endearment is one of [the] normal features [of Platonic love], though always subject to the constraint that terminal gratification will be denied."

10. As Nussbaum points out, this message from the *Symposium* (210bff.) is in effect reassessed in the *Phaedrus* (*The Fragility of Goodness,* 220ff.)

11. While it is true that sometimes he argues to the effect that it is wasteful not to make use of women's capacities—see, for example, Annas, "Plato's *Republic* and Feminism"—his argument presupposes his being able to see that women have such capacities.

12. See A. W. H. Adkins, *From the Many to the One* (Ithaca: Cornell University Press, 1970), 148: "The whole well-being of the *polis* depends on the ability of the rulers to distinguish these natural kinds."

13. See Erving Goffmann, *Asylums* (Garden City, N.Y.: Anchor Doubleday, 1961): "A basic social arrangement in modern society is that the individual tends to sleep, play, and work in different places, with different coparticipants, under different authorities, and without an over-all rational plan. The central feature of total institutions can be described as a breakdown of the barriers ordinarily separating these three spheres of life. First, all aspects of life are conducted in the same place and under the same single authority. Second, each phase of the member's daily activity is carried on in the immediate company of a large batch of others, all of whom are treated alike and required to do the same thing together. Third, all phases

of the day's activities are tightly scheduled, with one activity leading at a prearranged time into the next, the whole sequence of activities being imposed from above by a system of explicit formal rulings and a body of officials. Finally, the various enforced activities are brought together into a single rational plan purportedly designed to fulfill the official aims of the institution" (6). Total institutions are incompatible with the family (11). When spheres of life are "desegregated," a person's conduct "in one scene of activity is thrown up to him . . . as a comment and check upon his conduct in another context" (37).

14. Wood and Wood, *Class Ideology,* 53–54. See also Ernest Barker, *The Political Thought of Plato and Aristotle* (New York: Dover, 1959), 139.

15. While the philosopher-rulers of the *Republic* have to be able to distinguish between the well- and ill-born, the philosophers of the *Theaetetus* wouldn't bother: "Whether any fellow citizen is well- or ill-born or has inherited some defect from his ancestors on either side, the philosopher knows no more than how many pints of water there are in the sea" (173d). This suggests some ways in which the life of a philosopher who is not a ruler is quite different from the life of one who is; we might say that philosopher-rulers have to be interested in the particular historical identity of people in a way that mere philosophers are not.

16. Although Plato objects to certain types of men—sophists, tyrants, and so forth—his disdain for women is always expressed as disdain for women in general and not for any subgroup of women. Moreover, one of the ways he shows his disdain for certain types of men is to compare them to women. Children, slaves, and brutes also sometimes reveal the malfunctioning of the appropriate soul/body relation.

17. In passages like this we see Plato assuming that a certain kind of body implies the presence of a certain kind of soul. This is at odds with his explicit view elsewhere that what is really important about someone is that the person has a soul, no matter what kind of body she has.

18. In the *Phaedo* (82aff.), Socrates suggests that those who have led wantonly reckless and lawless lives are likely to come back as wolves, hawks, and kites, while those with the "ordinary goodness" of "self-control and integrity . . . will probably pass into some other kind of social and disciplined creature like bees, wasps, and ants, or even back into the human race again, becoming decent citizens."

19. For elaboration on the extent and significance of Plato's misogyny, see Spelman, "Woman as Body," 109–31.

20. In the *Menexenus* Socrates also expresses admiration for Aspasia as "an excellent mistress in the art of rhetoric" (235e). But there is serious doubt about whether Plato is the author of this dialogue. Moreover, Diotima may be a fictitious person.

21. In the examples from the *Laws* (944e) and *Timaeus* (42b–c, 91a), there is the suggestion that people are sentenced by the gods; in the Myth of Er at the end of the *Republic,* it is implied that people choose their next lives.

22. As should be clear already, Plato refers to the significance of reincarnation in a number of places throughout the dialogues; he doesn't always include ending up in a female body in his lists. See, for example, *Phaedrus* 248d ff.

23. The point is made less forcefully in the *Laws* (655a), when the Athenian legislator and Clinias agree that "a manly soul struggling with distress and a cowardly soul in the same or equal straits" will not express themselves in similar "postures . . . utterances . . . complexions." Later the Athenian suggests that a soul's "successive conjunction first with one body and then with another" is due to the power and responsibility of a god or gods "to shift the character that is becoming better to a better place, and that which is growing worse to a worser, each according to its due, that each may meet with its proper doom" (903d–e). See also Adkins, *From the Many to the One,* 134.

24. Necessary as long as you are alive; Plato would seem to believe that you don't need it after your soul is separated from your body, in death.

25. Barker, *Political Thought,* 145.

26. Annas, "Plato's *Republic* and Feminism," 183.

27. In connection with this, see Lynda Lange, "The Function of Equal Education in Plato's *Republic* and *Laws,*" in *The Sexism of Social and Political Theory,* ed. Clark and Lange, 3–15.

Eros and Epistemology

Christine Pierce

[handwritten annotation: how to make Symp? & Rep I consistent?]

What is it in Plato that so angers contemporary feminists?[1] Of the ancient philosophers, his views on women are the most enlightened, the most egalitarian. In Book V of the *Republic,* for instance, Plato says that women can in fact be philosophers; and this clear assertion has resisted decades of efforts by (mostly male) Plato commentators to argue it away. It is the *Symposium* and the *Phaedrus,* with their emphasis on homoerotic love as the necessary path to philosophic joy, that many feminist critics feel eliminate women from the search for wisdom and rational delight. But if Plato's thinking is consistent, the women he specifically includes as philosophers in the *Republic* cannot then be excluded by the *Symposium* and the *Phaedrus.*

Natalie Harris Bluestone, author of a 1987 book on Plato's *Republic* and gender[2], categorizes one hundred years of attempts to write women philosophers out of the *Republic,* from 1870 through 1970, as Seven Types of Hostility:[3]

1. Equality as a Non-Issue: Neglect of the Proposals
   The same period of scholarship that discoursed at length on Plato's proposals on the abolition of property and the family often ignored completely the Platonic text on female equality.

2. Women are Different: The Proposals as Unnatural
   Some of the most famous Plato scholars—Benjamin Jowett, Ernest Barker, A. E. Taylor and Leo Strauss—substituted their own views on women's nature and role for Plato's, asserting simply that Plato was blind to the facts of human nature or that he forgot the importance of the body. Barker is typical when he says: "The fact of [a woman's] sex . . . colors her whole being; it makes her able indeed to inspire noble enthusiasms, but not to direct a policy or drill a regiment, as Plato would require his woman-ruler or woman-soldier to do."[4]

25

3. Women Have Better Things to Do: The Proposals as Undesirable

   Richard Nettleship, for example, offers the opinion that Athenian women probably would have viewed Plato's proposal as "dragging them out of a position in which they would rather be left."[5]

4. Plato Didn't Really Mean It: The Proposals as Unintentional, Unwelcome or Comic

   Allan Bloom, for example, suggests that Plato's belief in competent women was a noble lie—a fabrication to cover up the truth that women are placed in the guardian class to reproduce guardians.

5. Other Ways of "Explaining Away" the Plan for Gender Equality

   Historical explanations which attribute the idea of equality of role to the historical Socrates and psychoanalytic explanations of Plato's motives tend to detract from the philosophical merit of Plato's claims.

6. Bias in Language: The Consequences of Hidden Assumptions

   Awkward and misleading translations include C. H. Hoole's "woman is the weaker man" and Jowett's phrase, "the female sex in man." Jowett also refers to female guardians as "helpmeets" and to pregnant women as "in the family way" even when there is meant to be no family. Cornford writes that wives must strip for exercise although it is men and not husbands who strip in the gymnasium. The just cause of equal education is not helped by talk of educating the young lad, and the ubiquitous "Philosopher-King" could have been "Philosopher-Ruler" all along.

7. As Long as They Don't Go Too Far: The Warnings of the So-Called Feminists

   These critics cautiously approve of some measure of women's equality while fearing that women will be unreasonable in their ambitions and excessive in their demands.

With the beginning of feminist commentary on Plato in the early 1970s, there was a turning away from the previous hostility to the idea of gender equality in the *Republic*. Today, with the notable exception of Allan Bloom, one rarely hears a challenge to the egalitarianism of the *Republic*.

What does Plato say in Book V of the *Republic?* The argument is this:

> Men are better in all pursuits including weaving and baking.
> Hence, women have no natural pursuits; there is no woman's place that is hers by nature.
> However, many women are better than many men in many things.
> Therefore, each woman must be judged on her own merits.

The argument is one for equal opportunity—a limited, but important type of equality. In short, Plato says that generalizations about the abilities of people as a class are not relevant in determining social roles or occupations in particular cases. The sentiment expressed by Allan Bloom in premise 1 (above)—that the class of men excel that of women in anything practiced by human beings— is especially interesting because believing it undercuts the notion that women as a class have a natural place. F. M. Cornford translates premise 1 a bit differently. Men, he says, are superior to women in any human occupation *except* things like weaving and watching over saucepans and batches of cakes. Although Plato's idea that the doctrine of natural place (or proper sphere) correctly applies to individuals rather than classes of persons is compatible with either translation, Bloom's version has the advantage that Socrates can grant as much as any misogynist could desire and still show the logical implication to be equal opportunity for both sexes. To some feminist commentators, Plato is labelled a sexist for having put forward any version of premise 1. Perhaps, instead, the assertion of this premise is an example of the common Platonic practice of having Socrates get his opponent to agree to some outrageous view only to pull the rug out from under him by showing where his views lead. If the argument is accounted for this way, Plato might be absolved of one instance of sexism.

Though Plato would not argue that either gender has a specific nature, he does insist that human beings as a class do. Plato believed that the nature of human beings is rationality. The nature of any class of things (humans, rocks—whatever) is its distinctive function, purpose or goal, i.e., the end that sets off the class being defined from all other classes of things. When function or purpose is part of what is meant by the nature of any "X" (or class of X's), standards for evaluating that "X" (or class of X's) are built into the use of the term; a good "X" is one that fulfills its function. So, the good life for humans is the rational life. To his credit, Plato took it for granted that women were human beings, and thus, in the *Republic,* he is not even tempted to suggest that child-bearing is the nature of women because as human beings, their nature is reason. Also, Plato could not remain consistent and claim that the natural end of human beings (or female human beings had he separated human beings into different classes as Aristotle later did) is child-bearing or reproduction because reproduction is not a function peculiar to human beings (or for that matter, female human beings).

Viewing the good life as the rational life means, of course, that the best life is the pursuit of philosophy, but rationality as the standard for good living is not limited to this implication. Plato's meritocracy in the *Republic* is built on the idea that humans are essentially rational creatures. Rational abilities or talents are dispersed among human beings in such a way that some individuals will be good at philosophy, some at carpentry, some at music, some at medicine. Hence, an individual's natural (read: rational) place is performing the task she or he does best. If only because of the variety of role choice, Plato's view is superior to that of Freud and others who thought there was something unnatural about and wrong with women who did not want to devote their lives to men and children. Of course, Plato would have thought there was something unnatural about and wrong with a woman (or a man) who was good at playing the tuba and didn't want to do it.

Perhaps sex roles do not need Plato to liberate them from the concept of nature for this is a task already (and finally) accomplished. Conventional sex roles used to be considered natural; today, conventional sex roles are considered conventional. Nonetheless, it may be worth noting that had Plato's view prevailed (rather than those of Aristotle, Aquinas, or Freud), the long fight for equal opportunity could have been largely avoided. Still, Plato's framework does not permit free choice with respect to social role; it merely expands the number of roles available to women that count as natural and makes life happier for those who are inclined to do whatever it is they are good at.

Some women are good at philosophy. They, along with the men who are similarly talented, should rule the State. Despite Plato's clarity on this point in the *Republic,* many feminist commentators still feel excluded from the philosophic life by the ties between philosophy and male homoeroticism that pervade the *Symposium* and the *Phaedrus.* Jean Bethke Elshtain's views are a case in point:

> [Plato's] debarment of women from the search for wisdom can be explained both by the social milieu within which the search occurred, including its sanctioned homoerotic attachments between older and younger men, as well as the particular *nature* of the truth at which Plato aimed. That is, a particular homosexual ethos, framed within a society rife with fear of, and repugnance towards, women, especially Mother, fused with what we call the Platonic metaphysic.[6]

Elshtain's position is presented by Bluestone as the most vicious and extreme against Plato insofar as she claims that Plato's substantive conclusions were "infected" by the homoerotic as part of the process of acquiring knowledge[7] and that "platonic metaphysics *in its very nature* excludes women."[8]

In truth, platonic metaphysics in its very nature excludes heterosexuals. Throughout the *Symposium* and the *Phaedrus* the eros which is required for the achievement of knowledge is homosexual. For Plato, reality consists of an eternal, changeless world of Forms of which the physical world is a mere copy. The particulars of our changing, material world (somehow) participate in the forms or essences or perfect exemplars of these particular things. In order to know these perfect exemplars, one must follow a certain process. We cannot, for example, know the Form of the Beautiful without first experiencing beautiful things. A key step in the ascent of knowledge is homosexual attraction. As Plato explains in the *Symposium,* the male philosopher begins by gazing upon beautiful boys. He goes on to contemplate beautiful souls and pursuits. Finally, the intense and powerful erotic charge of homosexuality is diverted from physical completion and the erotic energy is transferred from physical intimacy to an insight into imperishable beauty. As Michael Ruse puts it so nicely, "So, finally, having restrained ourselves in the physical (genital) realm, we come to be rewarded by what is almost literally a philosophical orgasm. As in the physical world, at the moment of climax we get a real sense of oneness with everything."[9] There is no reason that an analogous story cannot be told about women since platonic metaphysics does not in its nature exclude women. It does, however, require lesbian eroticism as a first step in the ascent of knowledge.

Even a critic as sympathetic to Plato as Bluestone is disturbed by his emphasis on the necessity of homoeroticism; she counters

Elshtain's infection thesis by arguing that homosexual eros is "only one devise among many."[10] Elshtain, she says, is "mistaken in her belief that homoeroticism is the only, or the chief, or in any sense, an essential element in the doctrine itself."[11] Bluestone maintains further that homosexual attraction has a "metaphorical function"[12] and that although the substitution of heterosexual eros would "detract from the particularity of a special ethos"[13] when the *Symposium* is considered as literature, when the *Symposium* is considered as philosophy just such a substitution can and usually has been made. Generations of Platonists have seen themselves as "followers of a doctrine essentially separable from . . . Athenian homosexual practice."[14] Quoting K. J. Dover approvingly to the effect that Plato *exploited* the homosexual ethos, Bluestone concludes that it is both possible and advisable "to consider Plato's theories independent of his . . . sexual preference."[15]

But the *Symposium* and the *Phaedrus* are not ambiguous on this point: homoeroticism is an essential element in the lover's upward path to the form of beauty. I will argue that Plato's choice of homosexuality over heterosexuality as the model for the ascent toward the knowledge of beauty is crucial, since it reflects his understanding of the nature of that ascent. First, however, I want to call attention to the clear and absolutely straightforward claims that Plato makes about hetero- and homosexuality and their relationship to knowledge and reality. He says that heterosexual eros is, from the point of view of metaphysics, i.e., knowing the forms, a dead end. Heterosexual eros is second-rate; it leads to making babies, not to philosophical achievement. In 211c *Symposium* Plato says, "So when someone rises by these stages, through loving boys correctly . . . This is what it is to go aright . . . "[16]

Susan Moller Okin is correct in her interpretation of Plato that the procreation of the soul which leads to poems, laws, and thoughts is achieved only in homosexual love and that homosexual love is a superior type of love. Even though she finds these views to be hostile to heterosexuality and to women,[17] Okin rejects efforts by Gregory Vlastos to temper Plato's devaluation of heterosexuality by labelling the very use of the image of procreation "a heterosexual paradigm." She says, "if [Vlastos] is implying . . . that there is any inclusion of heterosexuality in the theory of the higher type of love, his conclusion is unfounded. In spite of Plato's use of an image that, as Vlastos says, has 'a heterosexual paradigm,' it is clearly only the symbolic version of procreation—that of the spirit, which is only achieved in homosexual love—that is thought worthy of philosophical treatment."[18]

Okin is exactly right on this point; Plato is not espousing here—as Bluestone has suggested—some abstract notion of the erotic attraction and fecundity of minds which can be applied to any pair of lovers. Such a view misses completely the importance of the fact that a man's love is for one *like himself*. And though Bluestone, to her credit, admits lesbian attraction as a possible application of the abstract notion she takes to be Plato's, she still wants to include as well the possibility of some idealized heterosexual attraction, agreeing with Erich Segal that Dante's love for Beatrice is a "distinct parallel."[19] Elshtain and Okin are more accurate in arguing the necessity of homoeroticism to Plato's metaphysics, but they both infer wrongly that that eroticism must be male. Okin, in a statement reminiscent of Elshtain, says, "It is quite clear . . . that Plato's vision of love as a pathway to philosophic joy entirely excludes women."[20] Apparently, both Elshtain and Okin are following in the footsteps of Queen Victoria; for them, lesbians do not exist.

Thus current feminist criticism splits between views denying the importance of homoeroticism in Plato in order to include women in a conventionally acceptable way and views insisting on the necessity of homoeroticism but finding that it bars women from philosophy. Both sides of this unbefitting rift are heterosexist in their assumptions in that they make marginal or invisible the gay experience Plato took to be central. As we will see, feminist critics have reasons for thinking Plato's criteria for excellence sexist quite apart from the homoeroticism issue, but before looking at any of these, I want to present what I think is Plato's view on sexuality and knowledge.

Plato disapproved of sexual activity—whether heterosexual or homosexual— solely for the purpose of physical orgasm. But sexual activity is nevertheless important because knowledge of higher types of beauty is not obtainable without the lower level insights into beauty which sex provides. Its primary importance, according to Ellen Shapiro, is to establish the manner by which we know the Form. The reason homosexual experience initiates the ascent is because of its unique ability to provide human beings with a method of knowing analogous to the manner in which beauty is known.[21] The Form is known by acquaintance or direct experience—something very much like what Bertrand Russell called knowledge by acquaintance: "We shall say that we have *acquaintance* with anything of which we are directly aware, without the intermediary of any process of inference . . . things immediately known to me just as they are."[22] Homosexual experience best demonstrates the epistemological requirements for the ascent to knowing Beauty; it can provide the type of knowledge needed whereas heterosexual experience cannot.

The idea of beauty in the *Symposium* is not an abstract logical entity; it is absolutely and divinely beautiful, " . . . a love object par excellence . . . a paradigm Form so splendidly and shamelessly self-exemplifying that its own beauty outshines that of everything else."[23] The soul "throbs with ferment" and experiences a "strange sweating and fever" when it encounters (or better, recollects) the Form. Dover is getting at the connection between the direct experience of physical beauty and the direct experience of the Form when he says, "Why eros should play so conspicuous a part in a metaphysical system is not so obvious, but the most succinct explanation is to be found in *Phdr.* 250D, where it is observed that beauty is the only one, of those things . . . 'attracting eros,' which can be directly perceived by the senses so that the sight of something beautiful affords by far the most powerful and immediate access we have to the world of being."[24]

Plato claims that the Form of Beauty is itself beautiful. The self-predicative nature of beauty suggests the suitability of a particular way of knowing, namely, knowledge by acquaintance. Knowledge by description, to use another of Russell's terms, involves knowing that an object has a certain property, though the object itself is not directly known. It is clear from what Plato says that this is not the kind of knowledge one has of beauty. Beauty cannot be separated into constituents and known as a compilation of specific properties. " . . . it is not beautiful in part and ugly in part, nor beautiful at one time and ugly at another, nor beautiful in this relation and ugly in that, nor beautiful here and ugly there . . . "[25] Beauty is a self-referential whole, and to be known it must be experienced as such.

What are the epistemological features of homoeroticism that make it a standard for a method of knowing which in turn enables us to ascend to higher types of love? Simone de Beauvoir, in a passage on lesbian love, discusses relevant epistemological differences between homosexuality and heterosexuality that Plato saw before her:

> It is most important to emphasize the fact that refusal to make herself the object is not always what turns woman to homosexuality; most lesbians, on the contrary, seek to cultivate the treasures of their femininity. To be willing to be changed into a passive object is not to renounce all claim to subjectivity; woman

hopes in this way to find self-realization under the aspect of herself as a thing; but then she will be trying to find herself in her otherness, her alterity. When alone she does not succeed in really creating her double; if she caresses her own bosom, she still does not know how her breasts seem to a strange hand, nor how they are felt to react under a strange hand; a man can reveal to her the existence of her flesh for herself—that is to say, as she herself perceives it, but not what it is to others. It is only when her fingers trace the body of a woman whose fingers in turn trace her body that the miracle of the mirror is accomplished. Between man and woman love is an act; each torn from self becomes other: what fills the woman in love with wonder is that the languourous passivity of her flesh should be reflected in the male's impetuosity; the narcissistic woman, however, recognizes her enticements but dimly in the man's erected flesh. Between women love is contemplative; caresses are intended less to gain possession of the other than gradually to recreate the self through her; separateness is abolished, there is no struggle, no victory, no defeat; in exact reciprocity each is at once subject and object, sovereign and slave; duality becomes mutuality.[26]

In homosexual experience, separateness is abolished. The knowledge of the beloved, of how she is aroused, is not inferred because the experience of the lovers is, as de Beauvoir puts it, exactly reciprocal. The subject-object distinction breaks down: the miracle of the mirror. That image of a mirror was used by Plato to depict an important characteristic of homosexual relationships in the *Phaedrus* account of the special happiness that comes to lovers who—after much struggle—resist lust in favor of a life of philosophy together:

> He feels a desire, like the lover's yet not so strong, to behold, to touch, to kiss him, to share his couch: and now ere long the desire, as one might guess, leads to the act. So when they lie side by side, the wanton horse of the lover's soul would have a word with the charioteer, claiming a little guerdon for all his trouble. The like steed in the soul of the beloved has no word to say, but, swelling with desire for he knows not what, embraces and kisses the lover, in grateful acknowledgment of all his kindness. And when they lie by one another, he is minded not to refuse to do his part in gratifying his lover's entreaties; yet his yoke-fellow in turn, being moved by reverence and heedfulness, joins with the driver in resisting. And so, if the victory be won by the higher elements of mind guiding them into the ordered rule of the philosophic life, their days on earth will be blessed with happiness and concord.[27]

But that this swelling and calming of passion is more than physical attraction to some other is clear from Plato's account of the dawning of attraction: "so he loves, yet knows not what he loves: he does not understand, he cannot tell what has come upon him . . . he cannot account for it, not realizing that his lover is as it were a mirror in which he beholds himself."[28] The lover is aware of beauty in the same manner as he is aware of his own existence.

By contrast, heterosexual relationships—at their best—oscillate between subject and object. (At their worst, men are always subjects and women are always objects.) With respect to arousal, a woman knows that her lover desires her, but she does not know this directly. She infers it from his erected flesh, from his behavior. He may tell her so in words. But her experience must always be different and separate from his.

Homoeroticism provides the foundation for acquaintance with Beauty because the immediacy in homosexual encounters is akin to the way in which Beauty is known. Still, as Shapiro notes, it might be objected that the only genuine acquaintance or genuine knowledge is of the Forms, i.e., that knowledge of erotic properties is not really knowledge. We might then, she suggests, characterize homoeroticism as a kind of "psychological preparation" for genuine knowledge by acquaintance that will make possible the recollection of Beauty. It is clear that Plato intends that sexuality be the starting point for the ascent, and heterosexuality cannot provide the appropriate preparation because heterosexual "knowledge" of erotic properties must always be inferential.

Even if Plato's talk about homoeroticism is just talk about an image, a metaphor, an analogy or a model for knowledge, one must get one's images (or whatever) right. Evelyn Fox Keller, who compares various paradigms for knowledge in Western thought, takes this view. For Plato, she says, knowledge is a kind of communion—"a spiritual coupling between mind and form—a union of kindred essences."[29] Says Keller, "Plato's model for spiritual begetting is the love of man for man . . . the union of mind with 'the essential nature of things' is a union of like with like; accordingly, it is taken for granted throughout the *Symposium* and the *Phaedrus* 'that eros which is significant as a step towards the world of being is homosexual.' "[30] When Baconian science in the Renaissance invokes "a new set of images; homoerotic union is superseded by heterosexual conquest."[31] Our understanding of understanding shifts "with the shift from male to female object."[32] Nature is female for both Plato and Bacon but in the first instance she is abandoned, in the second, "seduced and conquered."[33] Since Plato clearly recognized (in Book V of the *Republic*) that women could be philosophers, the most we can conclude from this abandonment view is that being a philosopher requires that females (and males) forsake feminine characteristics associated with the earth in favor of abstractions associated with the masculine. But Keller thinks that Plato's conception of knowledge is not merely masculine, but male for she characterizes the Platonic Forms as "a rarefied distillate of male sexuality."[34] It is difficult to know what Keller means by this because none of the elements of Plato's model she emphasizes—the reciprocity, the importance of like with like, the lack of aggression, the egalitarian factors—in principle exclude women. She could mean that only men are erotically attracted by abstractions, but, of course, this is not true.

Still, Elshtain, Okin and Keller all feel excluded in some way by the homoerotic atmosphere of the dialogues. Only Elshtain and Okin, however, express anger at the exclusion, connect love in the *Symposium* with the belittling of women,[35] and attribute Plato's misogyny (in part) to his homosexuality. But women are neither excluded in theory from becoming philosophers or excluded in principle from participating in the process of knowing. Such points should not be lost on philosophers, i.e., those who normally value more highly matters of theory than practice. Why then the accusations by some feminists that Plato's criteria for excellence are sexist?

Plato in fact included women in the pursuit of philosophy, but only some women. He included those with exceptional intellectual gifts who also were devoted to masculine or manly values such as abstract thought and the rational control of passion. For Plato's academic world was not so very different from the contemporary one. Few women attended his Academy; one who did wore men's clothing. The historical existence of Diotima, the author of Socrates's speech on love in the *Symposium,* is questionable. As Elizabeth Spelman puts the point so nicely, "Misogyny has always been compatible with having high regard for 'exceptional' (and surely for imaginary) women."[36] Spelman focuses on the fact that Plato favors women who can be philosophers—that is, women who can be like the ideal man—and shows the typical Athenian woman—secretive, gossipy, and emotional—as the model of what to avoid. Men who act like the typical woman, Plato warns in the *Timaeus,* will be punished by becoming a woman in their next life. Although Plato was not impressed by the typical man either, he did not make continual derogatory remarks about them, the cumulative effect of

which is to make it harder for members of the disparaged class—
exceptional or typical—to gain equal respect with those who are
not similarly discredited. A variety of recent studies show that
academic women get less for their achievements even when their
achievements are objectively equal to men's.[37] In one such study,
for example, psychology chairs judged credentials accompanied by a
female name to be one rank lower than identical credentials accompanied by a male name.[38]

Plato's commitment to the so-called masculine virtue of abstract thought also implies much more than might first appear.
Luce Irigaray interprets Plato's attachment to reason as a denial of
the importance of our birth or, presumably, of giving birth, a denial
of our physical origin.[39] Birth, which is a non-rational event and the
beginning of a process of becoming can be conceptually obliterated
in a scheme that recognizes only eternal forms as real. Interestingly, recollection allows a philosopher to bypass birth and becoming altogether, for to recollect the forms is to join the realm of being
where one existed before birth:

> The recollection of "intelligibles" thus takes one back before the
> material, matrical conception. It is a matter to be settled "man to
> man." Really man to man? Where, in that case, is the mother? . . .
> Thoughts on divine truth are available to man only when he has
> left *behind* everything that still linked him to this sensible world
> that the earth, the mother, represents.[40]

Irigaray's point that the world of Forms rejects the material world
reiterates Keller's that for Plato the feminine "Nature" was to be
overcome and left behind. In Plato's thinking are perhaps still echoes of the great Earth Mother/Sky Father cultural struggle that
had occupied the Mediterranean world for centuries; and feminists
who argue that some "earth-connectedness" is central to their philosophy might ultimately find this rejection of the physical more
disturbing in Plato than any gender-typing of virtues. Thus, the anger is coming from different sources: some from those who find ob-
noxious the way in which the idea of the exceptional woman works
in society and in the academy; some from those who see mothers
rejected; some from those who extol the feminine and "earthy"
virtues; and some from those who in their implicit or explicit het-
erosexism take heterosexuality to be the norm.

Those commentators such as Elshtain, Okin and Irigaray who
fail to see that women are capable of Platonic knowledge because

they are capable of homoerotic relations are heterosexist even if they raise interesting points vis-à-vis Plato's idealism or other aspects of his epistemology. Those commentators like Bluestone who say that sexual preference does not matter to how we view reality trivialize the role that gay experience can play as a model for conceptions of knowledge. Keller is right in her view that alternative sexual models modify those conceptions of knowledge and of the relationship of mind to nature. Feminists should take the lead in exploring what new visions become available "[i]f we open up our ways of knowing and of sanctifying knowledge to understandings that are rooted in the phenomenology of being gay or lesbian in the world."[41]

At the very least the time has come for those who teach and write commentaries on Plato in the 1990s be more truthful. For generations Plato commentators have written and philosophy professors have taught or implied by their silence that platonic love is heterosexual and spiritual whereas, in fact, it is homosexual and quite physical. It is hoped that those who have worked hard to rid the pre-1970 Plato scholarship of its sexism will be particularly sensitive to the entrenched efforts in Plato scholarship to obliterate gay experience.

Notes

1. Some of the ideas in this paper were developed in correspondence with Ellen Shapiro in the late 1970s. In particular, the line of argument pursued in pages 31–34 was first suggested to me by her in "The Epistemological Significance of Homosexuality in Plato (*Symposium* and *Phaedrus*)," unpublished manuscript, Trinity College, 1977.

2. Natalie Harris Bluestone, *Women and the Ideal Society: Plato's Republic and Modern Myths of Gender.* Amherst: University of Massachusetts Press, 1987.

3. Summaries and examples of Bluestone's types are taken from her text, pp. 23–73. See also Christine Pierce, "Equality: *Republic* V, *The Monist,* 57.1, January 1973.

4. Ernest Barker, *The Political Thought of Plato and Aristotle,* New York: Russell and Russell, 1959; first published in 1906; reprinted as "Communism in Plato's *Republic*," in *Plato's Republic, Interpretation and Criticism,* ed. by Alexander Sesonske, Belmont: Wadsworth Publishing Company, 1966, 1968, p. 88.

5. Richard Nettleship, *Lectures on the Republic of Plato,* London: Macmillan and Co., Ltd., 1967, p. 173.

6. Jean Bethke Elshtain, *Public Man, Private Woman: Women in Social and Political Thought,* Princeton: Princeton University Press, 1981, p. 27.

7. Bluestone, p. 141.

8. Bluestone, p. 140.

9. Michael Ruse, *Homosexuality,* Oxford: Basil Blackwell, 1988, p. 181.

10. Bluestone, p. 146.

11. Bluestone, p. 141.

12. Bluestone, p. 146.

13. Bluestone, p. 146.

14. Bluestone, p. 141.

15. Bluestone, p. 144.

16. *Symposium,* 211c. Translated by Alexander Nehamas and Paul Woodruff, Indianapolis: Hackett Publishing Company, 1989, p. 59.

17. Susan Moller Okin, *Women in Western Political Thought,* Princeton: Princeton University Press, 1979, p. 25.

18. Okin, p. 25.

19. Bluestone, p. 142.

20. Okin, p. 25.

21. This is Shapiro's argument referred to in my introductory note. I am also indebted to her for pointing out the similarities between Plato and Simone de Beauvoir and the suggestiveness of Bertrand Russell's teminology for determining what Plato is getting at.

22. Bertrand Russell, *The Problems of Philosophy,* NY: Oxford University Press, 1959, pp. 46, 47.

23. Gregory Vlastos, "The Individual as an Object of Love in Plato," *Platonic Studies,* Princeton: Princeton University Press, 1973, p. 24.

24. K. J. Dover, *Greek Homosexuality,* Cambridge: Harvard University Press, 1978, p. 164.

25. *The Symposium* 211A, translated by Walter Hamilton, London, Penguin Books, 1951, p. 93.

26. Simone de Beauvoir, *The Second Sex,* NY: Bantam Books, 1961, p. 391.

27. *Phaedrus,* 255E, 256A, translated by R. Hackforth, NY: Bobbs-Merrill, 1952, pp. 105, 106.

28. *Phaedrus,* 255D, Hackforth, p. 105.

29. Evelyn Fox Keller, *Reflections on Gender and Sciences,* New Haven: Yale University Press, 1985, p. 27.

30. Keller, p. 24 quoting Dover, 1978, p. 162.

31. Keller, p. 31.

32. Keller, p. 30.

33. Keller, p. 31.

34. Keller, p. 30.

35. Bluestone, p. 145.

36. Elizabeth V. Spelman, *Inessential Woman: Problems of Exclusion in Feminist Thought,* Boston: Beacon Press, 1988, p. 30.

37. Virginia Valian, "The Evaluation of Women in Academia," unpublished manuscript, Hunter College, 1989.

38. L. S. Fidell, "Empirical Verification of Sex Discrimination in Hiring Practices in Psychology," in R. K. Unger and F. L. Denmark, editors, *Woman: Dependent or Independent Variable?* New York: Psychological Dimensions, Inc., 1975, pp. 774–782.

39. Luce Irigaray, *Speculum of the Other Woman,* trans. Gillian C. Gill, Ithaca: Cornell University Press, 1985. See pp. 246–247, 311, 352 as well as those cited in note 39.

40. Irigaray, pp. 317, 339.

41. Laura S. Brown, "New Voices and Visions: Toward a Lesbian/ Gay Paradigm for Psychology," Presidential Address, American Psychological Association, Atlanta, August 1988.

Feminist Dialectics: Plato and Dualism

Judith Genova

But if he failed in attaining this, at the second birth he would pass into a woman, and if, when in that state of being, he did not desist from evil, he would continually be changed into some brute. . . . [1]

Then there is no pursuit of the administrators of a state that belongs to a woman because she is a woman or to a man because he is a man. But the natural capacities are distributed alike among both creatures, and women naturally share in all pursuits and men in all—yet for all the woman is weaker than the man.[2]

Feminist philosophers and political theorists are having their difficulties with Plato.[3] Where does he stand on the question of the equality of women? On one hand, he is one of the few Western philosophers to recognize that sex is an irrelevant variable in the distribution of the Greek virtues of wisdom, courage, temperance and justice. In the famous passages of Book V of the *Republic,* he dramatically announces that women should be educated just like men and acknowledges the possibility of philosopher-queens. Throughout the Dialogues, truth and all the virtues are referred to as female and Goddesses invariably appear as the source of wisdom. Wendy Brown is so struck by this female coding of knowledge that she argues that Plato's vision of philosophy and the philosophical life undermines the agonistic masculine values of Greek society.[4] On the other hand, Plato continually adds that women are by nature weaker, less rational and ultimately a punishment for a soul's living less than a righteous life. Moreover, despite the place of honor accorded to some women like Diotima, women are excluded from the daily life of the polis and more importantly, for Plato, from the possibility of being lovers of beauty or wisdom. But, how can this be? How are men and women both equal and not equal? Why does Plato give with one hand what he takes away with the other?

Generally speaking, the majority of interpreters seem to settle for a deep-seated ambivalence on Plato's part as if logic and theory

41

pulled him one way, while culture and tradition pulled the other way. They tend to couple this with a tacit belief that if he had his choice he would argue for the equality of women. My reading of his works, however, sees a different dynamic. As I hope to show, women can never be the equal of men for Plato. Rather, femaleness, in his ontology, is a curse, the source of evil, chaos and dissolution. She is difference, otherness; an other who will never be the one or even the equal of man.[5] She is, by nature for Plato, antithetical to the life of reason and philosophy, even as she is the very condition of that life. While he educates her and argues that logically nothing prevents woman from equalling man, he never really believes this. Why does he bother with her at all then? I shall come to this question in time.

To see that Plato is no champion of women, one must turn from a reading of his political beliefs to a reading of his metaphysics and epistemology. All too often, political theorists fail to ground their understanding of his politics in his metaphysics resulting in the kind of confusion that surrounds Plato's ideas about women. Moreover, failure to understand how Platonic dialectics affects later ontologies, most notably, Hegel's understanding of the self-other dialectic, led no less a thinker than Simone de Beauvoir to wonder why Hegel's self/other dialectic broke down when it came to women, causing women always to be cast in the role of other.[6] She was stymied by the fact that the expected reciprocity between self and other never occurs in the relations between men and women. To the extent that Hegel's dialectics leans on Plato's, it becomes possible to see why otherness becomes the defining condition of women in this self/other dynamic. Given its long range effects on Western philosophy, one must finally recognize that only by overcoming Platonic dialectics and the philosophical/theological tradition it founded can women find equality and their potential as philosopher-queens.

The reading of Plato's ontology must begin with Pythagoras's famous table of opposites whose teaching Plato incorporated into his own:

Limit (péras)	Unlimited (ápeiron)
Odd (perittón)	Even ('ártion)
One (hén)	Multitude (plêthos)
Right (déxion)	Left (aristerón)
Male (árrehēn)	Female (thêlu)
Resting (eremoûn)	Moving (kinoúmenon)
Straight (euthú)	Twisted (kampulón)

Light (phōs)	Darkness (skótos)
Good (agathón)	Bad (kakón)
Square	Oblong
(tetrágōnon)	(heteromekes)[7]

For Plato and Pythagoras before him, the first pair of opposites, that between the Limited and the Unlimited, named the fundamental principles of all things. The other pairs of opposites were determined by the first and essentially functioned to name the basic dichotomous character of the world. Plato used different names in the dialogues to refer to this first, fundamental pair, "Limit and Unlimited," the "One and the Many" or the "One and Indefinite Dyad, also known as "the Great and the Small". Cosmologically the world is generated from the interaction of these two principles and ontologically the world is constituted by them.

In embracing Pythagorean dualism, Plato is rejecting the ontologies of two earlier thinkers: the pluralism (or apparent pluralism) of Heraclitus's ontology and the monism of Parmenides's ontology. For my purposes, this dualism seems to recognize the need for both the male and female in the founding and maintaining of the universe. The world would not be without the Indefinite Dyad, without the female. Hence, one might come to believe that in a dualistic ontology, the male and female are equally important and that the best state of the individual, the world or the state is when there is a balance of these two forces. Arleen Saxonhouse, for example, is taken in by this surface equality: "The Greek intellect is characterized by its penchant for dichotomization; division and classification run through both Plato's and Aristotle's works, but the diacritical method is moderated by an awareness of interdependence; public depends on private, as private depends on public . . . And so it is with the male and the female as well."[8] Yet, as it is important to see, these two principles were never of equal importance for Plato and balance between them was never the goal of either the harmonious individual, state, or cosmos.

First, that the female is not equal should be obvious from the association of the female with the bad, the dark, and, in general, with the world of Becoming, instead of the world of Being, the light and the good: "It [the table of opposites] is in the first place through and through axiological: the members on one side are 'good', on the other 'bad'. And the good members are in the main characterized by definiteness of nature and structure, while the bad are indefinite, sprawling, patternless, inchoate".[9] This statement points out not only the asymmetrical evaluation of the pair, but also begins to explain the reasons behind this asymmetry. The female is evil because she is indefinite, an unknown quantity. Her negative moral position is a function of her lack of fixed qualities. To be is to be something, some one thing, and thus to have some shape or other. Moreover, it is to be this something forever; if it changes then it becomes unclear what it really is. The Unlimited, however, is everything and nothing. It is a morass of qualities and determinations which as yet have no form. It is in movement and darkness since nothing is distinct. One gets the feeling that Plato would surely like to do without it; but, he cannot since no other ontology could explain both the simultaneous existence of the world of becoming and the possibility of knowledge which depended on the world of Being.

The key to understanding their unequal value is in their ontological roles and operation. In the *Philebus,* for example, The Unlimited provides an infinite continuum and thus always admits of more or less, and possibly excess and deficiency. Symbolically, Plato names the principle "The Great and the Small" to stand for all such continua. The limit is characterized by discrete, shaped and definite qualities allowing one to speak of things in its domain as equal, double "and any term expressing a ratio of one number to another, or one unit of measurement to another . . . "[10] The creation of all good and beautiful things is a result of the imposition of limit on the unlimited. Music, grammar, science, all systems of sense making, knowledge, are a result of the control of the Unlimited by the Limited. Knowledge and reason, the ability to say anything depends on the suppression of the Unlimited, female principle. She is the source of error and contradiction. Stable objects of knowledge are provided by the transformation of the irrational, relative continuum of more or less into the rational, determinate and definite, that which has shape and therefore limits. Without this shaping by the male, all would be chaos and knowledge would be impossible. Measurement cannot take place in the domain of the unlimited. The dual must always duel. This is no reign of equals.

To get a better grasp of what is being said, one can imagine an infinite domain, for example, of sound. Reason, in the form of Pythagorean ratios, delimits the possible harmonious, good sounds and calls this system music. The question, how does one know that the cuts and divisions made by these ratios are the true and good ones?, is circumvented by having a god, Theuth, the same God who discovered writing in the *Phaedrus,*[11] make the original divisions of nature.[12] The task of dialectics is to discover these proper ratios, to cut nature at her proper joints and thus obtain absolute and certain knowledge.[13] Other possibilities, shown by the music of other cultures or even contemporary Western music (Twelve tone scale) are eliminated given the Pythagorean method for obtaining the scale. They are noise, not music. All these other possibilities are contained in the infinite continuum of the Unlimited which is never used up but remains as a surplus and a continual threat to the sense systems erected by man. Things may be otherwise than the way our latest theories hold them to be; there are other possibilities, other ways of articulating the structure of nature. It is this thought that is most threatening and demands the suppression of the female.

The One, limited and odd, is the active member of the pair creating things by limiting the unlimited and making it a definite something. Things come to be through its action. They can be counted and measured. Aristotle took this to the literal level in biology by seeing the male as the creator of the child and the female as simply the petri dish. It is absolutely wrong to see these principles in a Yin and Yang fashion, each contributing their part in making a balanced androgynous whole: "Plato uses the feminine not because he cares about women as such, but because the feminine as part of human nature puts limitations on the masculine and allows for the creativity that the male alone lacks".[14] The female does not limit the male, nor is she the active, creative principle. The limit is male and brings order, rationality, meaning. It literally orders the limitless, the infinite and makes things be and then knowable. Thus, their roles are unequal. She is needed, but only as a foil for the One's actions, as something to act upon.

Later, Aristotle, depending most on the *Timaeus* will call this principle, matter. But for Plato, she is not quite matter or body yet. In the *Timaeus,* he refers to her as first the receptacle (hypodochē), then the nurse (tithēnē) of all being,[15] and then a few paragraphs later as space (chōra).[16] In this more mythical Dialogue, Plato openly likens this receptacle to the mother and the forms or intelligible principles to the father.[17] The scene of family metaphors which has been hiding behind the scene of abstract mathematical ones comes to the fore. In his own distinctive voice, Derrida draws the political consequences of her absence while reminding us of her continued presence: "It is all about fathers and sons, about bastards unaided by any public assistance, about glorious, legitimate sons, about inheritance, sperm, sterility. Nothing is said of the mother, but this will not be held against us. And if one looks hard enough as in those pictures in which a second picture faintly can be made out, one might be able to discern her unstable form, drawn upside-down in the foliage, at the back of the garden". [18] Her absence is guaranteed by her role in this scene. She can have no lines to speak since the main quality of the receptacle is that it must have no qualities, no characteristics of its own so that that which is to be made, the child, may more easily receive its pattern from the forms (eídēa). It must be as Luce Irigaray notes a great mirror, featureless in itself, yet able to take on all shapes: "Properly speaking, one can't say that she mimics anything for that would suppose a certain intention, a project, a minimum of consciousness. She (is) pure mimicry. Which is always the case for inferior species, of course. Needed to define essences, her function requires that she herself have no definition".[19] Ultimately, she remains for Plato incomprehensible and mysterious.[20]

The dialogue which best demonstrates the asymmetry of Plato's dualism is the *The Sophist*.[21] Under cover of wondering whether the sophist, statesmen and philosopher are three distinct kinds of beings, Plato poses the question of whether the principles of the universe are one, two or three. (If one includes the specter of the Gods raised in the opening sections, one can also include the possibility that they are four.) Ironically, however, the names "Limit and Unlimited" or any of their variations are never mentioned in this dialogue. Instead, Plato talks about forms, not first principles of Being. Yet, the discussion of the operation of these forms mimics those of the ontological elements so closely that one is entitled to read the drama enacted here as yet another statement of the interaction of the principles.

The forms in question are Being, or that which is or exists, the Same, and the Different or Other. In the process of answering his question, the first possibility that Plato eliminates is that the principles are three or a Heraclitean plurality. He does this by understanding the pair, same/different as another instance of the Indefinite Dyad. Accordingly, the choices reduce to two, or the opposition between Being (The Limited) and the Indefinite Dyad of The Same and the Different (Unlimited or Non-being). The question, then, becomes what is the nature and status of the Unlimited?

Plato's first discovery is that in order for us to discourse about anything and in order that falsity in both thought and speech be possible, non-being or that which is not, must in some sense be. In arguing that non-being must be, Plato rehearses an Oedipal conflict as he openly talks of patricide against Father Parmenides.[22] Parmenides was philosophy's first and most stubborn monist. He argued that non-being could in no sense be and that one could only speak of that which is, Being, the one. Much as he may have wanted to be a simple, straightforward monist, Plato recognized all the impossibilities of this position. First there are the logical problems that Parmenides cannot consistently speak of Being, pure unity, as one, that is, as a number, or as a whole, without admitting that there is something besides Being. Parmenides' speech, then, is at odds with itself. More generally, what Plato discovers is that if Being did not mix with other forms then nothing at all would be what it is. All discourse would be impossible. Accordingly, he concludes that there must be a plurality of forms and that they blend with one another.

His second and perhaps more important discovery is that there must be a logic, or structure to this blending; it must have a lawlike, rule-governed pattern detectable by reason. The goal of Dialectic or the science of the free is to discover this structure of how and which forms blend with one another. Because of this structure, which of course is eternal, the world is knowable. Dialectics is the method developed by Plato to guide reason in its discovery of the structure of the world. To know this structure is to know, have the truth, about the world.

As he begins to give the first example of the logic of blending, however, he discovers that in order to be able to count forms, that is to speak of a plurality of forms, he must be able to distinguish them from each other, that is to speak of one form as being the same as itself and different from other forms. He needs, in short, the forms of Sameness and Difference. But, as it turns out, to speak of something as different is to speak of that which is other than what is; it is then to speak of non-being, what is not. As Plato notes, that which is not is necessary if we are to recognize something as being what it is. Something is the same as itself only against the possibility that it may be other than itself. Sameness and otherness are relative. It is because we can say that x is different from y, that y is y and vice-versa. All forms partake of sameness and difference. Being needs otherness, difference. The dyad, Same/Different, then, becomes a way of talking about that which is not without supposing a form or category of non-being. Plato is thus able to uphold Parmenides dictum that Being alone is while at the same time arguing that non-being is in some sense.

At this point, it looks as if Being and Difference are equal cooperative factors in the production of discourse. Each thing is at the same time, the same as itself and other than other things. However, as we might have expected from seeing how the Unlimited is treated in the other dialogues, their equality is quickly compromised.

First, the analysis of non-being does not give it its own equally powerful domain; rather, in deference to Parmenides, Plato insists that non-being is not the contrary of being, but only that which is different from being. The other is not its own independent principle, but relative to what is. Its function is to reflect what is. The different is parasitic on the one and the same. Secondly, difference brings into the world the possibility of deception, falsehood, and chaos. The infinite distinctions it makes possible threaten to overwhelm all measures and rob us of the possibility of universal claims and thus the possibility of certain knowledge. Once again, otherness must be controlled, shaped and mastered. The other is the condition of discourse, but never the subject. Father Parmenides is not killed in this dialogue or anywhere in the Platonic corpus; he is just made to share an uneasy bed with Pythagoras. The principles are two, but one is always more important than the other, than two. As Plato might put it when he plays with Pythagorean number mysticism, 2 is only 1 + 1, the addition of two identical units, two unities, nothing more. It is unity or the one that is the more fundamental. The pair of unities, when looked at as the dyad, however, is something wholly different; it is indefinite and because it is infinitely divisible, dangerous. The different, the other may be necessary, but it is a necessary evil. Everything must be done to contain its power and render it tame. This includes educating the other's material presence in the world; namely, women. Earlier I posed the question, why does Plato even bother to educate women and say that they can be equal with man? The answer lies in the continued need for the one to control the other. Education, as Plato constantly reminds us, can have two conflicting goals: to liberate or to subjugate. I suspect that he was educating men for the former and women for the latter.

In answer to his original question in the *Sophist:* Are the principles of the universe one, two, or three, Plato answers two; but since the unlimited is but a shadow of the one, the answer is really one. And that one is male.

An unasked question that has been lurking in the background now asserts itself: Why does the male become associated with the limit and the good and the female with the unlimited and the bad in the first place? To answer that question, one would have to go back to another beginning. By the time of the Pythagorean table (sixth century B.C.), these connections are already solidified. The answer lies deep in myth, legend and cultural idiosyncrasies. One might try to make some sense of it by noting such things as that the female gives birth and is the symbol for plentitude and fullness. He is barren, alone, isolated; the odd phenomenon. She is many; she is two and multiple. One must control nature's production or it will get out of hand. On the whole, however, the answers are not philosophically interesting. Nothing about this ontology has seemed very rational anyway, despite its abstract, mathematical quality. Arbitrary, mythical decisions seem to guide fates. One can start only with the table and see how it has determined a history. For the philosopher, Derrida, this amounts to discovering how Platonic philosophy transforms mythos into logos; that is, how it rationalizes an earlier wisdom/ignorance and institutionalizes its beliefs on a new basis.[23] Dualism has never given equal weight and value to its two components, whatever they are. Dualism is simply monism masquerading as a plurality. But it is a sterile plurality which never reproduces anything but the one. Witness the history of philosophy and the monotonous repetition of this dualism in Descartes, Hegel, and every thinker until the present. Yes, there are two, but one is always better and more important than the other.

Another question, perhaps the most pressing, is how can one overcome this ontology and the conception of knowledge and rationality it has generated? In terms of the title of this chapter, I am asking what would a Feminist dialectics be like; that is, what would be the antidote to Platonic dialectics? What do feminists have to do to subvert its rhetoric and start anew? The answer, I believe, is contained in the contemporary practices of deconstruction and postmodernism. Because of its entrenchment in dualistic ontology, no reform of dialectics will do the job. It must be abandoned. First, dialectics assumes that there is one final description of reality, truth. Secondly, it assumes that there is a correct way for reason to proceed to be rational. As a method, it depends on collapsing phenomenal differences and then training reason to divide into twos to recreate a more controlled, artificial, list of differences. One brings together a dispersed plurality, a variety of instances and sees what is common to them, their essence. Then, one divides usually into halves and halves again, slowly gaining on the precise definition of the quarry: "We must divide only where there is a real cleavage between specific forms. . . . But it is dangerous, Socrates, to chop reality up into small portions. It is always safer to go down the middle to make our cuts. The real cleavages among the forms are more likely to be found thus, and the whole art of these definitions consists in finding these cleavages. . . . Surely it would be better and closer to the real structure of the forms to make a central division of number into odd and even or humankind into male and female".[24] Plato is constantly looking for "a true division into two groups each of which after separation is not only a portion of the whole class to be divided but also a real subdivision of it".[25] To subvert dialectics, then, the main strategy would be to multiply divisions in order to achieve a rampant pluralism. Refuse the first cut of humanity into males and females and begin with a wider, much wider, range of groups or individuals. While this will, as Plato feared, make it impossible to say anything in general about males and females, that is precisely what is wanted. As many feminists are discovering today, woman is not a category about which anything useful can be said. It leads to all kinds of stereotypes and discriminatory politics. Above all, by not hypostatizing these categories one will avoid the norms of absolute measurement that such dialectics was intended to secure: "Then we must posit two types and two standards of greatness and smallness. . . . The standard of relative comparison will remain, but we must acknowledge a second standard, which is a standard of comparison of due measure".[26] Isolating the form of something according to its necessary and sufficient conditions provided Plato with his ratio or absolute standard for judging everything else. To resist dialectics, then, is not to hypostatize a standard of our own making, all the while pretending the standard comes from nature and then measure everything and everyone against it.

Feminist dialectics, if one should still use the word, "dialectics," must produce a rich profusion of differences based not on truth but on pragmatic criteria of adequacy. This means feminists must abandon the project of knowledge as it has been conceived in the West. But that does not mean one ought to search for ignorance and falsity. No, that is already to grant dualism its power. There must be something else, some alternative between truth and falsity. However, this sounds strange. What I mean is that there must be some alternative concept of what it is to know something that does not depend on the concepts of true and false. As others have noted, it is almost impossible to talk about this alternative in any theoretical way since theory is so totally caught up in platonic dialectics. Nevertheless, we have been practicing alternatives ever since Nietzsche.

Deconstruction has surely been one tool developed recently to undermine the dichotomizing compulsion of dialectics. To a lesser extent, Hermeneutics has been articulating a different methodology for the sciences. All of post-modern thinking is basically aimed at undermining Platonic dialectics. What all these methods do is resist the universalizing inherent in the belief in essences by multiplying possibilities and distinctions so that things are not seen to be comparable, but incomparable. Feminism has been practicing these strategies as well. Recently there has been an attempt to stop speaking of Woman, as if there were something to be opposed to Man. There has also been a multiplication of feminisms and definitions of woman to head off the reduction to two. Pluralism and particularism, in all its messy varied forms, must grasp our allegiance and shake us and continue shaking us until we are no longer even tempted by dualism's facile dialectics.

Notes

1. *Timaeus* 42B in *Plato: Collected Dialogues,* eds. E. Hamilton and H. Cairns (Princeton: Princeton University Press, 1963). All further references to Plato's works will be from this collection.

2. *Republic* 455E.

3. Some of the more recent writings on Plato's would-be feminism are: Natalie Harris Bluestone, *Women and the Ideal Society: Plato's "Republic" and Modern Myths of Gender* (Massachusetts: University of Massachusetts Press, 1987); Arlene Saxonhouse, "Eros and the Female in Greek Political Thought," *Political Theory* 12, 1 (February 1984), 5–27; Arlene Saxonhouse, *Women in the History of Political Thought* (New York: Praeger, 1985); Wendy Brown, " 'Supposing Truth Were a Woman . . . ': Plato's Subversion of Masculine Discourse," *Political Theory* 16, 4 (November 1988), 594–616; Wendy Brown, *Manhood and Politics* (New Jersey: Roman and Littlefield, 1988).

4. Wendy Brown, " 'Supposing Truth Were a Woman . . . ': Plato's Subversion of Masculine Discourse," *Political Theory* 16, 4 (November 1988), 594–616. Too much is made of these facts. The main reason the words for these virtues are feminine and that powerful women appear to reveal ultimate wisdom has to do with the fact that in a more archaic Greek society women were the Gods. Aware that women's power lingers in the minds of the majority of Greek citizens, Plato turns to these cultural roots to help secure belief in his ideas.

5. Luce Irigaray was absolutely right when she titled her book, *This Sex Which Is Not One;* woman is not one, but two, the indefinite dyad.

6. Simone de Beauvoir, *The Second Sex* (New York: Random House, 1953), xv–xxxiv.

7. Plato scholars are continually debating the content of Plato's ontology, especially the influence of Pythagoras and whether there is a change in

Plato's beliefs from the middle dialogues to the later. For the purposes of this chapter, I shall avoid all reference to these debates and present his ontology as if it were a settled matter that Pythagoras has an enormous influence on the character of Plato's later ontology.

8. Arlene Saxonhouse, "Eros and the Female in Greek Political Thought: An Interpretation of Plato's *Symposium*," *Political Theory* 12 (1984): 10.

9. J N. Findlay, *Plato: The Written and Unwritten Doctrines* (New York: Humanities Press, 1974), 58.

10. *Philebus* 25A–B.

11. *Phaedrus* 274 D.

12. *Philebus* 18 B–C.

13. *Phaedrus* 265 D

14. Saxonhouse, 1984, 25.

15. 49B.

16. 52 D.

17. 55 D.

18. Derrida, 143.

19. Luce Irigaray, *Speculum of the Other Woman,* trans. Gillian C. Gill (Ithaca: Cornell University Press, 1985), 307.

20. *Timaeus* 51 B.

21. I am indebted to Seth Benardete's translation and commentary on the *Sophist* in *Plato's Sophist: Part II of the Being and the Beautiful* (Chicago: University of Chicago Press, 1986).

22. *Sophist* 241 D.

23. Jacques Derrida, "Plato's Pharmacy," *Dissemination,* trans. Barbara Johnson (Chicago: University of Chicago Press, 1981), 134.

24. *Statesman* 262 B–C. See also, *Phaedrus* 265–266, *Sophist* 253c–254.

25. *Statesman* 263.

26. *Statesman* 283 E.

Overcoming Dualism: The Importance of the Intermediate in Plato's Philebus

Cynthia Hampton

Introduction

One of the features of Western philosophy that many feminists have attacked is dualism, the conceptualization of reality in pairs composed of members which are mutually exclusive and yet supposed to be complementary. These pairs include not only those drawn from the observation of the cycles in nature, e.g., hot/cold, dry/wet, but also highly abstract metaphysical constructions such as one/many and limited/unlimited, and those used in explanations of the human world, e.g., male/female and soul/body.

Perhaps the most famous ancient instance of Western dualism is the sixth century B.C.E. Pythagorean Table of Opposites which is is headed by the opposition of the limited to the unlimited, and also includes: odd/even, one/many, right/left, male/female, rest/motion, straight/curved, light/dark, good/bad, square/oblong.[1] Some feminists, including Caroline Whitbeck[2] and Genevieve Lloyd[3], have suggested that not only was the first member of each dichotomous pair considered superior but that limit or form was associated with the masculine while unlimitedness or formlessness was linked to the feminine.[4]

Most feminists, including me, use the terms "feminine" and "masculine" in reference to socially constructed gender identities, not to the biological conditions of being female or male. Of course, there is no complete consensus about what counts as feminine or masculine even with a single culture or tradition. But since dualism is one of the hallmarks of the formal constructions of reality found in Western cultures which have been dominated by white men, it is fair to say that dichotomous thinking reflects a Western masculine worldview or ontology. For in the West, white men saw themselves as separate from anyone they perceived as significantly different than themselves, especially women. Yet at the same time these men needed to minimize the threat of women's "otherness" by channeling it in ways that would support their own positions of power, i.e., by encouraging the so-called complementary aspects of the "opposite sex". Not surprisingly, dualism emerged early in Western philosophy, prevailed in ancient Greek thinking, and indeed has permeated Western culture.

The dominance of masculinist ontology is problematic not simply because it underrepresents women's experiences but because the overemphasis on separation and opposition characteristic of dualistic thinking leads, as many feminists—including Carol Gilligan[5] and Sara Ruddick[6]—have pointed out, to alienation and violence. But if so, why should Western canonical philosophical texts continue to be studied? One answer is provided by French feminist deconstructionists such as Luce Irigaray. The goal of the deconstructionist project is to expose the pretensions of a text's claims to transcendent or extratextual truths and unitary meanings. One way of doing this is to read between the lines for hidden agendas or for ways the author subverts her/his own text. So by ferreting out masculinist assumptions and ways feminine views have been marginalized in canonical texts, the claims of the Western tradition to universality are undermined.[7]

I propose that there is another reason for reading the canon: for the purposes of reconstruction, not just deconstruction. There are conscious struggles against dichotomous thinking within the tradition.[8] Surprisingly enough, one of the philosophical texts where the struggle to overcome dualism is most marked is in Plato's late dialogue, the *Philebus*.[9] After some preliminary discussion of dualism in ancient Greek thinking before Plato as well as in his own earlier work, I shall focus on how the *Philebus* embodies Plato's struggle to overcome dichotomous thinking.

Although I do not think that Plato is altogether successful in his strivings, understanding his struggle is important as an example of how one's culture, let alone biology, is not one's destiny, at least not in any simple-minded way. Plato's resistance to masculinist dichotomous thinking is particularly noteworthy since as an aristocratic male he was the heir to a tradition where such thinking dominated. He was able to resist dualism not because he was a heroic feminist who championed the cause of women's liberation, but rather because he was attuned to feminine voices which his tradition could not altogether suppress.

The specific feminine strains I have in mind are those associated with a holistic worldview which sees the interrelatedness and harmony between individuals—be they persons or abstract terms—as the primary reality.[10] As I shall explain shortly, the holism that apparently abounded in the goddess-centered mythology of preclassical times began to give way, in classical mythology and presocratic philosophy, to an emphasis on separation and opposition. Nevertheless, the feminine influence never disappeared totally and in Plato's philosophy it leaves some rather strong traces. Following these traces should provide a better understanding that a feminine alternative to dualism is a part, albeit a neglected part, of Western heritage. If philosophies like Plato's can be interpreted so that it speaks meaningfully to contemporary audiences then this indicates that what is needed is not the wholesale rejection of the past, but a creative reshaping of it.

Dualism in Classical Greek Mythology and Presocratic Philosophy

Dualistic thinking, while formalized by the ancient philosophers, appeared in classical mythology where natural forces were personified as male and female deities who were both complementary and in opposition. While there are many examples, for the sake of brevity I shall concentrate on one: the poet Hesiod's version of the story of Gaia (earth) and Ouranos (sky or heaven) in his *Theogony*, written around 700–750 B.C.E.

The most famous part of this myth is the explanation of how the earth and sky, which were originally one, were separated. The sexual union of the two produced many children whom their father Ouranos hid within Gaia, concealed from the light. In revenge, Gaia made a sickle which she urged their son Cronos (Time) to use to castrate Ouranos.[11] Thus the opposition between Earth and Sky results in their separation, yet they continue to be complementary since it is the rain of the Sky that impregnates the Earth who then brings forth grain.

But there is more to the story. Of course, this myth—like most—leaves out many details and at times contradicts itself; for example, how could Ouranos impregnate Gaia **after** his castration? As most classicists acknowledge, Hesiod was weaving together different versions of the same myth and so a coherent narrative was unlikely to result.

Even so, there are aspects of Heisod's account that suggest that the feminine Earth was the older and more powerful deity, and so

Ouranos' crime was perhaps a form of rebellion. Besides Chaos (gap), Gaia was the first to emerge and Ouranos was simply her firstborn. Although Hesiod is quick to point out that Ouranos "matched [Gaia's] every dimension",[12] this seems unlikely, not only given the fact that she is his mother, but also that she (but not he) is able to produce children parthenogenetically; she bore the Sea (Pontus) "without any sweet act of love".[13]

These details of the myth suggest that parts of it are of pre-Hellenic origin. Although exact dating of pre-historical cultures is difficult to determine, the pre-Hellenic period was roughly between 2500 to 1000 or 800 B.C.E., from the flourishing of Cretan civilization to the time of the invasions of mainland Greece by the peoples of the north. During this time, Gaia was the ancient Earth-mother, a manifestation of the Great Goddess who was worshipped from India to the Mediterranean.[14]

If the Gaia myth does indeed contain fragments from the mythology of the Great Goddess, then certain details of the story such as why Ouranos hid the children, and why Gaia's revenge took the form of castration are more understandable. A closer look at the pre-Hellenic peoples who worshipped the Great Goddess and the mythology of those who invaded their lands is in order.

One reason pre-Hellenic people worshipped a female deity rather than a male might be that they assumed that females were the sole givers of life; they did not associate reproduction with sexual intercourse and so did not recognize paternity.[15] But unlike the Near and Middle Eastern peoples, the warrior peoples of the north, variously called Indo-Europeans, Indo-Iranians, Indo-Aryans or Aryans, worshipped a supreme male deity who was often portrayed as a storm god living on a mountain blazing with the light of fire or lightning. They also associated good and evil as light and dark respectively.

When these northerners invaded the Near and Middle East, they brought these ideas with them.[16] In classical Greek mythology, Ouranos' grandson Zeus is god of the thunderbolt and supreme king, and his name, like his grandfather's, means 'sky'. Even Ouranos as the personified sky is associated with rain and so is a variation of the northern thunder-god. So perhaps Ouranos' not letting his children "into the light"[17] symbolizes the struggle between the sky god of the northern peoples to overcome the pre-Hellenics' Great Goddess, who, from their point of view, is mysteriously dark and evil.

As far as Ouranos's castration is concerned, note that castration stories can be found in Hittite, Anatolian, and Egyptian mythologies, and there are references to eunuch priests in Summer, Babylon, Canaan and Anatolia.[18] Merlin Stone in her now classic book, *When God Was a Woman*, speculates that castration might have been one of the substitute rituals for the earlier human sacrifice of the young consort of the high priestess. The priestess and her consort symbolized the union between the Great Goddess and her son/lover.[19] So the Gaia myth is one which symbolizes the struggle between the very ancient matrifocal society which worshipped the Great Goddess and the patriarchial culture of the invaders. Although partriarchy had become thoroughly entrenched by the time of Hesiod, his retelling of this myth still contains fragments of the earlier stories.

The first Greek philosophers attempted to replace mythological explanations of natural phenomena with "rational" ones by adopting the focus on separation and opposition present in the classical myths and representing these forces in more abstract terms. The presocratic cosmogonies span three centuries, from the late seventh century figure Anaximenes to Anaxagoras who lived in the beginning of the fifth century. During this period, the Greek philosophers were concerned with the separation of the elements from the original undifferentiated source, and the subsequent "war of opposites" between the cold air, hot fire, the moist water, and the dry land.[20]

As scholars widely acknowledge, all their theories were addressing the same basic question: how is the diversity, "the many", of the natural world derived from one basic source? This question is known as the problem of [the] one and [the] many. The influence of mythological thinking is revealed most explicitly by the fact that most of the presocratics refer to the one source of all things as being "divine" or a "god".[21] By "divine" they, of course, do not necessarily mean a conscious being, let alone a person. Instead, the hallmark of divinity is simply its immortality. Yet even this practice perpetuates dualism since the contrast term for immortal is, of course, mortal.

The presocratics' tendency to think of one and many as mutually exclusive reached its logical extreme with Parmenides (b. 515 B.C.E.) who argued that there can be only the One, i.e., Being, so that the appearance of plurality is illusory. In his poem, written in imitation of Hesiod's *Theogony*, Parmenides describes the One as limited and unchanging (i.e., at rest), and associates its revelation to him with light. Thus Parmenides' description of the One echoes the limited (male) side of the Pythagorean Table of Opposites.[22] Parmenides' successors found his argument logically valid but rejected his conclusion as an outrageous assault upon common sense, even by philosophy's standards. In the attempt to find some place for ordinary experiences of time, change, and plurality there arose all subsequent cosmologies and ontologies, including Plato's Theory of Forms or Ideas.

Plato's Struggle With Dualism Prior to the 'Philebus'

Plato's general strategy for solving the problem of one and many was to distinguish between two groups. The first is a limited, unified group of immutable non-spatial and atemporal essences which are in no way qualified by their opposites. The second group is a manifestation of the first but is an unlimited collection of mutable, spatial and/or temporal sensibles which are throughly mixed with their opposites. The first group consists of Platonic Forms, the second, of sensibles or items of ordinary experience: trees, chairs, the color red, the patently false belief that the Cubs will win the pennant—ever.

A comparison between a Form and its sensible instances will highlight the differences between the two. Compare, for example, just laws with the Form of Justice. Through time and in many places, any number of just laws may be created and discarded, and none of them ever will be completely just; each one always will be unjust to some degree or in some respect.

In contrast, the Form of Justice is simply what it is—unqualifiably and unchangingly just—and thus may be used as the standard by which to judge the degree to which any given law, institution, action, person, etc. may be considered just. In this way, the Form's function as a standard is derived from its nature as the true reality which its sensible instances are able to approximate, by imitation or reflection, only in a partial way. For example, just persons try to embody the ideal of justice which is the Form but can never fully succeed because of the vicissitudes of human life and society. Not only are the Forms most fully real and thus most intelligible, they are also of supreme value. The scale of reality and knowledge is also a hierarchy of value with the Forms higher than their sensible instances, and one Form—variously referred to as the Good, the Beautiful, or the One—is the highest of all.[23]

Even with this bare bones sketch it appears that Plato's theory, while an attempt to bring the one and the many together, simply falls back on the same strategy as his predecessors: divide, or separate, to conquer the tensions between dualistic pairs of opposites. Indeed, in the *Republic* he talks as if Forms and sensibles belong to two completely separate worlds[24] and in the *Phaedo* this separation is mirrored in each human being as the dualism of body and soul.[25]

Yet Plato's dialogues dramatize the struggle against dualism even as they sometimes lapse into dualistic language. Throughout the Platonic corpus there is ample evidence, both implicit and explicit, of his striving to find intermediaries to bridge the gap between the one and the many, the Forms and sensibles, soul and body. Many scholars, including feminists, have called attention to some of this evidence. Genevieve Lloyd, for example, notes that in the *Republic*, Platonic psychology moves from a simple body/soul dualism to the more complex model of the tri-part soul.[26]

A most recent and provocative discussion of the role of the intermediate in the Platonic corpus is the one between Luce Irigaray and Andrea Nye on the subject of Diotima's method in the *Symposium*. Both feminists agree that the intermediary is the crucial element of the priestess Diotima's method which resists, if not overcomes, dualism. I agree that while all the speakers at the symposium identify *eros* as a fundamental force at work in both the mortal and immortal realms, only Diotima's method reveals that *eros* is the intermediary between the two realms. The following of erotic desire transforms ignorance into knowledge, need into plenty, longing into union, and in general, enables humans to approximate the divine as much as possible.[27] Diotima's language closely resembles that of the mystery cults, such as the Eleusinian mysteries in which the initiate comes to identify with, and even become, the earth-mother goddess Demeter.[28] As Nye also notes, Diotima's method is divine and fits within the Great Goddess tradition.[29]

On the other hand, Diotima's method is both feminine and demonic according to Irigaray, since the feminine subverts masculine logic and language.[30] I agree that Diotima stands the masculine Olympian tradition on its head; the god Eros is not beautiful, wise, or prosperous, but rather is in-between beauty and ugliness, ignorance and knowledge, poverty and plenty. Eros is not, strictly speaking, a god at all but rather a *daimon* (demon), a spirit who links mortal humans with the immortal gods.[31]

Although both Iragary and Nye have important insights, I disagree with some of the implications of their respective analyses. I don't think that Diotima leaps out of Plato's subconscious, like Athene out of the head of Zeus, in order to subvert her creator's conscious philosophical designs. Nor do I believe that Plato is trying to fit together, nilly willy, his philosophy with the Great Goddess tradition. Rather, I see him summoning non-dualistic images in

his struggle to articulate a way out of the central dualisms of
one and many, limit and unlimited, which he inherited from the
presocratics.

According to Plato, knowledge of ultimate reality is not just immediate insight but also is what can be accounted for in the prosaic
language of reasoned explanation or causality. For Plato, as for most
people who wish for both mystery and lucidity, the intoxicating images and symbolic language that abound in the *Symposium*—and
elsewhere—need to be accompanied by the more sober reflection of
philosophical discourse. Such reflection is found in Plato's late dialogue, the *Philebus*. I shall now turn to this text to show how Plato
uses what might now be called the feminine approach of the intermediate in one of his most sustained efforts to overcome dualism.

The Intermediate in the 'Philebus': The Divine Link to True Reality and Knowledge

In the *Philebus,* the intermediate—what lies between the one
and the many—plays a key role. The gist of the ontology or worldview depicted in the dialogue is this: there is an ultimate One—the
Good—which unifies all things *via* its intermediate aspects. Here—
in marked contrast to Parmenides' One which made plurality illusory—the Good in the *Philebus* is a One which itself contains
plurality.

However, as I shall explain shortly, the Good encompasses the
plurality of the sensible world only indirectly since sensible plurality is infinite in extent and indefinite in character[32] and so not fully
real or knowable. What can be known are the Forms which are the
intermediates between the infinite plurality of sensibles and the
all-encompassing Form of the Good. The Forms, unlike sensibles,
are inherently limited and definite in nature. Since, as previously
noted, sensibles approximate Forms, when one understands the
Forms one will learn all that there is to comprehend about sensibles: the structure which "underlies" them.[33] Like contemporary
chaos theorists, Plato believes that behind the apparent random-
ness of sensible phenomena lies order.

But how does one come to know these intermediate Forms and
so solve the puzzle of one and many? As an answer to this question,
Socrates—as the Platonic speaker of the dialogue—[34] introduces
"the Divine Method". This method is grounded on the assumption
that all is from one and many and everything has within it definite-

ness (or the limited) and indefiniteness (or unlimitedness). So the very foundation of the Divine Method is the assumption that one and many are expressed in the combinations of limit and unlimited that are an inherent part of the nature of all things.[35]

The realization that limit and unlimited are combined in all things enables Plato to transform the traditional dualistic pairs of Hot/Cold and Wet/Dry into continua of Hotter-and-Colder, and Drier-and-Wetter.[36] Plato retains the usual Greek view of seeing Hot and Cold as equally real, i.e., Cold is no more the absence of heat than vice versa[37] but he now depicts sensibles as being neither hot nor cold per se. Instead, each has some particular temperature which can be expressed as some point along the Hotter-Colder continuum.

The Divine Method not only enables Plato to break out of the dualisms concerned with the strictly material aspects of the sensible world, but it also provides a non-dualistic model for how ultimate reality is related to sensibles. This model is illuminated by the illustrations of the Divine Method: linguistic and musical sound. In the case of learning to pronounce the letters of the alphabet, for example, one realizes that although the sounds that can be vocalized are infinite, the rules of grammar which determine the number and nature of distinguishable linguistic sounds—vowels, semi-vowels, mutes—make linguistic sound one comprehensive unit.[38]

One cannot learn to pronounce the letters in isolation from one another, but must do so by combining them. Thus the role of grammar is crucial in that it reveals the proper ways to unite the letters.[39] Presumably, letters form syllables, then nouns and verbs, then sentences.[40] What is true of language is true of everything else. Knowledge takes place when one can discern and express the pattern "behind" the indefiniteness and infinite variety of sensible phenomena.

Plato's insights into the nature of language studied by linguistics are remarkably similar to those of the contemporary language philosopher, Noam Chomsky, who believes that all languages exhibit a universal grammar.[41] In his discussion of the knowledge of a language, he says that:

> ... knowledge of a language is mentally represented as a 'grammar'—that is, a finite system of rules and principles that interact to determine ('generate') an infinite class of expressions, each with a phonetic form, meaning, and associated structural properties (for example, an organization into words and phrases).[42]

Plato and Chomsky would agree that the mind is not a blank slate, and that knowledge of universal grammar is innate. But Chomsky considers this innate knowledge to be part of peoples biological endowment while Plato believes that the universal features of language point to the nature of ultimate reality. As the *Philebus* makes clear, the reason one and many are perennially present in all utterances is because language—at its deepest, most universal level—reflects the structure provided by the Forms.[43] It is the business of the Divine Method to reveal this structure.

The focus of the Divine Method on the intermediates indicates that the goal of knowledge is neither contemplation of the absolute, indivisible One nor the experience of infinite variety, but the articulation of unity as it is expressed in multiplicity. That Plato uses linguistic and musical sound as his illustrations of the Divine Method is no accident, for such examples depict the basic structure of reality as an organic whole rather than a mere aggregate of individuals. Parts are not discrete units but elements that blend together like sounds that form spoken syllables or musical scales.

Plato's use of auditory examples also presents an alternative to the model of knowledge which relies on the analogies of sight and/or touch. Such a model is prevalent in Plato's earlier works such as the *Republic*.[44] The visual/tactile model suggests that the soul directly encounters the Forms as the eyes or hand must be in the immediate presence of the sensible in order to see or grasp its properties. Such a model suggests that the ultimate objects of knowledge, the Forms, are absolute simples with no parts: they can be seen all at once or grasped in their entirety. But the auditory model suggested by spoken and musical sound emphasizes the interconnections of the Forms which must be articulated as a system in order to be understood.

Plato's striving to overcome dualism is evident not only in his description and illustration of the Divine Method but also in the story he tells of this method's origins. According to Socrates in the *Philebus,* the Divine Method is "thrown down by the gods in a blaze of light from some Prometheus".[45] In Plato's earlier version of this myth[46] Prometheus (whose name means "forethought"), a brother of Cronos and son of Ouranos, was the Titan who helped humankind overcome their initial condition of utter helplessness by giving them fire and wisdom in the crafts or skills. These skills include religious rituals by which we mark our kinship with the divine as well as the means for providing for our material needs (food, clothing, and shelter), and language. In the *Philebus,* Prometheus' gift is responsible for **any** skill that humans possess.

The origin of the Divine Method clearly indicates that there is continuity between divinity and human community. The Divine Method is given by the gods to be learned and taught among all people. It is part of a tradition handed down from the pious ancients.

Later in the dialogue, Socrates alludes to another aspect of the Promethean myth: the Titan's role in bringing about victory for the gods in their war against the other Titans and in the subsequent crowning of Zeus as king. This part of the myth is brought up when Socrates is discussing causality as one of the main forces at work in universe. He credits the Cause (which is here personified) with ensouling human bodies and giving them medicine and other devices, and also for implanting a kingly soul and intellectual intuition (*nous*) in Zeus.[47]

In this passage, the personified Cause assumes Prometheus' role and expands it. Whereas the Titan provided for human intelligence, the Cause is responsible also for divine intelligence. The Cause, as becomes clear later in the dialogue, is identical with the causal power of the Form of the Good. So Plato appropriates the Promethean myth in order to give mythic expression to his own conception of the good.

The main point Plato makes by using this myth is that the Divine Method can impart god-like power to mortals. This is symbolized by Prometheus' gift of fire, which, having been stolen from the gods, brings enlightenment to humankind. One noteworthy detail of this myth is the fact that humankind's benefactor is a deity who is older than the Olympian gods of classical Greek mythology. This fact suggests that human development depends on getting in touch with an older source of divinity, the spirit of inventiveness. As I shall explain shortly, this spirit ultimately leads to knowledge of the basic structure of reality provided by the Cause, the ultimate One or Good.

Such knowledge is possible not by contemplation of the One by itself but by identifying the presence of the one within the many. In other words, the recognition of the intermediate is what is called "divine", not the isolation of the one from the many. This recognition is not simply intellectual but includes the ability to act on the awareness of the intermediate even in securing the basic necessities of physical existence. Plato, by appropriating the Prometheus myth for his own purposes, stresses the idea that the Divine Method played a key role in the foundation of civilization. Of course, Plato's version of the myth is still androcentric in its reliance on male warrior gods and their symbols: the fire and blaze of light, which are reminiscent of the lightning of the thunder-god. But at least he

manages to use the myth to illustrate the concept of the intermediate which is feminine in its inspiration.

The Importance of the Intermediate in the 'Philebus' Conception of the Good and the Good Life

A. *Intermediates of the Universal Good:*
Truth, Proportion, and Beauty

The importance of the intermediate is most apparent in the discussion at the end of the *Philebus* where the universal Good—the
Form—is linked to the good life for humanity. At the end of the dialogue, Plato reveals that through the causal agency of certain intermediate aspects of the Good—Proportion, Beauty, and Truth—
the good human life becomes possible. True to the general emphasis
on interrelations in this dialogue, Socrates and his interlocutor
Protarchus agreed early on that the good life consists of neither
pleasure nor knowledge by themselves but the right mixture of
the two.[48]

But the question of which is the best element, knowledge or
pleasure, is one that they do not consider to be answered in full even
after lengthy discussion about each. The reason is that in order to
make clear whether knowledge, including practical reasoning, i.e.,
phronesis, or pleasure contributes more to the goodness of the good,
mixed life "we must get a clear conception, or at least an outline of
the Good".[49] The outline of the Good emerges when Truth, Proportion or Measure, and Beauty are considered in terms of how they
cause the mixed life of pleasure and knowledge to be a good one.[50]

Truth is said to enable the good life—or any other mixture—to
come into existence[51] as well as to become intelligible. As has been
widely noted,[52] truth here clearly is not simply a property of a
statement which obtains if it describes something that really is the
case. For example, the statement, "The cat is on the mat" is true if
in fact the cat *is* on the mat. If this were all Plato meant by truth
then it would be a form of knowledge. However, since he has already
included forms of knowledge in the good mixed life earlier in the
dialogue[53] the present discussion indicates that truth is something
distinct from knowledge.

In fact, truth is more important than knowledge since it must
be present in order for the good mixture even to exist. Truth, like
sunlight, not only illuminates but is also the source of energy.[54] If it

were not for Truth, there would be no knowledge and pleasure to mix together and form the good life. There would be no reality at all, at either the universal or the human level.

Proportion, or Measure, is likewise essential. Since Proportion brings unity it enables the components of the good life to compose a mixture rather than a jumbled heap. Once unified, the mixture may admit of beauty as a higher level of organization. Thus Proportion and Beauty are intimately related though Plato is not very explicit about the nature of their relationship.

Perhaps a clue is given in his allusion to a connection between Beauty and excellence.[55] Beauty seems to bring the perfect order that something displays once it has fully realized its function or achieved its excellence. The idea that every type of thing—a knife, tree, or human—has a function, i.e., work it alone can do or do better than anything else, is one of the most important points Plato developed earlier in such dialogues as the *Republic*.[56] What enables something to function fully or perform its work well is its excellence and the good life is the one characterized by such excellences or virtues.

In this passage in the *Philebus*, Plato is applying his previous analysis of function and excellence to Proportion and Beauty. Using the example of the human body, one which Plato often employs elsewhere, will help clarify the relations between Proportion, Beauty and excellence. The human body is composed of proportions of hotness and coldness, wetness and dryness, etc. A diseased body is one where at least some of these proportions are out of kilter; nevertheless, some degree of order is maintained. But the diseased body has lost, at least temporarily, its excellence: health. And certainly it has lost its beauty for only the well-functioning body could be truly beautiful.

Plato, naturally enough, saw his aesthetic standards as carved in stone, like in the Greek original of the Apollo Belvedere. His aesthetics, like his ethics, is grounded on his idea of function. He would explain that people in their prime are physically more beautiful than those who are not by pointing out that only the former are fully realizing the body's true nature.

The body's good therefore consists in its realization of its function or true nature and in this way it manifests truth, proportion, and beauty. What is true of the body would extend also to the other dimensions of human existence so that the ideal life would be one in which pleasure and knowledge are combined in a manner which exhibits all three aspects of the Good.

B. Application of the Intermediates to the Good Life: The Ranking of Pleasure

B. Application of the Intermediates to the Good Life:
The Ranking of Pleasure

Of course, Plato's claim that the ideal human life is truthful, proportionate, and beautiful seems rather platitudinous. What makes all the difference is how pleasure and knowledge are to be combined in such a life. Readers of Plato's earlier work would know that he takes a dim view of the pleasures of the flesh and of flashy worldly glories. So much so that one often gets the impression, especially in the *Phaedo*, that Plato is more priggish than the most scrupulous Puritan. In this light, the fact that there is any role at all for pleasure in the good life is remarkable. In fact, as I shall demonstrate shortly, pleasure and knowledge do not simply parallel the dualism of body and soul. There are bad psychic pleasures and pure bodily ones. These are just a few foretastes of what is to come.

Let those who anticipate a total salvaging of earthly delights in the *Philebus* be forewarned. In the contest between pleasure and knowledge, the latter is found to be the most like the Good in all three of its aspects: Truth, Proportion (Measure) and Beauty. Hence knowledge is declared to be the more honorable among both humans and gods.[57]

Worse yet, the contest seems rigged. Pleasure as a class is not compared to knowledge as a class, but to the highest type of knowledge, *nous* (intellectual intuition) and *phronesis* (practical reasoning). The comparison reveals that *nous* is either truth itself or the most like it while pleasure is the greatest of impostors.[58] Likewise, nothing is more in harmony with measure than *phronesis* while the opposite is true of pleasure. Finally, *phronesis* and *nous* are never unseemly whereas the most intense pleasures are ridiculous or disgraceful.[59] So in each case, the comparison is between the most extreme and disruptive pleasures and the highest type of knowledge.

This contest will turn out not to be as unfair as it seems. For Plato considers most pleasures to be mixed with pain and therefore contingently good at best while all types of knowledge must rest ultimately upon the foundation of *nous* and *phronesis*. In other words, pleasures by and large do not unambiguously reflect Truth, Proportion, and Beauty while knowledge of whatever type does to a greater or lesser extent. This contest is simply a summary of the entire analyses of pleasure and knowledge respectively.

Before turning first to the classification of pleasure and then to knowledge, a word needs to be said about the final competition at the very end of the *Philebus*. In "the final ranking"—a kind of academy awards ceremony for what is valuable in life—the presenter, a personified "eternal nature" (i.e., the Good)[60] does not give top honors to knowledge. Instead, first place goes to measure, the mean, fitness and their kin while the second spot is taken by proportion, beauty, completeness and sufficiency, and all of their ilk. Trailing at a mere third place come *nous* and *phronesis,* while the lower forms of knowledge take fourth prize and the painless pleasures bring up the rear.[61]

The reason why knowledge, even in its highest form, does not claim first prize is that the order of the final ranking is determined by how humans can express the Good by realizing their proper place within the order of reality. This task requires an awareness of how human needs for both pleasure and knowledge can be structured so that they reflect what is objectively good, i.e., what the "eternal nature" would choose.

Earlier in the dialogue, Plato made it clear that limit and measure, as well as purity and truth, should be used as criteria in distinguishing between higher and lower pleasures and forms of cognition. To examine how Plato used these criteria is thus important in understanding how he fleshes out his ideal of the good life.

During the classification of pleasure, two basic kinds emerged. First are the mixed pleasures, so called because they are mixed with their opposite, pain. These pleasures are classified differently depending upon what aspects of them are being considered. In regard to their inherent capacity for extension in degree of intensity, magnitude and number, the mixed or impure pleasures are indefinite.[62] This aspect of the mixed pleasures is experienced when a pleasure originates from abnormal and/or inordinate desires, be they physical or psychological.[63] The pleasures of the profligate, the homosexual prostitute, and the emotionally distressed would all fall into the indefinite category.[64] As mentioned earlier, pleasures of the soul do not necessarily fare better than those of a more physical nature. Excesses of emotion are condemned along with the usual catalogue of bodily vices.

In contrast, when limit is imposed on the mixed pleasures through intelligence, then they are considered members of the class where the indefinite is mixed with the definite.[65] The limited aspect of these pleasures would be experienced in connection with health and strength.[66]

The second main type of pleasure consists of the pure pleasures which are by their very nature limited. These include not only ones

free from pain, e.g., the smell of a rose, but also those whose objects
are relatively simple: the formal representations involved in geometry, music, and art. These latter pleasures are considered to be
"divine"[67] because they are the closest link to the Forms the experience of pleasure can afford. Note that even the physical sensation
of smelling can be a pure pleasure, although not a divine one.

The key to the classification of pleasure is to compare the different varieties according to the criteria of limit, purity, and truth.
Those that are inherently unlimited are hopelessly impure, being
mixed with their opposite, pain. These pleasures Socrates also considers to be false because their unlimitedness and indefiniteness inevitably lead to distortions of reality in one of three basic ways.

The first way pleasure distorts reality is when the agent acts as
if what is at best extrinsically valuable were intrinsically so, e.g., a
miser who lives as if the acquisition of currency has value in itself.
The second way involves the agent exaggerating the pleasure of
satisfaction, e.g., when someone breaks his or her diet and, in an
attempt to rationalize what she or he knows is a poor choice, exag-
gerates his or her enjoyment while eating the forbidden sweets.[68]
The third type of distortion occurs when what is really in itself neither pleasant nor painful is experienced as pleasant because one
has just escaped from pain and this freedom seems pleasant by comparison to the pain just experienced. An example of this is the belief
someone might have that she or he is experiencing pleasure because
the dentist has stopped drilling.

All three of these types of distortions have as their source the
inherent indefiniteness of the pleasures involved. That is, the confused mixture of pleasure and pain in these situations will inevitably confuse the agent the true value of the objects involved.

By contrast, the pleasures that are intrinsically limited and
pure are true, i.e., accurately reflect reality. Not surprisingly, in the
final ranking the true and pure pleasures are admitted into the
good life while the inherently indefinite pleasures are barred.[69]
These latter are a hindrance to the pure pleasures and prevent the
higher types of intelligence from coming about at all.[70]

Although the fact that the pure and true pleasures are superior to the impure, mixed ones is obvious enough, exactly how truth
and purity are related is not clear. Throughout most of the classification of pleasure, Plato uses the words "purity" and "truth" as
more or less equivalent terms. But at one point[71] Socrates asks
whether pure or impure pleasures are more closely related to truth.

To help explain what he means by "purity", he gives an example: unmixed white.

Clearly, there is a sense in which unmixed white is more white than that which is mixed with other colors. But Socrates goes on to conclude that it is also the truest and most beautiful of all whiteness. Although he does not explain the relations between purity, truth, and beauty explicitly, he does say enough to convey the general point.

Purity is valuable, even highly valuable, in its own right and not just as the absence of impurity. For something to be what it is and nothing else is to be a clear reflection of the definiteness of the basic structure of reality. Even in our experiences of pleasure we may affirm our connection with the beautiful and well-proportioned whole of reality of which we are a part. This is the significance of the pure pleasures, which are true because they unambiguously exemplify the definiteness, proportion, and beauty that underlie the surface of human life.

C. Application of the Intermediates to the Good Life: The Ranking of Knowledge

Purity is likewise used as a criterion in the classification of knowledge, for it is equated to exactness[72] and related to truth.[73] These criteria first are used to rank different kinds of skilled work according to the extent to which they employ arithmetic, the science of measurement and weighing. Music (i.e., playing by ear), medicine, agriculture, piloting, and generalship are all examples of imprecise skills, while building is more exact because it uses a good number of measurements and instruments.[74]

Furthermore, within both arithmetic and the science of measurement are two distinct kinds: those of the many and those of the philosophers. Concerning arithmetic, some reckon unequal units, e.g., two armies, while others insist on units that are all equal to one another. Likewise, calculation and measuring used in building and trade differ from the geometry of philosophers.[75]

The "philosophic" arithmetic and metrical arts surpass the more pedestrian varieties in purity, exactness and truth[76] just as some pleasures are purer and truer than others.[77] The truest form of knowledge is the dialectic, defined as " . . . that knowledge which has to do with being and reality and that which is always the same".[78] It is called *nous* and *phronesis*, "the contemplation of true

Being".[79] So, the extent of truth or purity involved in the various forms of skills and knowledge depends upon the definiteness of their respective objects.

Insofar as all forms of cognition are limited or definite to some extent, all are included in the final ranking of the good life. Such inclusion does not mean that all types of knowledge are on the same level, however. The objects of divine knowledge, as well as those of divine pleasure, are clearly objects of a higher ontological status— are more fully real—than those of the less pure types of pleasure and knowledge. The divine circle, sphere, etc. are at least closer than sensibles to true reality if not fully real themselves.

At any rate, the knowledge of divine mathematical objects, along with *phronesis* regarding Justice itself and *nous,* are more important than the lower forms of knowledge which are needed for the practical purposes of life, so that one may "find ... [the] way home".[80] But practical types of knowledge are truly good only if one has divine knowledge.[81] The latter, *nous* and *phronesis,* is put into a separate class from the lower varieties of cognition. The point is that divine knowledge or the dialectic, which earlier was identified with the Divine Method,[82] differs significantly from the lower types of cognition. Only the dialectic directly aims at the discovery of ultimate reality.

Put differently, this last aspect of the ranking is important as an instance of where an appeal to the universal, and not just the human, Good is being made. Although recognition of the crucial importance of limit in terms of obvious human goods such as health and excellence may be easy, the superiority of the dialectic to all other forms of cognition takes us beyond what we can value in strictly practical terms.

The dialectic is superior in terms of both knowledge and value simply because its objects are ontologically superior. The objects of the dialectic are contrasted to those of the skills in terms of stability, purity, and truth. The dialectic's objects are "cognitively dependable",[83] but are so, as I have argued elsewhere[84] because they, unlike sensibles, are real without qualification.

The great chain of Being is also a scale of value. "True Being" is no mere description of ultimate reality; it is an honorific title. For one to fully appreciate the truth involves according to everything its proper value as an expression of a true understanding of reality, both distributively and collectively. The dialectic or the Divine Method makes this understanding possible by revealing the basic structure of the realm of the Forms which in turn explains the underlying order of the sensible world. In fact, the dialectic as the Divine Method ultimately leads to the Good.

D. Summary: The Role of the Intermediates in the Good Life as Imitation of the Divine

In terms of the good life, the types of pleasure and knowledge that are part of its mixture are those which admit of some measure or proportion and truth, while those pleasures that are inherently indefinite are left out. Measure or limit, as well as purity and truth, are used to rank the various types of knowledge and pleasure. The highest types are called "divine" because their objects belong, or are most akin, to the Forms which are aspects of the Good. So when pleasure and knowledge are compared in terms of three of the Good's aspects—Truth, Proportion, and Beauty—knowledge, in particular the highest type, is once again shown to be the more important element in the good life.

The fact that the highest type of knowledge is referred to as *nous* and *phronesis* is also significant. *Nous* is related to *noesis*, the intuitive apprehension of the Forms.[85] Although, as has been already noted, Plato is moving away from the visual/tactile model of knowledge in the *Philebus*, the term *nous* still might refer to a type of knowledge which, once realized, is self-evident.

But what is of particular interest is the fact that *nous* is coupled with *phronesis*, practical reasoning. This coupling suggests that the highest knowledge is the most complete; it is what makes human imitation of ultimate reality and value possible by combining insight and activity. Small wonder that both these capacities are crucial for human imitation of the divine since the Cause itself, later identified with the Good, is described[86] as the producer and governor of the cosmic order according to *nous, phronesis,* and wisdom.[87]

Thinking of the Good as the Cause or Creative agent,[88] rather than as an abstract pattern set up in Platonic heaven, is more efficacious for human imitation of the divine. In a sense, human beings are co-creators with the Good. Those who mix what is limited, pure, and true within themselves enhance the organic unity of their lives. In so doing, they touch the divine.

Conclusion

In sum, the *Philebus* depicts the universal order, including the ideal life for humanity, as a unity of distinct but interrelated aspects.

Rigid dualism definitely loses ground in Plato's thought. Admittedly, though, most feminists still would find Plato's philosophy too masculine. After all, Plato persists not only in making abstract distinctions between different types of things but also in elevating what is more definite, limited or measured, pure and true, over what is less so. These criteria he takes to be objective: built into the nature of things.

I agree that for Plato—or anyone—to speak about the real nature of things is problematic, and that masculinist and intellectualist biases often parade under the banner of objectivity. But Plato is less guilty than it seems. He never makes a direct claim to absolute knowledge. The very fact that he writes dialogues indicates an openness to truth as it is revealed from the different perspectives voiced by the characters[89] although this feature is more prominent in earlier dialogues than it is in the *Philebus*. But even in the *Philebus*, only an "outline" of the nature of the Good is given. Plato's main concern is not arcane metaphysics as an end in itself. Rather, he urges his interlocutors, including his readers, to realize that human life is most meaningful when it points to what is beyond—and yet within—itself: the divine.

The longing for the divine is, I believe, at the root of Plato's holism, and perhaps all holistic "visions".[90] Recall that for the ancient Greeks, divinity is not limited to a conception of specific deities. "Divine" means immortal, what is not mortal. Plato's Forms are divine in this sense. To long for union with the divine, then, is to desire to participate in divinity, to be god-like. For Plato, as I have shown, this requires human beings to shape the human world so that it reflects more clearly the universal order which "underlies" all experiences.

I believe that a worldview ultimately needs to be judged in terms of the values it expresses. The religion of the Great Goddess is attractive to many feminists because it embodies and exhalts the feminine values associated with embracing diverse forms of life, welcoming and nurturing them as one's own. Yet as I have mentioned, Plato—like many people—yearns for plainer prose in addition to symbolic language. Here Plato's holism has much to recommend it since it too affirms the importance of connectedness and celebrates the presence of divinity in the natural and human world but does so in a more abstract form (or Form!) Plato's dialogues exhibit a kind of holistic thinking which combines symbolism with abstract reasoning.

All and all, I find that Plato's holism provides a good antidote not only to dichotomous thinking but also to the modern masculine values that accompany dualism: aggressive egoism in all its manifold guises. Feminists searching for ways to conceptualize human experiences in a non-dualistic fashion might do well to pay closer attention to the all-embracing, spiritually charged holism of Plato.

Notes

I would like to acknowledge Pat Lull, Candice Blocker, and Bat-Ami Bar On for their comments on earlier drafts of this chapter.

1. There are no complete texts from the presocratics (so-called because with Socrates came a definite change of interest from what is now called natural philosophy to more humanistic concerns). At best, there are quotations from their works perserved in the writings of later authors (these are often referred to as "fragments"). For the fragments of the Pythagoreans and the other presocratics, as well as an excellent running commentary, see G. S. Kirk, J. E. Raven, and M. Schofield, eds., *The Presocratic Philosophers,* 2nd ed., (Cambridge: Cambridge University Press, 1983).

2. See Whitbeck, "Theories of Sex Difference", repr. in *Women and Values: Readings in Recent Feminist Philosophy,* Marilyn Pearsall, ed. (Belmont, CA: Wadsworth Publishing Company, 1986), and "A Different Reality: Feminist Ontology", in *Beyond Domination: New Perspectives on Women and Philosophy,* Carol Gould, ed. (Totowa, NY: Rowman & Littlefield, 1984).

3. See Genevieve Lloyd, *The Man of Reason: "Male" and "Female" in Western Philosophy* (Minneapolis: University of Minnesota Press, 1984), pp. 2–9.

4. See also Nancy Tuana, "The Weaker Seed: The Sexist Bias of Reproductive Theory", *Hypatia,* vol. 3, no. 1, 1988.

5. See, e.g., Gilligan's "Moral Orientation and Moral Development", in *Women and Moral Theory,* Eva and Kittay and Dianan Meyers, eds. (Totowa, NJ: Rowman and Littlefield, 1986), pp. 19–33.

6. See, e.g., Ruddick's "Maternal Thinking", in *Women and Values,* op cit., pp. 340–351.

7. French feminist deconstructionists are applying the views of the philosopher Jacques Derrida, and sometimes those of psychoanalytic theorist Jacques Lacan, for feminist purposes. For a brief overview of deconstructionism, especially as practiced by Luce Irigaray, see Andrea Nye,

"The Hidden Host: Irigaray and Diotima at Plato's Symposium", *Hypatia*, vol. 3, no. 3, winter 1989), pp. 45–61, esp. pp. 49–53.

8. Of course, I do not mean that Plato saw his struggle against dualism in terms of feminine vs. masculine ways of thinking, or even that he considered dualism per se as the enemy. Most likely, he was himself battling against the materialism of some of his predecessors and the relativism of the sophists. All I am suggesting is that he was deeply committed to a holistic worldview despite the strong dualistic elements within this own tradition, including certain strains within his own theory.

9. Plato's dialogues are divided into three periods: early (from the execution of Plato's teacher, Socrates, in 399 B.C.E. to Plato's first trip to Italy and Syracuse in 388–87), middle (between his second and third trips to Syracuse at 367 and 361 respectively) and late (after his third trip to Syracuse until his death in 348–47). Exactly which dialogues belong to what period is a matter of perennial debate since there is little evidence from ancient sources to indicate their order of composition. Various methods of dating have been used. [For a brief overview of these methods, see the Introduction to R. E. Allen's *The Dialogues of Plato*, vol. I (New Haven: Yale University Press, 1984).] The vast majority of scholars, however, agree that the *Philebus* is a late dialogue, probably the second to last Plato wrote (the *Laws* is the last).

Most editions of the dialogues, including translations, use a standard pagination—Stephanus pages—in the margins; these pages are subdivided according to the letters A, B, C, D, and E, according to the divisions in the original folio page. In this paper, I shall follow the customary practice of referring to the Stephanus pages in the Platonic corpus. Usually, I shall only allude to passages but when I quote directly from the *Philebus*, I shall translate from the Greek text found in John Burnet, *Platonis Opera*, vol. II (Oxford: Oxford University Press, 1979).

10. Many feminists might agree with me that the feminine worldview is a holistic one but object that it cannot be identified with such an abstractly rational theory as Plato's. But I believe that Plato's holism—like any which tries to live up to the name—seeks to encompass as much of human experience as possible, and thus includes his inevitably clumsy attempts to capture the spiritual dimensions of life in abstractions and then explore them through reasoning. Perhaps he sometimes gets a little lost in his own abstractions but this fact does not in any way diminish his holistic aims.

11. See Richmond Lattimore, tr., *Hesiod: The Works and Days, Theogony, The Shield of Herakles* (Ann Arbor: The University of Michigan Press, eighth printing, 1973), pp. 130–135.

12. Ibid., p. 130, 1. 126.

13. Ibid., p. 131, 1. 131.

14. See Charlene Spretnak, *Lost Goddesses of Early Greece: A Collection of Pre-Hellenic Myths* (Boston: Beacon Press, 1984), pp. 17–27. Worth pointing out is the fact that the importance of the Great Goddess religion is recognized not only by feminists but also by more traditional archeologists and Classics such as E. O. James (*The Cult of the Mother-Goddess*, 1959), B. C. Dietrich (*The Origins of Greek Religion*, 1974), and R. F. Willets (*The Civilization of Ancient Crete*, 1977).

15. See Merlin Stone, *When God was a Woman* (San Diego, New York, London: Harcourt, Brace, Jovanovich, 1976), pp. 10–11.

16. Ibid., pp. 66–67.

17. *Theogony*, op cit., p. 132, 1. 158.

18. Stone, op cit., pp. 148–149.

19. Ibid., pp. 129–130.

20. The concept of opposed natural phenomena occurs in Anaximander, Heraclitus, Parmenides (who rejects it, see n. 21), Empedocles, Anaxagoras, and in the Pythagoreans as early as Alcmaeon. See *The Presocratic Philosophers*, op cit., p. 119ff.

21. Examples of presocratics who refer to the ultimate source (*arche*) as divine or a god include: Thales, Anaximander, Anaximenes, Xenophanes, the Pythagoreans, Heraclitus, and Empedocles. See *The Presocratics, op.cit.*

22. In Parmenides' poem, he journeys past the Gates of Night and Day which alternate by way of Justice (i.e., the world of ordinary experience where opposites alternate) to a highway (i.e., path of thought) which leads him to two mutually exclusive paths: the Way of Truth (of true changeless Being) and the Way of Seeming (what mortal opinion holds as real: the changing world of empirical experience). Parmenides' cosmology *does* stress the interaction of the opposite powers of light and night but of course, this is only the Way of Seeming. In truth, Being is limited, unitary, and at rest. See ibid., pp. 239–262.

23. The Theory of Forms is characterized differently in various dialogues (and sometimes even within a single work, e.g., the *Phaedo;* see n. 24 and 25 below). For example, in the *Symposium,* the highest Form considered is the Beautiful, while in the *Republic* it is the Good, and in the *Parmenides,* the One. According to my reading of the *Philebus,* the Good turns out to be the ultimate One, and Beauty is one of its important aspects.

24. Here I am thinking of the famous Sun, Line, and Cave passages in Books VI and VII which are often cited as evidence of Plato's "doctrine of the Two Worlds". There is also evidence in these passages that the so-called Two Worlds are continuous because the Forms encompass their sensibles, but the more popular interpretations emphasize their separation. For a

useful recent summary of the standard interpretations of the Theory of Forms in the middle dialogues and elsewhere, see William J. Prior, *Unity and Development in Plato's Metaphysics,* (La Salle, IL: Open Publishing Company, 1985).

25. Although there are passages in the *Phaedo* that suggest that the Forms are immanent in sensibles (in the account of causation at 100C–105C; see Prior, ibid. pp. 12–17), throughout most of the dialogue, the arguments for the immortality of the soul depend on recognizing the kinship of the human soul with the Forms while the human body is relegated to the sensible realm. Thus the body/soul dualism is simply one aspect of the Two Worlds doctrine (see Prior, ibid., pp. 33–41).

26. See Lloyd, op cit., pp. 18–22.

27. See *Symposium* 202B–205E.

28. See, e.g., "Mystery Religions", Kurt Randolph, in *Religions of Antiquity,* ed. Robert M. Seltzer (New York: MacMillan Publishing Co., 1989), esp. pp. 276–277.

29. See Andrea Nye, op cit., pp. 53–58.

30. See Luce Irigaray, "Sorcerer Love: A Reading of Plato's *Symposium,* Diotima's Speech", Eleanor H. Kuykendall, trans., *Hypatia,* vol. 3, no. 3, winter 1989, pp. 32–44.

31. See *Symposium* 202D–203A.

32. The Greek word *apeiron* is ambiguous; it may mean infinite or indefinite. I maintain that it means both. As will become evident in my discussion above of true knowledge vs. opinion, true Being vs. Becoming at *Philebus* 58C–58D, sensibles are indefinite *because* they are infinite in magnitude and intensity. For further details about this and all passages of the *Philebus* mentioned in this paper, see my *Knowledge, Pleasure, and Being: An Analysis of Plato's Philebus* (Albany: State University of New York Press, 1990).

33. This point will become most apparent in my discussion of the Divine Method above.

34. Although there is controversy about the extent to which Socrates is the spokesperson for Plato's views throughout the dialogues, I think that Socrates does speak for Plato in the *Philebus.* Or, at the very least, Socrates' role of main speaker indicates that Plato is once again focusing on his Socratic interests in the good life rather than on the epistemological and metaphysical puzzles discussed in the preceding triology of the *Theatetus, Sophist* and *Statesman* where Socrates was completely absent and the main speaker was the Stranger from Elea.

35. Although clearly the purpose of the Divine Method is to help us untangle the knots of the problem of one and many, the exact nature of the

problem (stated as a series of "puzzles", i.e., *aporiai*) is not easy to discern. The key passage is 15B1–8 which is rather ambiguously worded and thus much controversy surrounds how to interpret the puzzles and even how many (two or three?) of them there are. For a brief overview of the controversy, see R. M. Dancy, "The One, The Many, and the Forms: *Philebus* 15B1–8,", *Ancient Philosophy*, vol. 4, 1984. Fortunately, for the purposes of this paper, this issue need not be explored.

I also think that the units (which Plato calls "monads") are Forms which are ontologically prior to their sensible instances but to argue for this would go beyond the scope of this paper.

36. See *Philebus* 23C–26D.

37. As noted by Philip Wheelwright, *The Presocratics* (New York: The Odyssey Press, Inc., 1966), p. 11.

38. Robin Waterfield notes that the Greek classification was based on how much breath it took to sound a particular letter; vowels took the most, mutes (our 'stops') took the least, with the semi-vowels (our nasals, sibilants and continuants) in-between. See Waterfield, *Plato Philebus* (Harmondsworth, Middlesex, England and New York: Penguin Books Ltd, 1982,) p. 63, n. 2. Perhaps Plato sees the letters, as well as musical notes, forming a continuum. When making the same division of letters in the *Cratylus,* Plato does draw a parallel between this division and the one of musical sound into rhythms (see 423E–425A; cited by Waterfield, *ibid.*). For our present purposes, the details of this account need not be determined.

39. See *Philebus* 18B–D.

40. Cf. *Cratylus* 424D–425A and *Theatetus* 203E–204A. In the latter, Socrates explicitly claims that the syllable is a single entity with a character of its own different from the letters that make it up; it is an example of a whole which is different from the aggregate of its parts.

41. See Chomsky's summary of his theory in his entry, "Language: Chomsky's Theory", in the *Oxford Companion to the Mind,* ed. Richard L. Gregory (Oxford: Oxford University Press, 1987), pp. 419–421.

42. Ibid., p. 421.

43. See *Philebus* 15D–16B.

44. The fact that that the visual/tactile model is used throughout the middle dialogues is noted by Henry Teloh, *The Development of Plato's Metaphysics* (University Park and London: The Pennsylvania State University Press, 1981), pp. 100–118.

Consider how this model works in the Sun Analogy where Socrates gives an outline of the Good by comparing it to the sun. The analogy works on two levels: epistemological and ontological. The epistemological comparison is as follows. As the presence of the sun's light enables us to see and visible objects to be seen, so the Good enables us to know and for intelligible objects to be known. The ontological comparison I consider below (see n. 54). See *Republic* Bk. VI, 506E–509D.

45. *Philebus* 16C.

46. See *Protagoras* 320C-322A. The Promethean myth is merely alluded to in the *Philebus*, and there are, in fact, some important differences between the version in the *Protagoras* and the one in the *Philebus*. See my "Virtue, Knowledge, and the Necessity of Divinity: Plato's Use of the Promethean Myth", in *Rereading the Greeks*, ed. Gary Kessler, forthcoming. But for my present purposes, these differences are not crucial.

47. See *Philebus* 30B–D.

48. Ibid., 18E–22C.

49. Ibid., 61A.

50. Ibid., 65A.

51. Ibid., 64B.

52. I agree with Bury and Hackforth in emphasizing the close tie between truth and reality or Being. See R. G. Bury, *The Philebus of Plato* (Cambridge: Cambridge University Press, 1897), Appendix F., pp. 201ff.; and R. Hackforth, *Plato's Examination of Pleasure* (Cambridge: The University Press, 1954), p. 133. For a different view, see J. C. B. Gosling, *Plato Philebus* (Oxford: The Clarendon Press, 1975), pp. 134–135; pp. 212 seq.

53. See *Philebus* 55C–59D.

54. That is, the sun's energy that enables things to generate and grow is analogous to the Truth that sustains Being. See the Sun Analogy, *Republic* 507A–509C.

55. See *Philebus* 64B.

56. See *Republic* 353A–B.

57. See *Philebus* 65A–B.

58. Ibid., 65C.

59. Ibid., 65E–66A.

60. I am translating "the eternal nature" although the text here is uncertain, as Gosling notes (op cit., pp. 137–138). The Greek supports my translation (as well as alternatives) and in context, I think "the eternal nature" refers to the Good as it did at 64C. The personification of the Good occurs elsewhere in the *Philebus*, notably in the discussion of the Cause at 26E–31A where it is depicted as the creator of all (30E1–2), including the mixed kind (26E–27C). As I have argued elsewhere, there is no need to take the talk of the Cause's generation and production literally. (See Cynthia

Hampton, "Plato's Late Ontology: A Riddle Unresolved", *Ancient Philosophy,* vol. VIII, no. 1, spring 1988, p. 110–111; 115, n.16.) As I point out below, one reason Plato might have in using such language and for personifying the Good as a creator is to give us a representation of the Good which makes it clearer to us how we can model our own activities in imitation of the Forms.

61. See *Philebus* 66A–C.

62. Ibid.

63. Ibid., 44B–51A.

64. Unfortunately, Plato is not terribly forthcoming with clear examples of abnormal and inordinate pleasures. One example he gives is the pleasure an invalid experiences when scratching an itch caused by a disease (44B–46B). He also alludes to a sexual experience at 46D–47A but does not indicate whether the pleasures here are abnormal, inordinate, or both. The example of the passive homosexual (the *kinaidos*) whose passivity may include 'being kept' or even being a prostitute, and whose life is compared to one of perpetual scratching, I have borrowed from *Gorgias* 494E. The life of such a one is clearly thought by Plato to be disgraceful, and perhaps abnormal. As examples of pleasures that arise from psychic abnormalities and/or excesses he refers to those involving anger, fear, yearning, mourning, love, jealousy, envy, etc. (46B–48B). The only emotions he actually analyzes here are those aroused by comedy: the mixture of the pain of malice with the pleasure of laughing at the misfortunes of others (48B–50E). But discussion of this complicated case would take us too far afield from our present purpose.

65. See *Philebus* 31Aff.

66. Somewhat confusingly, Plato refers to both the pleasures that are mixed with pain, and those which are limited by intelligence, as being mixed, measure, or limited. But I take the mixture with pain to be the broader category, including both the inherently indefinite pleasures and those limited by intelligence. For the pleasures limited by intelligence still include pain, e.g., the pleasures of health involve the restoration of bodily imbalances.

67. See *Philebus* 51B–52C.

68. For more on these two types of false pleasure, see Cynthia Hampton, "Pleasure, Truth and Being in Plato's *Philebus:* A Reply to Professor Frede", *Phronesis,* vol. XXXII, no. 2, 1987, pp. 253–262, and *Pleasure, Knowledge, and Being: An Analysis of Plato's Philebus,* op. cit.

69. There remains the problem of where the pleasures which are limited by intelligence (i.e., the necessary pleasures attending health, strength, etc.) are supposed to fit in the final ranking. A. E. Taylor and R.

Hackforth speculate that the reference to a sixth class at 66C–D is meant
to encompass the necessary pleasures while Gosling explains the omission
by pointing out that the prize-giving is not between all elements of the good
life but only those which contribute to its goodness. [See Taylor, *Plato Philebus and Epinomis*, R. Klinbansky, G. Calogero, and A. C. Lloyds, eds. (London: Thomas Nelson & Sons, 1956) p. 91; Hackforth, op cit., pp. 139; 140, n.
3; and Gosling, op. cit., p. 224.] Perhaps Taylor and Hackforth are right but
it is still puzzling that there is no explicit reference to what comprises the
sixth class. I find Gosling's suggestion unsatisfactory because the necessary pleasures include those which promote fitness, health and virtue
(62E–63A, 63E), and these elements (especially virtue), surely contribute
to the goodness of the mixed life.

70. See *Philebus* 63D–64A.

71. Ibid., 52Dff.

72. Ibid., 57B.

73. Ibid., 57D.

74. Ibid., 55E–56C.

75. Ibid., 56D–57A.

76. Ibid., 57D.

77. Ibid., 57B.

78. Ibid., 58A.

79. Ibid., 59D. As Hackforth notes (op. cit., p. 124, n.1), Plato does not
always restrict the meaning of the terms *nous, phronesis* and *episteme*. But
the context strongly suggests that the first two terms refer to a specially
elevated form of knowledge. The reference to 'contemplation' simply means
knowledge of the Forms which includes intuiting them (i.e., *nous*), but also
involves knowing how to embody them in our lives (i.e., *phronesis*). I shall
discuss this more later.

Concerning the use of the Greek term for knowledge, i.e., *"episteme"*, it
is used in the *Philebus* in a general sense as something roughly equivalent
to "cognition", the term I use above. In this general sense, it is sometimes
used in conjunction with *techne* (craft, skill, or art). Roger Shiner in his
monograph, *Knowledge and Reality in Plato's Philebus* (Assen: Koninklijke
Van Gorcum & Comp. B.V., 1974), p. 55, points to the interchangability of
the terms *episteme* and *techne* as evidence of the radical shift in the *Philebus* from the epistemology in the *Republic*. But as Richard Mohr has
pointed out [in *"Philebus* 55C–62A and Revisionism"*, New Essays on Plato,*
ed. Francis Jeffry Pelletier and John King-Farlow, (Guelph: Canadian Association for Publishing in Philosophy, The University of Calgary Press,
1983), p. 166] Plato does not consistently use technical language even in the

Republic. Note *Republic* 533B1–6 where the dialectic is called a *techne.* In response to Mohr, Shiner claims (in "Knowledge in *Philebus* 55C–62A; a Response", *New Essays on Plato,* p. 172) that the language in the *Republic* suggests that the dialectic is the only way to knowledge whereas the *Philebus* does not. But it seems to me that in both dialogues, the dialectic is the highest form of cognition and hence knowledge in the full or true sense, and the lower forms, including *techne,* presuppose it. But to settle this question here would take us too far afield.

80. See *Philebus* 62B.

81. Ibid., 62B; D.

82. Ibid., 17A.

83. "Cognitively dependable" is a phrase used by Gregory Vlastos. See his "Degrees of Reality in Plato", repr. in *Platonic Studies,* 2nd ed., (Princeton: Princeton University Press, 1981), p. 64.

84. See Hampton, "Pleasure, Truth and Being in Plato's *Philebus:* A Reply to Professor Frede", op. cit., pp. 256–57.

85. See the Divided Line passage in the *Republic* at 509D–511C.

86. See *Philebus* 28D–30E.

87. A similar reason might also help explain the use of the Divine Artisan or Demiurge in *Republic* Book X and in the *Timaeus.*

88. See *Philebus* 26E.

89. Plato, both in the *Phaedrus* and his seventh letter, notes the limitations of written language for conveying truth. See *Phaedrus* 274Cff. and seventh letter, 341B–344D.

90. Although Plato's philosophy is holistic, I hesitate to call it mystical. As I pointed out above, direct communion with ultimate reality, *nous,* is supposed to be coupled with the ability to realize this intuition in action through *phronesis.* In other words, rational intuition and practical reasoning are two moments or aspects of the same capacity. Intuition is not "superrational", much less irrational. Instead, *nous* is part of the highest type of reasoning or knowledge.

Diotima Speaks Through the Body

Susan Hawthorne

Diotima's speech in *The Symposium*[1] makes philosophical use of the female body as a metaphor for understanding the nature of love. The female body and the processes associated with its renewal, change, and demise become a filter for Diotima's perception of the world. Through her understanding of her own body's function she creates a vision of the world that is distinctively 'feminine'[2], and from that vision argues for a particular way of understanding the nature of Eros.[3]

Although Socrates is the mouthpiece of the speech, and Plato is the scribe, on the basis of the structure of the speech and the specifically feminine view of the world presented, the originator of the speech, it is argued, is Diotima.[4]

Interestingly, in spite of the marked social and political differences in rights between women and men in Ancient Greek culture, Socrates presents the teachings of Diotima in a way that make it very clear that he held her in high regard. To what extent Plato's judgement accords with Socrates' is unclear, and must remain so, given that he maintains his role as scribe to Socrates, rather than the more personalized role of commentator (undoubtedly, the very act of writing down involves selection and perception, but this is an indirect and invisible commentary). In this regard the speech serves only to contribute to the contradictory stances held by Plato on the position of women. In spite of Socrates' praise of Diotima, she is not present at the dinner, nor are any other women. Instead, they are made invisible, although they do provide some services behind the scene. What the speech does point to, however, is the acknowledgement that some women were held in high esteem for their wisdom. And although this goes against much of what is known about fifth century Athens, the fact that there were pockets of women's culture is important.

Part of its importance is its prior invisibility. Making visible the contribution of women is not always a straightforward task, and decoding the evidence of men is fraught with hidden dangers. The analysis that follows highlights the particularly feminine nature of the speech, both in terms of its structure and its use of language, specifically the metaphors used in the speech.

The metaphors, attributed to Diotima by Socrates, draw heavily on female experiences associated with the body, and with being a woman. In this respect, the speech differs markedly from the other speeches in *The Symposium,* and it is surprising that this feature has not been remarked upon sooner.[5] The metaphors used by Diotima include pregnancy, birth, becoming, death and transformation through mediation.

Diotima's Metaphors

Pregnancy

Diotima, in her speech uses the following expression:

> *hoi en tais psuchais kuousin eti mallon he en tois somasin . . .*
> *. . . those who are pregnant in their souls still more than in their bodies . . .* [6]

Using the metaphor of pregnancy, Diotima[7] challenges the listener (reader) to think about bodies and souls in equivalent ways and impute similar characteristics to them. Whereas, in common discourse the two are considered to have very different attributes—souls are not said to be 'pregnant'. In fact there is almost something shocking about this idea, since the soul, in most treatises, is posited as incompatible with bodily comparisons. Indeed, in *The Symposium* speech that precedes Socrates', Agathon, a tragic poet and the host of the party, notes the difference in substance between bodies and souls, and points out how delicate Eros must be, because he resides in the most delicate of substances—namely, the soul. So it is revealing, in this context, to see Diotima attributing such a physical event as pregnancy to the soul.

Diotima's use of metaphor in this instance, parallels the first part of Aristotle's definition of a metaphor insofar as souls and bodies are treated as though they belong to the same class of entities:

> Metaphor (*metaphora*) consists in giving the thing a name that belongs to something else; the transference (*epiphora*) being either from genus to species, or from species to genus, or from species to species, or on the grounds of analogy.[8]

As for the last phrase of Aristotle's quotation, analogy, particular use is made of this kind of metaphor with regard to the notions of *metaxu*—'between', and *gignomenos*—'becoming'.[9] These words point to a concern with mediation and with process, both of which can be shown to be important cultural expectations for women.[10]

Metaphors direct our attention to similarities between different things, or in the case of analogies, to similarities between structures and processes. The metaphors used by Diotima highlight particular events in the lives of women, thus drawing our attention to these events in her discussion of the nature of love, delivered through Socrates. The irony of this is that men, since that time, have used Socrates' (Diotima's) insights to draw the analogy between creations of the mind (art) and creations of the body (children) to exclude women from the field of artistic creation. It has been argued that the reason there have been no great women artists is that women create through the body and therefore do not need (or are unable) to create through the mind. Although it is clear from the way in which the metaphors are used by Diotima, that creativity in one sphere was not exclusive of creativity in other spheres.[11]

Birth

The metaphors used by Diotima emphasize certain aspects of the world which can be related to her perception of the world as a woman. Throughout the speech there are a great number of metaphors which relate to the process of birth: from conception, to pregnancy, to giving birth; then to processes of becoming; to initiation, to death and to rebirth.[12] Considered together these metaphors show a concern for the ongoing process of life—a view much more in keeping with women's experience of the world, than with men's.[13]

The most important section on conception and birth begins with:

> birth (*tokos*) can be according to the body or according to the psyche.[14]

This is reiterated a little later with:

> 'there are those who are pregnant in their souls—they are, she said, those who conceive in the soul rather than in the body, who bear and give birth to those things proper to the soul.'[15]

These individuals are those whom she calls 'creative poets: artists and inventors'.[16] She claims that all people desire to procreate, but that this is only possible when there is beauty. But having given beauty such an important place, she goes on to deny that beauty is the object of love[17] (as Agathon would have us believe). Instead she says that the object of love is:

tis genniseos kai tou tokou ev to kalo

the conceiving and bringing forth in beauty.[18]

Her reason for saying this is, she argues, that humans can approach immortality only by means of procreation, and all creatures desire immortality. However, humans have an alternative, which is to bring forth children of the soul/psyche through works of art, such as those produced by the originators of poetry and other crafts. Her reference to the makers of crafts[19] is explained in an earlier section in a discussion of poiesis, creation.[20]

> You know that creation is a broad notion. For when anything whatever passes from non-existence into existence, the whole cause is creation, so that even the works made by the crafts are acts of creation and all the makers of these are poets.[21]

Although the birth metaphor is extended to all people, it comes from a view of the world that takes the female principle as its starting point, and by analogy and metaphor, extends it to the male population.[22] Diotima speaks from her experience of the body, as a woman, and it is from this experience that her perceptions, and her metaphors, derive. But for men the experience of giving birth must remain foreign, hence her attempt to universalize understanding through the analogy of *poiesis*. It is interesting that Diotima draws no hierarchy of distinction between poetry and the creation of objects, but uses the same word, *poiesis*, creation for both.

Becoming

The 'becoming' metaphor occurs in two contexts: as processes of change; and in the 'ascent' passage[23] which outlines the process involved in attaining knowledge of the mysteries of love through contemplation of perfect beauty. It ends with the following sentence:

> 'For the right way to approach the things of love (erotic matters), or to be guided by another, is to begin with beautiful things, and from these things of beauty to ascend continually, as if up steps on

a stair, from one example to two, and from two t
ies, and from beautiful bodies still to beautifi
tices), and from activities to beautiful learning
from different kinds of learnings to that ultim;
is nothing other than itself, learning of beau
know finally that which is beauty itself."[24]

Diotima draws analogies between the physical process of growth and replenishment of parts of the body (hair, flesh, bones, blood);[25] and then she extends it into the mental sphere[26] when she talks of the process of coming to know things: recollection (through experiences of custom, belief, desire, pleasure, pain and fear). In neither case is it a static arrangement, rather there is a continual process of change in both realms.

Diotima returns to the metaphor of becoming in the ascent passage,[27] again making reference to the love of physical beauty (of boys and daily activities), to the mental (knowledge) and to the spiritual. The process of spiritual enlightenment culminates in:

[a person] having brought forth and nurtured true virtue, it is possible for that one to become dear to the god, [Eros] and if ever immortality is given to any of humankind, it will be given to that one.[28]

A part of this process of spiritual becoming is initiation into the mysteries. Initiation is a type of second birth during life, a spiritual rather than a physical birth. It is one of the steps towards spiritual enlightenment. Thus, we have another intersection between giving birth and becoming, the former providing the image in helping us to understand the spiritual form.

Death

Diotima also turns her intellect to death, or rather dying, not as an ultimate end, but as a means to immortality. Again the notion of rebirth is linked with dying. Speaking of Eros, Diotima says:

and he is neither immortal nor mortal, but on one and the same day he is a young shoot and alive, whenever he is prosperous, and then he dies, but he returns to life again because of the nature of his father.[29]

Apart from the reference to physical and mental 'loss and reparation'[30] the other reference to death is in relation to

...lf-sacrifice.[31] Alcestis, Achilles and Codrus are said to have died for others because they:

> believed there would be an immortal memory concerning their virtue.[32]

Their reasons for sacrificing themselves are the same as those who give birth physically or spiritually—that is, because:

> they are in love with immortality.[33]

Death, therefore, becomes just another form of birth. It is necessary for regeneration (physical), recollection (mental) and immortality (spiritual). Death and birth are the two transformative processes that ensure the continuity of life, and both may be regarded as different aspects of the same process.

Transformation

Birth is a central theme of Diotima's speech. Around it hover other concepts (such as becoming, death and transformation). The events of birth, growth, death and regeneration indicated in these words are processes that repeat themselves cyclically. The cyclical process is one that is familiar to all women—how much more familiar would it be in a culture in which the moon (*he mene*) and month (*ho men*) are tied to the word for menstrual cycle? Diotima also makes some reference to analogous natural cycles. Some of these concepts are aired in earlier speeches by others, but not in such abundance, nor are they as central. Moreover, the manner in which Diotima presents her speech is markedly different. For one thing, there is no dualistic battle taking place in Diotima's speech, even between such different events (to us) as birth and death. They are represented as part of a continuum which always returns to its point of departure.

This is reflected in Diotima's use of another metaphor, *metaxu*—between. *Metaxu* is conceived of as a point on a continuum, a bridge between things that are separated, or between qualities that appear irreconcilable:

phronesis—thoughtfulness	*amathia*—ignorance
kalos—beauty	*aischros*—ugliness
athanatos—immortality	*thnetos*—mortality[34]

What Diotima attempts, through the use of the *metaxu* metaphor, is to establish links between separated elements, by doing so she breaks down the separation,[35] and thus enables humanity to commune with the divine. This is precisely the role of Eros—as the bridge, the intermediary, the *metaxu.*

Simone Weil expressed the relationship embodied in the term *metaxu* in the following way:

> Two prisoners whose cells adjoin communicate with each other by knocking on the wall. The wall is the thing that separates them but it is also their means of communication. It is the same with us and God. Every separation is a link.[36]

The metaxu, therefore, is a concept liked to connectivity, or the feminist 'ethic of inseparability'.[37] For Diotima there is no separation, and what she is recommending to her listener (Socrates) is that he reflect on the nature of the mysteries and the interconnectivity of all.

Structure

The metaphors used by Diotima in her speech lead to integration in every dimension. The speech proceeds as a series of cycles or spirals, all impinging on different aspects of one another. The result is a pulling together rather than a cleaving apart, not into something static and detached, but a point on a continuum, linked by the *metaxu.*

What Diotima achieves in this speech, and what I consider to be her central mode of argument, is the philosophical use of the female body as a metaphor. In using the body in this way and in identifying the life processes as a starting point for an inclusive philosophy about the nature of love, she challenges the other speakers in *The Symposium* to think about the subject in a very different way. For example, her speech does not reveal a dependence on dualistic thinking, namely by creating separations between the processes of birth and death. Nor does she have the problem which Eryximachus[38] faces in his conclusion, of battling binary oppositions. Instead we have a unity. The unity, the divine beauty itself, is one point on a continuum between birth and death, or possibly, between death and birth. This resembles the 'ethic of nonseparability'[39] found in some recent feminist philosophy.

The structure of the speech itself reflects this sense of a continuum. Several times Diotima returns to speak about a subject she has already mentioned, but each time she deals with it in a slightly different way (rather like the process of becoming). Each part of the process is dealt with on the three levels: physical, mental, spiritual. The ascent passage repeats this structure yet again, briefly touching on almost everything that has preceded it in the speech.

At the beginning of the speech Diotima challenges Socrates' absolutist dualistic divisions, by rejecting the notion that if something is not beautiful then it must be ugly, if not wise then ignorant, and so forth. Diotima recognizes degrees of change, rather than simply seeing only those qualities at each end of the spectrum. She then moves on to a discussion of creation. Creation is examined through metaphors relating to the body, mind and soul. Each section is roughly half the length of the preceding section. Visually represented it would resemble the spiral that emerges from the Golden Rectangle—a spiral formed by tracing a curved diagonal line through progressively halved rectangles.[40] Both in structure and content, then, the speech reveals a connection with the life processes (and metaphorically with its abtract representations). The only exception to this occurs at the very end, where in two places she speaks of the ultimate experience of perceiving beauty:

> being itself, by itself, with itself, unique, eternal.[41]

And:

> what might we suppose about someone's state if it were possible for them to see beauty itself, clear, pure and unmixed, and not defiled by human flesh and colour and other perishable nonsense, but who is able to perceive the singular divine beauty itself.[42]

In order to get into such a state, however, one must go through a process of 'becoming,' and once there, one engages in 'bringing forth and nurturing'. So that, in fact, one is connected to the same cycles and processes, even there.

Conclusion

The interpretation being offered here could, I believe, open the way for a re-examination of the work of other women philosophers, from antiquity to the present, and could lead philosophers to look again at the assumptions of what constitutes the basis for a feminist ontology and epistemology.

Susanne Langer describes metaphor as 'the source of generality'.[43] For Diotima the source of her metaphor, and hence of her ability to generalize about the world, is herself. Her ontological perspective differs from that of her fellow speakers because her experience in the world is affected by her experience of the female body: menstrual cycles, pregnancy, and experiences of 'becoming' (perhaps through the growth of the foetus or the development of language, memory and so forth in growing children).

In addition, I believe that Diotima's speech shows a way forward for feminist philosphers. Her speech provides a model for a structural mode of argument very different from the standard linear logical mode usual in Western philosophy. She may even be the earliest named woman philosopher[44] to 'think through the body',[45] or to 'write the body'.[46]

Notes

1. Plato, *The Symposium,* ed. Kenneth Dover (Cambridge: Cambridge University Press, 1980). Diotima's speech is the section between 201 d1– 212 c2. The above Greek version is the one used as the basis for all translations in this article. Other versions used are: *Great Dialogues of Plato,* trans. W.H.D. Rouse, eds. Eric H. Warmington and Philip G. Rouse (New York: New American Library, 1984). Also see Plato, *The Symposium,* trans. Walter Hamilton (London: Penguin Books, 1988). The translation by Rouse is recommended by this writer, as it is closer to the spirit of the original Greek and is less likely to introduce the value laden, often sexist, terms that Hamilton resorts to.

2. The word 'feminine' is hardly ideal. In using it I do not mean to attribute conventional connotations, I mean simply 'pertaining to the female.' Sharon Magnarelli has introduced a useful term 'feminive', which she defines in the following way: 'I use the word etymologically in reference to literature written by women, and more specifically, I use it to evoke literature that is subversive in that it breaks with at least some of the traditional canons of literary standards . . . These canonical subversions or breaks with tradition exist on the level of theme, in the style or structure, or even both.' Sharon Magnarelli, 'An Overview of Some Recent Hispanic "Feminive" Prose, *Occasional Paper 8* (Melbourne: Centre for Women's Studies, Monash University, 1989).

3. The word *eros* in Greek is masculine and is personified by the spirit, Eros. Eros is a male spirit.

4. The different ways in which women and men use language has been studied by, among others, Robin Lakoff, *Language and Woman's Place* (New York: Harper & Row, 1975) and Dale Spender, *Man Made Language* (London and Boston: Routledge & Kegan Paul, 1980). Based on cultural differences between women and men, these researchers have pointed to a number of variables including vocabulary, sentence structure and imagery. And Carol Gilligan, *In a Different Voice: Psychological Theory and Women's Development* (Cambridge, MA: Harvard University Press, 1982), has pointed to the different ways in which women and men understand and make moral decisions. Gilligan writes:

> '. . . the morality of rights differ from the morality of responsibility in its emphasis on separation rather than connection, in its consideration of the individual rather than the relationship as primary.' (ibid., p. 19).

The notion of connection, rather than separation, is an important one in Diotima's speech. See my discussion in the section, Transformation.

The world of ancient Greece was a highly divided one in terms of the roles played by women and men in that culture. And one would expect women's and men's language to reflect the cultural divisions. Obviously there are many grammatical differences between Ancient Greek language and Modern English, and the analysis that follows does not take such differences into account. Instead the focus is on the structure of the argument put forward in the speech by Socrates in *The Symposium,* and the preoccupations expressed. The cultural differences, including experiences and expectations, are reflected in the preoccupations of Diotima's speech. Conventionally, Diotima is regarded not as a real woman who taught Socrates these things (although he claims this), but rather as a mythical figure fabricated by Socrates for the purpose of this speech. See the comment by Dover, op. cit., p. 137.

5. The analysis may also go some way towards affirming the existence of the real woman, Diotima, and hence giving her the status of one of the earliest women philosophers we can name, a woman with her own developed philosophy and not just simply the woman whose words Socrates reports. For some other recent discussions of Diotima's speech, see Eleanor H. Kuykendall 'Introduction to "Sorcerer Love," by Luce Irigaray'; Luce Irigaray, 'Sorcerer Love: A Reading of Plato's Symposium, Diotima's Speech; and Andrea Nye, 'The Hidden Host: Irigaray and Diotima at Plato's Symposium' in *Hypatia: Special Issue. French Feminist Philosophy,* vol. 3, no. 3, winter 1989.

6. Op. cit. Dover, *Symposium,* 209 a1. Translations from The Symposium throughout this article are by the author. For a published translation see op. cit. Rouse, p. 103.

7. Although Socrates speaks the speech, I will refer to it as Diotima's speech, since Socrates claims to be merely repeating what Diotima has said to him on another occasion.

8. Aristotle, *Poetics*, 1457, quoted from Colin Murray Turbayne, *The Myth of Metaphor* (Columbia, S.C.: University of South Carolina Press, 1971) p. 11.

9. Op. cit. *Symposium*, 207 d7 and 208 a1.

10. I elaborate on this later in this paper.

11. Misogynist translations have exacerbated this tendency. See, for example, the difference between the following two translations of 208 e1–e3: Rouse accurately translates, 'those who are pregnant in body . . . turn rather to women' (op. cit., p. 103.); Hamilton, on the other hand, translates it as: 'Those whose creative instinct is physical have recourse to women' (op. cit. p. 90.).

12. The variety of terms employed is an indication of this:

he gennesis	a begetting/a producing
ho gennetor	father
he genna	descent/offspring
gignomai	to become/to happen/to be born/to be
tikto	to bring into the world/to bring forth/to bear
he kuesis	pregnancy
to kuema	that which is conceived, embryo, foetus
egkumon	pregnant
kueo	trans. to bear in the womb/to be pregnant of/intrans. to be pregnant/to conceive
anabioo	to come to life again/to return to life
he poiesis	a making/a forming/a creating II the art of poetry/a poem
ho tokos	a bringing forth/birth/the time of delivery/ 2. offspring
paidogonos	begetting children
empoieo	to make in/to produce/to cause

13. See Riane Eisler, *The Chalice and the Blade* (New York: Harper & Row, 1988) for an elaboration of this. I am not suggesting some mysterious essence here, simply the observation that women experience their bodies and (like men) use them as the basis for synthesizing theories about the nature of the world around them. The other side of this is women's response

to experiences constructed by their societies, in particular patriarchal constructions.

14. Op. cit., *Symposium,* 206 b7.

15. Ibid., 209 a1.

16. Ibid., 209 a4–5.

17. One could well see this as an early objection to identifying love and objectification.

18. Op. cit., *Symposium,* 206 e5.

19. *'Demiourgos'*—worker, craftsman (sic), maker, author. Craftsman is the standard translation given in sources such as Liddell and Scott, *Greek–English Lexicon* (Oxford: Oxford University Press, 1986).

20. Op. cit., *Symposium,* 205 b8–c2. In Greek, *poiesis*—maker, creator, also means specifically, poet.

21. This is used as an analogy to clarify her point about love.

22. One could speculate that she has done this for the benefit of her male audience (Socrates) in order to make her metaphysics applicable to them. At 209 e5 she says to Socrates: 'Perhaps even you could be initiated into these mysteries; but whether you grasp the perfect revelations . . . I do not know.' This might indicate a belief on her part, that men have difficulties in understanding the more profound aspects of the mysteries—particularly as this seems to be a reference to the Eleusinian Mysteries which were connected with the fertility of both women and the land.

23. Op. cit., *Symposium,* 210 e1–211 d1.

24. Ibid., 211 b6–211 d1. For a translation, see also op. cit., Rouse, pp. 104–6.

25. Ibid., *Symposium,* 207 d6.

26. Ibid., 207 e5.

27. Ibid., 210 e1–211 d1.

28. Ibid., 212 a5–7.

29. Ibid., 203 d8. Eros' father is Hephaestos which means resourcefulness.

30. Ibid., 207 d6 and 207 e5 respectively, See also the discussion under Becoming.

31. Ibid., 208 d2 ff.

32. Ibid., 208 d5–6.

33. Ibid., 207 e1.

34. The source of these words is op. cit. Liddell and Scott.

35. For a contemporary example of this, see Susan Griffin, *Woman and Nature: The Roaring Inside Her* (New York: Harper & Row,1980). Also see Robin Morgan, *The Demon Lover: On the Sexuality of Terrorism* (New York: W. W. Norton & Company, 1989.) Robin Morgan summarizes the conventional wisdom of patriarchy and feminism in a way that, interestingly reflects the argument put forward in this paper. She writes:

> 'If I had to name one quality as the genius of patriarchy, it would be compartmentalization, the capacity for institutionalizing disconnection. Intellect severed from emotion. Thought separated from action. . . . The personal isolated from the political. Sex divorced from love. The material ruptured from the spiritual.' (ibid., p. 51).

And:

> 'If I had to name one quality as the genius of feminist thought, culture and action, it would be *connectivity*. (ibid., p. 53).

See also Robin Morgan's chapter, 'Beyond Terror: The Politics of Eros' (ibid., *The Demon Lover*), and the work of philosopher, Mary Daly, with her concept of the 'biophilic' in *Gyn/Ecology: The Metaethics of Radical Feminism* (Boston: Beacon Press, 1978).

36. Simone Weil, *Gravity and Grace* (London: Routledge & Kegan Paul, 1972) p. 132.

37. Catherine Keller, 'Feminism and the Ethic of Inseparability' in Judith Plaskow and Carol P. Christ (eds.) *Weaving the Visions: New Patterns in Feminist Spirituality* (San Francisco: Harper & Row, 1989), pp. 256–265.

38. Op. cit, *Symposium,* Eryximachus' speech precedes Socrates', 185 e6–188 e7.

39. Op. cit., Keller, in *Weaving the Visions.*

40. The golden rectangle and the subsequent nautilus-shaped spiral are forms that would be familiar to ancient Greek philosophers through the teachings of Pythagoras.

41. Op. cit., *Symposium,* p. 211 b1–2.

42. Ibid., 211 d8–e4.

43. Susanne K. Langer, *Philosophy in a New Key: A Study in the Symbolism of Reason, Rite and Art* (New York: Penguin Books, Inc., 1942), p. 111.

44. The themes and overall structure of the speech are so different from the other speeches in *The Symposium,* and display such a strong female influence that I find it difficult to believe in the mythical status of Diotima.

45. Adrienne Rich, *Of Woman Born* (New York: Bantam Books, 1976), p. 290. For commentary on this, see also: Naomi R. Goldenberg, 'Archetypal Theory and the Separation of Mind and Body' in Judith Plaskow and Carol P. Christ (eds.) *Weaving the Visions,* pp. 244–255.

46. See Luce Irigaray, *This Sex Which is Not One* (Ithaca, NY: Cornell University Press, 1985); *Speculum of the Other Woman* (Ithaca, NY: Cornell University Press, 1985); and *le corps-a-corps avec la mere* (Montreal: les editions de la pleine lune, 1981).

PART TWO

ARISTOTLE

Who's Who in the Polis

Elizabeth V. Spelman

When you read about Black women being lynched, they aren't think-ing of us as females. The horrors that we have experienced have ab-solutely everything to do with them not even viewing us as women.

Barbara Smith

How shall we go about investigating a philosopher's views about women? The most logical and straightforward approach would seem to be to focus on whatever the philosopher says about women, in particular on the differences he draws between women and men, and then to see what social and political implications he takes such differences to have.

Hence in recent years we have been directed to Aristotle's de-scriptions of the biological differences between males and females—in particular, their roles in reproduction—and to his description of the different rational capacities of males and females.[1] Aristotle be-lieves that both kinds of difference bespeak the natural superiority of men to women: biologically, women provide simply the matter in which the seed, bearer of the purer and more important element of form provided by the male, can grow; and while women are not without reason, their reason hasn't the power or authority of that found in men.

In what follows I take a different tack in trying to get at Aris-totle's views about women. Instead of focusing simply on his discus-sions of the differences between men and women, I begin by asking about another and very closely related distinction he makes: the distinction between women and slaves. This distinction cuts across that between male and female, since slaves can be either male or female.[2] The importance Aristotle attaches to the difference be-tween "women" and "slaves" raises serious difficulties for any read-ing of his views about "woman's nature" based only on the distinction he draws between "men" and "women." For in Aristotle, the significance of the distinction between men and women varies according to whether the men and women we are talking about are free or slave. There is no simple distinction in Aristotle between men and women. Although he almost always thinks of people as gendered, he does not think of them only in terms of gender. And if we don't see that, we can't fully capture what he says about gender differences: that is, we have to refer to what appears to be something other than gender to describe his account of gender.

What Aristotle says about the nature of free women is quite different from what he says about the nature of slave women. An account of "Aristotle's views about women" that doesn't inquire seriously into what he says about slave women not only announces that the position of slave women is theoretically insignificant, it also gives a radically incomplete picture of what he says about women who are not slaves.

I

It is mainly in the *Politics* that Aristotle talks about the political significance of the distinction in kind between male and female, between master and slave, and also between woman and slave. People come together, Aristotle says, out of the mutual need they have of each other for human life to be reproduced and maintained. But what makes a life a characteristically human one, and what makes that form of human community called the city-state or polis something different from cattle grazing together, is the end for the sake of which the polis exists: the possibility of a good life, a life lived in accordance with the highest human virtue.[3] The household, consisting of husband, wife, children, and slaves, is the place where basic life-sustaining activities take place. The polis, consisting of citizens deliberating about and executing public affairs, is the forum in which men can engage in the noblest activities of which humans are capable.[4]

In a well-ordered city-state, women and slaves are not parts of the polis, but they are the conditions of it. Without their work, the polis could not exist, but they do not participate in the activities of the polis.[5] They are not capable of living lives that exhibit the highest form of human excellence, though it would not be possible for others to live such lives without them. In a "well-ordered state the citizens should have leisure and not have to provide for their daily wants" (*Politics* 1269a34–35).[6] The work that women, slaves, and other laborers do is not the kind of work the good man or good citizen should perform, for "no man can practice human excellence who is living the life of a mechanic or laborer" (*Politics* 1278a22; see also 1328b38–1329a2). It is not simply that one needs leisure to develop such excellence (*Politics* 1329a1) and that performing menial duties would be degrading and disgraceful for good men and good citizens (*Politics* 1273a32ff.); there is a danger of masters becoming too much like slaves or other laborers, or in any event ceasing to be able to do their proper work well, if these good citizens "learn the crafts of inferiors" (*Politics* 1277b6).[7] It also would be dangerous for statesmen to do women's work—for example, carding wool—for the contempt their subjects would have for them is just the kind of trifle that can cause revolution (*Politics* 1312a1ff.).

According to Aristotle the relation between a man and a woman—in the *Politics,* as we shall see in more detail below, this means the relation between husband and wife, or more specifically, between a man who is a citizen and his wife—is quite different from the relation between master and slave, even though both are relations of those who are by nature fit to rule and those who are by nature fit to be ruled. This difference respects the different functions, virtues, and natures of women and slaves.

All things, including human beings, are defined by their special function—that which nature intended them and their kind alone to do well—and people are capable of performing their different functions well to the extent that they have the appropriate virtues (see e.g., *Politics* 1253a23, 1252b3). Both women and slaves are fit by nature to carry on activities and provide services within the household that make is possible for the man who is their natural ruler to do the work he is fit to do outside the household in the polis. Again, their function in the household is to make life possible, his function in the polis is to make a good life. Women are suited by their nature to bear children and be companions to their husbands, and to "preserve" what their husbands "acquire" (*Politics* 1277b25–26). Slaves are suited by their nature to "minister to the wants of individuals" (1287a12); "with their bodies [they] minister to the needs of life" (1254b25) and do menial labor under the direction of others.

These differences in function, virtue, and nature between women and slaves are reflected in the kind of relationships and kind of rule masters have over women on the one hand and slaves on the other. The relation between master and slave, Aristotle sometimes says, is very much like that between soul and body: the slave is the bodily instrument of the master and is the possession of the master. As the soul rules the body despotically, so masters rule slaves (*Politics* 1254b5). Insofar as both friendship and justice require a kind of common moral and legal status, neither is really possible between masters and slaves (see *Nicomachean Ethics* 1161b4–5), though sometimes Aristotle speaks of a kind of friendship (see *Politics* 1255b14) and a kind of justice (see *Nicomachean Ethics* 1134b8 ff.) that is possible between them.

The relationship between the ruler and his wife is between two free people (*Politics* 1256b1), not one free and one slave, and the rule here is more like that between intellect and appetite than between soul and body (*Politics* 1254b5).[8] Intellect and appetite are both parts of the soul, so are closer than soul and body, but still intellect is superior to appetite.[9] While both men and women in this instance are free, that is, neither is a natural slave (a reminder that "woman" or "wife" in this context of Aristotle's thought does not include slave women), nevertheless the man is superior to the woman and so ought to rule her. Their relationship, Aristotle seems to be saying, is more equal than that of master and slave, but it is still far from being one between equals. Thus while there is a kind of friendship appropriate for husband and wife, it is different from both a friendship between equals and from that between master and slave (*Nicomachean Ethics* 1158b12ff.). Similarly, there is a kind of justice obtaining between husband and wife different from that between political equals but nonetheless "more fully realized" than the justice between master and slave (*Nicomachean Ethics* 1134b15–17). At one point in the *Poetics*, Aristotle describes the difference between a woman and a slave in this way: while a woman is "inferior," the slave is a "wholly worthless being" (1454a20).

This attempt to describe a relationship somewhere between radical inequality and full equality is reiterated in Aristotle's desire to call the rule of husband over wife constitutional as opposed to despotical. The rule of men over women can't really be constitutional, since the women don't get a turn to rule, but it is less one-sided than that of masters over slaves. For example, the man may hand over some of his affairs to his wife (*Nicomachean Ethics* 1160b35) but presumably not to his slaves. Similarly, Aristotle insists that the rule of husband over wife is for the sake of the wife, while that of master over slave is finally for the sake of the master (*Politics* 1278b31 ff.); but rule among those who are equal is for the common interest (*Politics* 1279a18 ff.).[10]

In sum, women and slaves have certain things in common: both do the work that makes the life of the polis possible and both have natures that exclude them from the ranks of those who are fit to rule. But the function, virtue, and nature of women differ from those of slaves; nature, Aristotle says, intended that.

II

Not all the women Aristotle knew about were free women, and not all the slaves he knew about were men. What about female slaves? Does he even note their existence? He does indeed, right at the beginning of the *Politics:*

> Now nature has distinguished between the female and the slaves. For she is not niggardly, like the smith who fashions the Delphian knife for many uses; she makes each thing for a single use, and every instrument is best made when intended for one and not for many uses. But among barbarians no distinction is made between women and slaves, because there is no natural ruler among them: they are a community of slaves, male and female. (*Politics* 1252b1–7)

While the passage begins by distinguishing between female and slave, it ends with a reference to female slaves.[11] What is Aristotle getting at here?

First of all we need to remember that in book 1 of the *Politics* Aristotle distinguished between those people who were slaves by convention and those who were slaves by nature. It is one thing, he said, to be enslaved by others in consequence of being defeated by them in war; it is another thing altogether to be fit by nature to be the slave of someone who is by nature your superior (we shall return to Aristotle's grounds for this distinction below). Now we only see what nature really intends for things or individuals or communities when such things are in their most perfect state.[12] In a community of natural slaves, we cannot see human excellence in its full flowering: excellence is found only in those who are natural rulers, and only when they are living in communities in which they can function as rulers. While nature distinguishes between the woman and the slave, we see the distinction at work only in the well-ordered state, not in a community of natural slaves.

Aristotle's point seems to be this: If you *are* a slave—a slave by nature and not by convention—then you can't also *have* slaves, people who are naturally subject to your rule. To put the point a slightly different way: if the entire population is a slave population, then in one sense there are slaves, in another there are not. According to Aristotle, a population is slave because by nature it is fit to be ruled by others; but the same population cannot contain slaves within it because it has no natural rulers among its members.[13] Where everyone is a slave (and hence where no one can be anyone else's slave), there is no distinction between slave and anyone else.

But even if all are slaves, some are women and some are men, as Aristotle himself says. So there is still a conceptual distinction between woman and slave, even though in a population of natural slaves, all the women are slaves. In the context of the *Politics*, it is clear that by "woman" Aristotle means the female companion of a natural ruler, that is, a free woman, not a slave woman. The function performed by a free woman who is a wife of a citizen is different from that performed by the citizen's slaves, male or female. The wife's function, again, is to be a companion of sorts and to reproduce, not just any children, but children who will be citizens.[14] Indeed, as is argued in the *Generation of Animals* (767b), best of all she produces males just like the father. The slaves' function is to otherwise minister to his needs and presumably to a certain extent to the needs of his wife and children. A "woman" is the female who will have the citizen's legitimate children; a "slave" is a person, male or female, who does the menial work in the household.[15]

Thus Aristotle does not allow for the possibility of slaves who are women, but only for slaves who are female—for he draws a distinction between woman and slave in such a way that "woman" can only mean free woman, not slave woman. When Aristotle talks about women, he doesn't mean us to be thinking about slave women.[16]

In sum, then, there is only a category of "woman" distinct from that of "slave" under the following conditions: There is a community that exists for the sake of the good life, not just for life itself, in which the ruling men lead lives exhibiting the ends for which such communities exist. The free woman and the slave make the best life possible, even though neither participates in it. Without women, new citizens could not be born; without slaves, "everyday wants" could not be provided for: "Those who are in a position which places them above toil have stewards who attend to their households while they occupy themselves with philosophy or with politics" (*Politics* 1255b35–37). This division of labor also exempts the woman of the house from some tasks:

> A man's [i.e., a citizen's] constitution should be inured to labor, but not to labor which is excessive or of one sort only, such as is practised by athletes; he should be capable of all the action of a freeman. These remarks apply equally to both parents. (*Politics* 1335b10–11)[17]

For the purposes of a well-ordered state, the distinction between male and female is important only for citizens; for slaves it is irrelevant. That is, when a people are a slave people, it doesn't matter—

for the purposes of their function in a well-ordered political community—whether they are male or female.

Hence biology—in the sense of one's reproductive capacities— only makes a political difference, according to Aristotle, in concert with the difference between citizen and slave.[18] Though a slave may be female, what defines her function in the state is the fact of her being a slave, not the fact of her being female. Some females are meant by nature to be "slaves," others to be "women," free women. Moreover, since there are no natural rulers among slaves, a man who is a slave is not the natural ruler of a woman who is a slave (and surely not of a free woman). Thus a male slave isn't really a "man" insofar as Aristotle uses the term in the *Politics* to refer to natural rulers: maleness signals the superiority a man has over a woman only if the male in question is a natural ruler. This means that one of the marks of inferiority of a male slave is that he is not a better specimen of humanity than his wife.

What are said by Aristotle to be the prerogatives and functions and natures of "men" and "women" don't apply to males and females who are natural slaves. This is hardly an unfamiliar state of affairs. For example, notions of man as citizen, provider, and head of household, of woman as delicate and in need of protection, were supposed to be applicable to the men and women of the white slave-holding class in the United States, but not to the black men and women who were their slaves.

III

It is clear from Aristotle's argument that something other than simple reproductive role decides one's role in the state, no matter what he says elsewhere about the natural biological superiority of male to female.[19] He never argues (and we wouldn't expect him to) that there is a difference in reproductive biology between a male who is a citizen and one who is a slave. Nor does he argue that there is any other bodily fact that reliably differentiates the two. The bodies of men who are citizens and men who are slaves are the same— reproductively they are the same, and they quite often look the same in stature and strength, to Aristotle's dismay:

> Nature would like to distinguish between the bodies of freemen and slaves, making the one strong for servile labor, the other upright, and although useless for such services, useful for political life in the arts both of war and peace. But the opposite often happens—that some have the souls and others have the bodies of

freemen. And doubtless if men differed from one another in the mere forms of their bodies as much as the statues of the Gods do from men, all would acknowledge that the inferior class should be slaves of the superior. And if this is true of the body, how much more just that a similar distinction should exist in the soul? But the beauty of the body is seen, whereas the beauty of the soul is not seen. It is clear, then, that some men are by nature free, and others slaves, and that for these latter slavery is both expedient and right. (*Politics* 1254b34–1255a2).[20]

In this way, whatever biological superiority male slaves have to female slaves, they are inferior to the wives of male citizens. And as we saw above, there are crucial differences, in Aristotle's view, between slave women and free women, even though presumably both have the same reproductive biology.[21]

While we might expect to find Aristotle making a strong connection between the kind of soul one has (of which the mind is a part) and the kind of body one has, we have already begun to see why there cannot be a simple and reliable correlation between them: one can't tell from the fact that there is a female body whether one is in the presence of a "woman" or a female slave, nor can one tell from the fact that there is a male body whether one is in the presence of a "man" or a male slave.[22] Even strength or bulk of body isn't a sure guide, as we have seen. What, then, does differentiate among all these kinds of persons?

Aristotle sometimes speaks as if the inferiority of women to men, slaves to masters, were due to the fact that women and slaves are essentially bodies without souls and are hence in need of the direction and command of the souls of natural male rulers. For example, in *Generation of Animals* (732a, 738b), Aristotle describes the relative worth of the contributions of male and female as determined by the relative worth of soul to body, or of form to matter: the male provides the more divine element of soul, or form, while the female only provides the body, or the matter. As we saw earlier, Aristotle also sometimes speaks of the relation of master and slave as being just like the relation of soul and body; the rule of master over slave is a despotical one, just as is the rule of soul over body.

But in the *Politics,* Aristotle is thinking of women and slaves as members—in however attenuated a fashion—of the human community. Females of the human species are different from other females, and slaves are different from mere brutes, insofar as they have not merely a soul (all living things have a soul in some sense, according to Aristotle) but a human soul. While Aristotle is untroubled by the idea that humans are to rule animals, because he believes that animals' lack of reason establishes their inferiority to humans and disqualifies them from eligibility to rule, he seems to believe that all humans *qua* humans have reason and "share in the rational principle" (*Politics* 1259b27). On what grounds, then, can he argue for the inferior and subordinate status of women vis-à-vis men, slaves vis-à-vis masters?[23]

Fortunately, according to Aristotle, "the very constitution of the soul has shown us the way" (*Politics* 1260a5). The soul has two main parts or elements, the rational and the irrational, and it is "natural and expedient" for the rational to rule over the irrational (*Politics* 1254b4ff.).[24] Just so, men are to rule women, for in women the deliberative capacity of the rational element is without authority—it is easily overruled by the irrational element.[25] Masters are to rule slaves, for while slaves, in virtue of the rational element in their souls, can hear and obey orders, they really don't have the capacity to deliberate. Indeed, all that distinguishes slaves from nonhuman beasts of burden is that they, unlike beasts, have just enough reason to understand the results of masters' deliberations.[26]

To twist a phrase from Nietzsche, Aristotle holds that women and slaves are human, but not too human. As humans they have at least a minimal level of reason—just enough to enable them to perform well their functions in the state. Because their work in the state is conditional for the expression of human excellence in the lives of the natural rulers, they must perform their functions well, that is, in accordance with the kind of excellence appropriate to those functions. Hence women need training (see *Politics* 1260b15), slaves need looking after (see *Politics* 1260b8). Women and slaves need at least some power of reasoning, but only that appropriate for the kind of activities they would be engaged in in the well-ordered state. Nature tossed them a dash of reason—enough to make them members of the same species as male citizens—but clearly not the kind of reason found in the souls of their natural rulers.[27]

IV

According to Aristotle, a well-ordered state respects, indeed expresses, what nature intended in the creation of different kinds of human natures. Some people are intended to rule, others to be ruled. We have been asking how, according to Aristotle, we can tell the kind of nature people have. Two criteria come to mind: (1)

whether a person is male or female and (2) whether a person has the body of a freeman or the body of a slave.

We have seen that for Aristotle neither criterion alone, nor both together, is a sufficient indicator of the kind of nature people have: Point 1 will not hold because both male citizens and male slaves have male bodies, but their natures are not the same; both free women and slave women have female bodies, but their natures are not the same; and male and female slaves have different bodies but their natures are the same. Point 2 won't work, since as Aristotle ruefully admits, you can't always tell what kind of soul or nature someone has from the size or shape or appearance of his body.[28] We do know that a necessary condition of belonging by nature to the ruling element is being male.[29] But there is a further condition that obtains: (3) whether one is the kind of person in whom the rational part of the soul rules (indeed is meant to rule) the irrational part.[30]

Again, there is no simple correlation between having a male or female body and having a particular kind of psychic capacity or nature.[31] The kind of person you are, the kind of human nature you possess, is determined by the combination of biological and psychological characteristics you have.[32]

Biological/Psychological Description	Nature
female body/deliberative capacity without authority	"woman" (free female)
female body/no deliberative capacity	"slave" (female)
male body/deliberative capacity with authority	"man" (male citizen)
male body/no deliberative capacity	"slave" (male)

In Aristotle the distinction between men and women crosses the distinction between master and slave.[33] Even though typically his language (and, as we shall see below, that of his commentators and critics) suggests that women constitute one natural class, slaves another, we've seen that this obscures the fact that some females are slaves. Similarly, even though his language typically suggests that men constitute one natural class, women another, this obscures the fact that some males and some females are slaves. In Aristotle's scheme of things, then, one is never simply male or female, simply master or slave. We thus can't talk simply about the relationship between men and women or between masters and slaves. For what is true of the relationship between the male citizen and his wife (i.e., that he is her natural ruler) is not true of that between the male slave and female slave. What is true of the relationship between the male citizen and his wife (i.e., that he governs her in accordance with a "constitutional rule") is not true either of the relationship between the male citizen and the female slave or of that between the male slave and the free woman. At the same time, the difference between the male citizen and male slave does not exactly mirror that between the free woman and the female slave: the first is a difference between those with the full power of reason and those with scarcely any at all; the second is a difference beween those with only an unauthoritative power of reason and those with scarcely any at all.

Whenever Aristotle speaks of the differences between "men and women," he is in fact distinguishing between men and women of a particular social class, the citizen class. Being female is not a necessary condition of belonging to the part of humanity meant to be ruled: males who are by nature slaves belong to that part also. Being female is a sufficient condition of belonging to the part of humanity meant to be ruled, but in importantly different ways for different females. It would be highly misleading to present Aristotle's views as if the similarity of being male outweighed the dissimilarity between being master or slave; and it is only slightly less misleading to present his views as if the similarity of being female outweighed the dissimilarity between being a free woman (or wife) or a female slave.[34]

Moreover, we've seen that it is differences in rationality to which Aristotle turns to ground his claims about relations of superiority and inferiority among all categories of persons. Hence it would be misleading to describe Aristotle simply as holding that rationality is male. For while it is true that Aristotle says that *only* men are fully rational, he clearly does not say that *all* men are fully rational, nor does he hold that all females lack rationality in the same way. Indeed, the difference is enough in Aristotle's mind to make him exclude female slaves from his discussion of the difference between "men" and "women." In order to understand what Aristotle believes about the nature and place of "women," then, we have to ask not only about the nature and function of citizen-class women vis-à-vis their men, but also about the nature and function of citizen-class women vis-à-vis slave men and slave women.

V

One of the methodological devices feminists have introduced into the study of human societies and of political and social theory has been to keep at the forefront questions such as: What about the women? What are women's lives like in such a society? How is their work assessed and valued? What are the prevailing attitudes about women? What notions are there of "women's nature"? Those of us who are feminists have quite rightly been annoyed by accounts of Aristotle's view of human nature that ignore or fail to appreciate the fact that what he says about "man's nature" isn't meant to describe "woman's nature" and that Aristotle's political views clearly incorporate a distinction between the sexes. But we have not been equally attentive to the fact that when Aristotle talks about "woman's nature" versus "man's nature" he isn't talking about all women, nor have we thought about how our own analyses of Aristotle's views of "women" might have to be revised if we investigate what he had to say about slave women as well as citizen-class women.

For the most part Aristotle's terminology, like that of much contemporary feminist inquiry, employs the concepts of "woman" and "slave" in a way that simply dismisses the existence of female slaves. If we don't explicitly ask what he has to say about female slaves, then like him we take the class of woman to include only free women. In my own earlier work on Aristotle and in that of many other feminist investigators, the status of female slaves has been either ignored or taken to be of no real significance for the understanding of the place of "women." For example, in an earlier essay I examined in some detail Aristotle's attempts to argue that "women are naturally subordinate to men."[35] But while the language I use replicates Aristotle's, I ignore the fact that according to his catalog of persons, functions, virtues, and natures some men are naturally subordinate to some women (or in any event not naturally superior to those women); some women are not naturally subordinate to some men; and some women are naturally subordinate to some other women.

We find in Susan Moller Okin's very important work the claim that "Aristotle's assumption that woman is defined by her reproductive function and her other duties within the household permeates everything he has to say about her."[36] But as we've seen, the reproductive function of a female slave does not determine what Aristotle has to say about her. Okin refers to slaves and even alludes to the fact that not all women belong to the same class, but she does not talk about where the female slave fits in, simply reiterating Aristotle's view that "women" and "slaves" have different functions.[37] Moreover, she complains when Aristotle retracts the distinction between the kind of justice between men and women and that between master and slave: "We are left with the impression that, so far as justice is concerned, Aristotle has relegated woman to an altogether sub-human position."[38] This almost sounds like the complaint found quite commonly in feminist thought that women have been treated like slaves—a complaint that challenges the position of "women," but not the position of "slaves," a group that includes females. When we attend to the fact that by "women" Aristotle means free women, then Okin's concern amounts to saying that one of the objectionable aspects of Aristotle's treatment of citizen-class women was that he didn't always respect the distinction he drew between them and those men and women who were slaves.

Sarah Pomeroy's very useful work describes in some detail the actual differences between classes of women in Athens around the time of Socrates, Plato, and Aristotle. Athenians of the Classical period, she says, "applied different standards to different economic and social classes of women and men, according to the categories of citizens, resident foreigners (metics), and slaves. Behavior appropriate to one group of women detracted from the status of another group.[39] These class differences were not unrelated: Solon's regulations enabled women of the citizen class to enjoy advantages "predicted on the status loss of lower-class women: the slaves who staffed the brothels."[40] But Pomeroy's own language works against these reminders that all women did not have the same status. For example, she talks of scholars "who considered the life of an Athenian woman little better than that of a harem slave" without noting that the "harem slave" is also presumably a woman; she speaks of how protective Athenians were of "their women," even though in the context of her chapter she makes it quite clear that "their women" could not possibly include slave women, of whom they were not protective.[41]

Jean Grimshaw's recent exciting contribution to the literature on feminism and the history of philosophical thought implicitly recognizes that the contrast in Aristotle between those who are fully rational and those who aren't can't be described simply as a contrast between men and women. It is rather between "free males," on the one hand, and "women and slaves," on the other.[42] But she does not argue as a consequence that if the distinction between master and slave in Aristotle means that we must indicate what category of male we are referring to, then it also means we must indicate what category of female we are referring to, or that we must explain why distinctions among women aren't significant.

In short, feminist scholars have not taken the place Aristotle assigns female slaves to be theoretically interesting—at best, female slaves are mentioned in small addenda standing in unclear relationship to what is taken to be the heart of the analysis of women's position. So let us ask instead what would happen if we began an investigation of the relevant parts of Aristotle's work by asking what he said or implied about slave women.

We've learned that there are a number of things we can't say about female slaves: (1) We can't say that their social and political position are determined by their biological or psychological difference from men. (2) Nor can we say their position is similar to that of slaves.

The first statement is misleading because female slaves' status as slaves complicates Aristotle's account of why any particular female ought to be excluded from full participation in the polis. For Aristotle, a female slave's biological difference from a male slave makes no difference to her function vis-à-vis the polis; and she is psychologically different, not from slave men, but from citizen men. The second statement is outrageous, since the women in question *are* slaves.

There is nothing problematic for many feminists about the fact that roughly half of the population Aristotle defined as "slaves" were women. Perhaps we assume that we can generate an account of the nature of slave women by adding together what Aristotle says about free women and what he says about slaves. But if it is possible to generate an account of Aristotle's views about female slaves by extrapolating from what he says about "women" and about "slaves," then it ought also to be possible to generate an account of his views about "women" by extrapolating from what he says about free men and slave women. What does it tell us about feminist methodology that while the former seems perfectly logical, the latter seems terribly confused?[43]

We can begin answering this question with the reminder that because Aristotle insists on the distinction in function and nature between "women" and "slaves," the only way to construct what he says about the place of female slaves is to see into which of the two mutually exclusive categories he puts them. It should be clear by now that he takes their function to be that of a "slave," not a "woman." But is there any particular reason why feminists should be more concerned about females who are "women" than about those who are "slaves"? Is there any reason why we should take what a philosopher says about one group of women as what he said about all women?

VI

The following response might at first seem reasonable: that Aristotle didn't think of slave women as "women" is simply a reminder that slave women were oppressed as slaves, not as women, and if we want to understand the sexism present in a philosopher's work as distinct from, for example, the classism or racism to be found there, we have to look at what he says about those women whose main identifying feature in his eyes is their womanhood.[44]

Janet Radcliffe Richards has explicitly endorsed just this methodological principle. A feminist *qua* feminist, Richards insists, cannot be interested in any and all harm that is done to a woman, but only in the harm that is done to her as a woman; a feminist by definition must focus on sexism, not on racism or classism or any other form of oppression:

> If, for instance, there are men and women in slavery, it is not the business of feminism to start freeing the women. Feminism is not concerned with a group of people it wants to benefit, but with a type of injustice it wants to eliminate.[45]

Richards might therefore argue that however disturbing slavery is, it has nothing to do with gender; indeed, she might try to use Aristotle on behalf of her position, since he took a female slave's status as a slave, not as a woman, to be the definitive fact about her.

A similar view appears in the recent work of Eva Cantarella on the place of women in the Greek polis: "The exclusion of the female slave [from the polis] was not linked specifically to her sex so much as to her servile status. She was 'different' from both free men and free women and equal to slaves of the male sex."[46] Cantarella thinks it therefore "more useful to concentrate on free women and the [legal] codification of their difference" in order to "follow the course that led to the exclusion of women" from the polis.[47] Cantarella's decision to concentrate on free and not slave women may seem perfectly appropriate, for the reasons Richards gives: If we want to understand how women are treated on account of being women, then let's look at women who were excluded on account of being women and not on account of being slaves. If it is their gender that explains their exclusion rather than their servile status, and we want to understand the role of gender in how women are treated, then surely it makes sense to focus on their case.

But we ought to examine this apparently straightforward methodological decision: if it is sound, it tells us that the proper, or anyway the prime, focus of feminist inquiry is how a particular group of women are treated. The idea is that however unjust and disturbing "racism" is, it is different from sexism.[48] Feminists, on this view, don't have to hold that sexism is in some sense more "fundamental" than any form of oppression, only that the analysis of sexism is what feminism is centrally about. Both Richards and Cantarella are saying that it is sexism—discrimination, exploitation, oppression on the basis of sex or gender—not classism or racism or any other form of oppression, that feminism wants to unearth and undermine. The clearest examples of sexism are found in the lives of women who are subject to no other form of discrimination, abuse, oppression, or exploitation. So no wonder, when we are reading Aristotle, we look at what he says about free women, not slave women. No wonder, if we area examining contemporary life in the United States, we look at the lives of white middle-class women. For if we want to understand how sexism functions in the treatment of women, then first we examine the lives of women whose class or racial or religious or other identity doesn't complicate their situation: if they are mistreated, it must be because of sexism, not anything else. And then we will have begun the account of other women's lives, too, insofar as they are subject to sexism, whatever other forms of oppression they might endure.

According to Richards and Cantarella, then, feminists interested in Aristotle should be first and foremost concerned with his treatment of free women. The study of how Aristotle regarded free women leads to an account of how he thought of any woman *as a woman*, even though knowing this does not yet give us his account of every woman's nature. That is, there is a difference in Aristotle (and most anyone else) between his account of "woman's nature" and that of "women's natures." His account of "woman's nature" is his account of woman as woman, while his account of "women's natures" is whatever account he gives of various kinds of women. This implies that slave women have a different nature as slaves than they do as women; that the total picture of their nature is a combination of them as women and as slaves.

VII

We have asked whether there is any particular reason why feminists should be more concerned about what Aristotle said about free women than what he said about slave women or why we should take what he says about free women to be his account of "woman's nature." The answer we have found in Richards and Cantarella goes something like this:

1. Feminists as feminists are centrally concerned with sexism, the oppression women face as women.
2. The most paradigmatic examples of sexism are to be found in the lives of women who are subject only to sexism and not to other forms of oppression, for the treatment of these women has to do only with their gender and nothing to do with their class, race, nationality, servile status, etc.
3. Hence feminists as feminists are centrally concerned with the lives of women who are subject to sexism but not to other forms of oppression.

Now it is important to see that proposition 2 is flawed: women who are not oppressed on account of their "race" are nevertheless not without a "racial" identity, and this identity has as much to do with their position as their gender—indeed, it is part of what shapes their gender identity. For if their "racial" identity were different, they would be called "slave" instead of "woman," despite their femaleness. A female has the status of "woman" in Aristotle only if she is not a slave. We cannot ignore her status as a free woman simply because she is not a slave and hence not oppressed on account of it—anymore than we could ignore the sex of a natural ruler because he is not a woman and hence not oppressed on account of it.

Point 2 fails to ask what it is about this group of women that makes it true that they are subject to just one form of oppression. In general we have no trouble asking and answering the question of why some women are subject to many forms of oppression—because of their race, we say, because of their class, as well as their gender. The same answer applies to the question of why some women are subject to just one form of oppression—because of their class, because of their race. That is, no woman is subject to any form of oppression simply because she is a woman; which forms of oppression she is subject to depend on what "kind" of woman she is. In a world in which a woman might be subject to racism, classism, homophobia, anti-Semitism, if she is not so subject it is because of her race, class, religion, sexual orientation. So it can never be the case that the treatment of a woman has only to do with her gender and nothing to do with her class or race. That she is subject only to sexism tells us a lot about her race and class identity, her being free or slave, and so on. For her, being subject only to sexism is made possible by these other facts about her identity. So rather than saying she is oppressed "as a woman," we might more accurately say she is oppressed as a citizen-class woman is oppressed.

What would be the Richards/Cantarella account of why slave women are excluded from the polis? We might pose their view as follows and add it to our list above:

4. The treatment of some women has to do only with their "race," with their being slaves; sexism is not a factor here, because it is not as women that slave women are excluded.[49]

They thus provide what appears to be a very sound reason for attending only to what Aristotle says about free women if we want to know what role gender plays in his political views: If we want to know how a woman's gender identity affects her position vis-à-vis the polis, there's no point to examining how her "racial" identity affects her position. In Aristotle, slave women are excluded from the polis not because they are women but because they are slaves. Slave women's exclusion might well be disturbing, but analyzing it can't tell us about the role of gender as an obstacle to citizenship. An inquiry into the position of slave women does tell a different story than one into the position of free women—but that is what we'd expect, if slave women and free women are excluded from the polis on different grounds: the former because of their "race," the latter because of their gender.

But what appears to be a principled methodological reason for focusing on free rather than slave women obscures the essential role of "race" in the determination of the free woman's position. Her "racial" identity is as crucial in making possible her exclusion simply on the basis of gender as is the slave woman's "racial" identity in making her gender identity irrelevant to her exclusion (and remember that Richards and Cantarella insist that the slave woman's gender identity is irrelevant here). The free woman is not excluded on account of her "racial" identity, but she couldn't be excluded on the basis of her gender unless she had the "racial" identity she does, that is, unless she were a free woman. The situation of slave women makes us see that if not all women are excluded from the polis on account of sexism, then it is not your gender identity alone that subjects you to sexism. If it is true, as Richards and Cantarella propose, that some women are not subject to sexism, we have to look to factors other than sexism to explain the case of those who are.

VIII

Our examination of the distinction Aristotle draws between "women" and "slaves" leads to the recognition that for him one's gender identity is inseparable from one's "racial" identity: only certain males and females count as "men" and "women." But we can set out the following argument about an important way in which we can and should talk about gender independently of race or class.

The crucial distinction in Aristotle and others is not exactly male versus female. Although male slaves certainly are not without maleness, this does not mean for Aristotle that therefore they are the natural rulers of any woman all. But what is crucial is an explicit or implicit concept of masculinity: what slaves and women lack are characteristically masculine traits. Rationality is not male—but it is masculine. And masculinity is a gender concept. What finally separates those meant to rule and those meant to be ruled, in both Plato and Aristotle, is being characterized as masculine.

For example, one of the things that separates philosopher-rulers from everybody else is whether their souls are masculine. The traits philosopher-rulers must have are traits of masculinity. In Aristotle, what characterizes natural rulers is a form of rationality that is masculine. Plato and Aristotle are alike in presenting an ideal of humanity that is above all else a masculine ideal. They only differ with respect to who could exemplify such an ideal: while Plato apparently can imagine females with masculine souls, Aristotle says that is impossible: there is no imaginable way for male excellence to be expressed in a female body.

This is to argue that both Plato and Aristotle have a normative notion of humanness that is inseparable from a notion of masculinity (which is of course normative). Aristotle arrogates both the notion of real manliness and of real humanness to male citizens. But to say simple this ignores the fact that the concept of masculinity is at once a gender and a "race" concept—for as is clear, even if only males can be masculine, not all males can be masculine. One must not only be male but be of a particular "race" to be masculine. Moreover, it is not as if the only possible way not to be masculine is to be feminine. In Aristotle, male slaves are not masculine, but they certainly are not feminine either; that is part of Aristotle's insistence on the difference between "women" and "slaves." Female slaves fail to be masculine in quite different ways than free women do. So "masculine" and "feminine" are not exhaustive political categories: that is, being masculine or feminine won't necessarily indicate where you belong within the polis.

It's true that for Aristotle being male is not a sufficient condition of being human, while being masculine is; but this just tells us what we knew before—that only certain kinds of men are really human. Interestingly enough, there are more alternatives to being masculine than to being male: if you are not male you are female,[50] while if you are not masculine that doesn't mean you are feminine. Gender possibilities are more numerous than sexual ones, as we have seen in the various configurations possible for soul and body. In Aristotle, while citizen men who are not masculine are probably considered effeminate (which is not the same as being feminine), male slaves are not effeminate, because they can't fall from the grace of masculinity. And while women can fail to be feminine, that doesn't mean they are masculine, even though being masculine is one way to fail at being feminine. Female slaves, as we've said, aren't feminine in Aristotle's scheme, but they clearly aren't masculine either. Attention to the treatment of female slaves in Aristotle leads us to see that "masculinity" and "femininity" are not simply gender concepts since gender is in part a function of "race" and "class."

IX

Whatever else feminism includes, central to it are investigations into how a person's sex and gender affect his or her place in the world. It would seem, then, to be an unexceptionable principle of any inquiry into someone's views about gender to focus on how he or she distinguishes between men and women. And yet we've seen in the case of Aristotle that this produces a very skewed account of his views about gender. To capture the distinction in Aristotle between sex and gender, it is not enough to observe that the gender "woman" is what females, the gender "man" what males, are expected to become. For this leaves out two startling conclusions we draw from Aristotle's account: (1) To have a gender identity is itself a "race" privilege.[51] (2) It is thus misleading to say that we have to look at both gender identity and "race" identity—free or slave—in order to see one's function vis-à-vis the polis.

In Aristotle a person's gender identity is determined by sexual and "race" identity and hence is not something added to "race" identity. Slaves are without gender because, for Aristotle's purposes, their sex doesn't matter. In any world in which for some people sex is made to matter—positively for males, negatively for females— then it also matters a lot if your sex doesn't matter. This suggests another reason why feminists like Richards and Cantarella might think it out of our jurisdiction as feminists to concern ourselves with female slaves: if the sex of female slaves doesn't matter—for the purposes, anyway, of someone with a lot of power and authority to determine where slaves "belong"—how can a theory premised on the argument that sex does matter find room for them?

The assumption that gender is isolatable from "race" will blind us to some very important elements of Aristotle's views about gender: though no one can have a gender identity without having a sexual identity, having a particular "racial" identity is a necessary condition of having a gender identity at all. We can't understand Aristotle's views about gender without looking at those males and females he took to be neither "men" nor "women."

Notes

1. See, for example, Okin, *Women in Western Political Thought;* Saxonhouse, *Women in the History of Political Thought;* Spelman, "Aristotle and the Politicization of the Soul." See also notes 34–36, 39, 42, and 46 below.

2. The shift in terminology here from "women" and "men" to "male" and "female" is significant (see pp.41–43 below).

3. See, for example, *Politics,* book 1, chap. 2; book 3, chap. 8; *Ethics* 1170b13: What "living together means in the case of human beings" is "conversing and exchanging ideas"; it does not mean "being pastured like cattle in the same field."

4. *Polis* is not univocal in meaning: see, for example, H. D. F. Kitto, *The Greeks* (Hammondsworth: Penguin, 1951), 64–79; Barker, *Political Thought,* 411ff.

As is well known, there is some ambivalence in Aristotle about just what activities constitute the most noble of all human activities. Is a life of contemplation, away from the fray of politics, a nobler life, finally, than one in which one does the kind of thinking and acting characteristic of statesman? (See, for example, Thomas Nagel, "Aristotle on Eudaimonia," and J. L. Ackrill, "Aristotle on Eudaimonia," both in *Essays on Aristotle's Ethics,* ed. Amélie Oksenberg Rorty (Berkeley: University of California Press, 1980), 7–14 and 15–33). Either form of the noble life is made possible by the existence of the household, in which everyday necessities are taken care of by those who are not capable of leading the highest form of human life. (On this point, see below.)

5. In the well-ordered state, Aristotle says, "farmers, artisans and laborers of all kinds" (*Politics* 1329a36) ought not to be slaves but neither ought they to be citizens. Aristotle thus thought it a grave mistake for Athens to include traders, artisans, and workers in the citizen assembly (on this see Austin and Vidal-Naquet, *Economic and Social History,* 107).

6. From *The Complete Works of Aristotle,* ed. Jonathan Barnes (Princeton: Princeton University Press, 1984), vol. 2. All references to works by Aristotle are to this two-volume set and will be cited parenthetically in the text.

7. Austin and Vidal-Naquet note the existence in Athens of laws trying to undermine such judgments about the meaning and effects of plying a trade (*Economic and Social History,* 107). M. I. Finley notes the difference between Benjamin Franklin's concern about slavery threatening the virtue of the children of white slaveowners because it offered them idleness, and ancient moralists' ideal of freedom from industry (*Ancient Slavery,* 100).

8. Referring to the woman as "free" seems bizarre, since women surely were not the social or political equals of free men and since Aristotle says that it is the "mark of a free man not to live at another's beck and call" (*Rhetoric* 1367a32). Nevertheless, as discussed below, some women were slaves, others were not slaves, that is, were free.

9. This is somewhat misleading, since soul and body aren't so distinct in Aristotle as in Plato. See, for example, *De Anima* 403a15, 412b6, 414a20.

10. Aristotle waffles a bit about for whose sake the master rules the slave. See, for example, *Politics* 1255b14. His struggles to find the appropriate language for describing the kind of rule of husband over wife, master over slave, may have to do with his using terminology geared to describe a variety of possible relationships in the polis in order to talk about relationships within the household.

11. In this passage, Aristotle uses completely separate words to refer to females and female slaves: *thēlu* for "female" and *doulē* for "female slave" (the latter being simply the feminine version of *doulos;* Aristotle often uses the neuter *doulon*).

12. Thus though the soul is intended by nature to rule the body, in corrupt or evil men it appears that the body rules the soul. See, for example, *Politics* 1254a35–37.

13. For a recent argument that Aristotle probably thought that no enslaved people of his own time met the criteria he lays out for a people being natural slaves, see Wayne Ambler, "Aristotle on Nature and Politics: The

Case of Slavery," *Political Theory* 15, no. 3 (1987): 390–410. Ambler, like many authors referred to below, speaks as if "female" and "slave" were mutually exclusive categories.

14. According to Austin and Vidal-Naquet, the Periclean law of 451–450 decreed that in order to be a citizen one's parents both had to be citizens; relations between citizens and slaves were not legally sanctioned (*Economic and Social History,* 89).

15. Aristotle says little if anything about public slaves, that is, slaves who did not work only in the household.

16. See Austin and Vidal-Naquet, *Economic and Social History,* 184: "The distinctions between men and women, and adults, and children, are relevant for the author of the *Politics* only within the body of free citizens."

17. See *Politics* 1258b37–40: "Those occupations are most truly arts in which there is the least element of chance; they are the meanest in which the body is most maltreated, the most servile in which there is the greatest use of the body, and the most illiberal in which there is the least need of excellence." Also see *Rhetoric* 1361a8ff., where it is said that the excellences of women include "self-command and an industry that is not sordid." In Demosthenes there is an account of a man whose citizenship was questioned because his mother was engaged in the unbecoming trade of selling ribbons in market (quoted in Austin and Vidal-Naquet, *Economic and Social History,* 178ff.).

18. Aristotle doesn't really say very much about free men and women of the metic class.

19. See, for example, *Generation of Animals* 728a17ff., 732a1ff., 775a15.

20. As Finley (*Ancient Slavery,* 118) and others remind us, stigma did not attach to skin color in ancient Greece.

21. Has women's capacity to reproduce ever been taken to be significant in isolation from the kind of children they can produce? To what extent has men's concern about women's reproductive capacities been a concern about producing children of their own kind? We need to explore the extent to which the sexism at work in the attempt to control women's bodies through legislation about contraception, abortion, and so on, is linked to explicit or implicit eugenics projects.

22. See note 9 above.

23. Or, for that matter, of children vis-à-vis fathers.

24. Cf. *Nicomachean Ethics* 1102b30, in which that irrational part or element of the soul called the desiderative or appetitive is said to be "submissive and obedient" to the rational part.

25. Austin and Vidal-Naquet say that the idea here is that "a woman is capable of deliberation but cannot give the force of law to her deliberations" (*Economic and Social History*, 183). See also Saxonhouse, *Women in the History of Political Thought*, 74. As Martha Nussbaum point out, this most likely is not what Aristotle meant, even if that is what the Greek seems to mean (see *The Fragility of Goodness*, 499). Aristotle is not concerned about obstacles that prevent the realization of women's well-thought-out deliberations, but about a kind of incapacity in women's reasoning ability.

26. Fathers are to rule children, because although children—male children, presumably; more specifically, male children who are not born of natural slaves—have the capacity to deliberate that is associated with the rational element of the soul, this capacity is immature (*Politics* 1260a6–15).

27. "The difference between ruler and subject is a difference in kind, which the difference of more and less never is" (*Politics* 1259b36–37).

28. As evident in the passage from the *Politics* comparing women and slaves (1252b1–7), Aristotle seemed to take barbarians to be natural slaves (although Ambler, "Aristotle on Nature and Politics," argues against this view). Thus, while he didn't think one's status as slave was reflected in bodily appearance, he perhaps did take one's speech as an important clue: a barbarian was "a man whose speech was unintelligent and sounded like 'bar-bar-bar'" (M. I. Finley, *The Ancient Greeks* [Hammondsworth: Penguin, 1963], 18).

29. Aristotle mentions that some women are "exceptions to the order of nature" and may be more fit for command than their husbands (*Politics* 1259b2–3).

30. On this see Spelman, "Aristotle and the Politicization of the Soul," 17–30.

31. Aristotle suggests that while most states of the soul take place in and involve a body (e.g., *De Anima* 403a15, 412b6, 413a4), there is no connection between any activity of reason and bodily activity. See, for example, *Generation of Animals* 736b29, and *De Anima* 413b26, 430a16ff.; see also Lange, "The Function of Equal Education in Plato's *Republic* and *Laws*, 6. If there is a kind of reason that needn't be embodied in order to exist, having a male body could not be a necessary condition for its presence.

32. It also would be misleading to say that Aristotle's views about the biological differences between men and women are parallel to his views about the psychological differences between them. The psychological differences complicate and confuse the biological ones because of Aristotle's insistence on the distinctions between "men" and "women" and between "master" and "slave." If not all males are natural rulers, something other than reproductive biology is going to have to ground the distinction between

them and those who are the naturally ruled; if nature distinguishes between "women" and "slaves," something other than reproductive biology is going to have to ground the distinction between the women who are appropriate companions for natural rulers and those who are fit to be slaves.

33. As noted earlier, Aristotle doesn't talk much about a class of free men and women who are neither citizens nor slaves. There was such a class in Athens, but it does not fit neatly into Aristotle's categories: the dichotomy of the rulers and the ruled is supposed to be exhaustive, and it may be unclear where free men and women belong. Aristotle does say at one point that a person is by nature a master or a slave but not by nature an artisan or a farmer (*Politics* 1260b3ff.), leaving it unclear how we could tell whether artisans are by nature rulers or ruled.

34. As we note below, the kind of work one did was not always a reliable indicator of man's status as free or slave in Classical Athens, even though those free men who were citizens may have shared Aristotle's concern about the bad effects of engaging in certain kinds of activities. Free women and slave women spent much time together and may have done some of the same kind of work: "Women of the upper class, excluded from the activities of males, supervised and—when they wished—pursued many of the same tasks deemed appropriate to slaves. [Slave and free women] spent much time together and their lives were not dissimilar" (Pomeroy, *Goddesses, Whores, Wives, and Slaves,* 71). Hannah Arendt refers to work showing "that women and slaves belonged and lived together, that no woman, not even the wife of the household head, lived among her equals—other free women—so that rank dependent much less on birth than on 'occupation' or function" (*The Human Condition* [Garden City, N.Y.: Doubleday Anchor, 1959], 321). Now if these characterizations of the lives of free and slave women are accurate, does that mean that there was no significant difference in their position, no matter Aristotle's views on the matter? The messages from Pomeroy and Arendt are confusing: Pomeroy says that perhaps the lives of free and slave women were not dissimilar even though she has just said that the free women were in a position to supervise the slaves and that whether they performed the same tasks depended on whether they wanted to. Surely, then, their work conditions could not be said to be the same. Arendt says in one breath that free women do occupy a particular rank, and then in the next suggests that really their rank depended on the kind of work they did, as if being free really didn't finally matter. It seems obvious from these brief attempts to describe the relative positions of free and slave women that we need to give much more attention to the matter than we have heretofore. Moreover, if there is no significant distinction between the treatment of free and slave women, then there is something quite odd about the claim that we can best understand the position of "women" by focusing on free rather than on slave women.

35. Spelman, "Aristotle and the Politicization of the Soul," 17–30.

36. Okin, *Women in Western Political Thought,* 86.

37. Ibid., 89, 90.

38. Ibid., 87.

39. Pomeroy, *Goddesses, Whores, Wives, and Slaves,* 60.

40. Ibid., 58.

41. Ibid., 58, 59.

42. Grimshaw, *Philosophy and Feminist Thinking,* 41.

43. Another way of asking this question: What would happen if we took the primary reference of the word "woman" to be slave women, not free women? Whenever we talked about the status of free women, we'd have to make sure to include the qualifier "free." Why can't I say "whenever I use the word 'woman' without a qualifier, I am referring to slave women; so whenever I want to refer to free women I will use 'free women' "? What kind of implicit rules for the use of the unqualified "woman" am I breaking?

44. A note on terminology: there is no easy way to categorize that aspect of a person's identity by virtue of which, according to Aristotle, one is free or slave. Both "class" and "race" are likely to be misleading. Slaves in ancient Greece can't be said to constitute a class in terms of their position in relations of production or in terms of shared consciousness. In Aristotle's time, the kind of labor one did was not always a reliable indicator of one's status as a citizen, free noncitizen, or slave (see, e.g., M. I. Finley, *Economy and Society in Ancient Greece* [New York: Penguin, 1983], chap. 7 and passim). This is a fact of Greek life that might have been of concern to Aristotle, since, as we've seen, he thinks that with the difference between master (citizen) and slave ought to go the difference between kinds of activities people are engaged in (whether he would insist on this distinction between free and slave is not clear). But "class" better describe Aristotle's discussion of relations among citizens (as, for example, in book 5 of the *Politics*) than those between citizen and slave (see Austin and Vidal-Naquet, *Economic and Social History,* 22).

Moreover, reference to "racial" differences is likely to lead to misunderstanding as well, because we saw above, Aristotle didn't think the distinction between master and slave or between free and slave corresponded to a difference in skin color or any other physical difference. On the other hand, as we've also seen, Aristotle thought of natural slaves as distinctly and irretrievably different from natural rulers—as if they were a different breed of humans. Hence some scholars such as Finley, insist on the word "racism" to describe the "ideological expressions . . . formulated around 'barbarians' " such as we find in Aristotle (*Ancient Slavery,* 118). "Race," then, is probably less misleading than "class." I shall use "race" in quotation marks to refer to that dimension of the identity of persons by which, according to Aristotle, rulers/citizens and their wives are distinguished from those males and females who are "by nature" slaves.

45. Janet Radcliffe Richards, *The Sceptical Feminist* (Boston: Routledge and Kegan Paul, 1980), 5.

46. Cantarella, *Pandora's Daughters,* 39.

47. Ibid.

48. See Footnote 44 above for an explanation of why "racism" is used in this context.

49. I've actually suggested that there may be two different accounts in Richards and Canterella of the position of slave women. One could be described as follows:

> 4. The treatment of some women has to do only with their "race," with their being slaves; sexism is not a factor here, because it is not as women that slaves are excluded from the polis.

The other is suggested in my extrapolation on p. 49:

> 5. The treatment of some women has to do with their gender and their "race"; their treatment is a combination of their status as slaves and of their being women.

Now we need to notice that propositions 4 and 5 contradict each other if they are taken to apply to the same women. That is, we can't say (even apart from the question of what Aristotle's opinion on the matter is) that the treatment of slave women in Aristotle has to do *both* with their gender and "race" and *simply* with their "race"; we can't say that they were subject *both* to sexism and "racism" and *only* to "racism." Which will it be? If we go with proposition 5 and say that they were excluded on both counts, then we lose the rationale for focusing on free women: if any and all women are excluded from the polis as women, then we can take any woman as an example. If we go with point 4 and say they were excluded on the single count of "race," then we can't maintain the idea that there is a form of oppression to which all women are subject as women. Alice Paul insisted that the disenfranchisement of Black women was due to their race rather than their sex, even though she also assumed that suffrage was a "purely feminist" issue around which women could unite despite their differences. See Nancy Cott, *The Grounding of Modern Feminism* (New Haven: Yale University Press, 1987), 70–71.

50. This argument obscures the existence of those who are neither male nor female.

51. The males and females who are slaves are from Aristotle's perspective without a gender identity (or anyway without the gender identity of "man" or "woman"). Cf. Angela Davis's description of Black female slaves as "genderless" in chapter 1 of *Women, Race, and Class* (New York: Random, 1981).

Women, Slaves, and "Love of Toil" in Aristotle's Moral Philosophy

Eve Browning Cole

In Plato's *Meno*, Socrates asks his conversation-partner to say what virtue is. Meno responds eagerly as follows:[1]

> It is not hard to tell you, Socrates. First, if you want the virtue of a man, it is easy to say that a man's virtue consists of being able to manage public affairs and in so doing to benefit his friends and harm his enemies and to be careful that no harm comes to himself; if you want the virtue of a woman, it is not difficult to describe: she must manage the home well, preserve its possessions, and be submissive to her husband . . . And there are many other virtues, so that one is not at a loss to say what virtue is. There is a virtue for every action and every age, for every task of ours and every one of us—and, Socrates, the same is true for wickedness.

The variation of virtue which occurs to Meno first of all is that between male and female virtues. It is unsurprising, given what is known of Greek culture (and alas of most cultural history since this period), that the sphere of male virtue is not restricted to the home and the marital relationship, but ranges throughout the political universe. Women's virtues, however, can be exercised only within a special "indoors" provided by the male head of the household, which is dependent upon his favor for its maintenance. There is no balanced situation of separate spheres, each of which counts equally, but rather a circle inscribed within a much larger circle. The interior circle represents women's moral domain, and the exterior embracing circle represents the male moral domain defining and including that of the female.

But this tidy duality of political and domestic virtue-spheres quickly gets muddled in Meno's response; for he steps off from it to embrace a radical pluralism about virtue: there are separate types of virtue not only for males and females, but also for "every action

127

and every age, for every task of ours and every one of us", in short for every conceivable variant context.

In the ensuing pages of the dialogue, Socrates points out the multiple problems he finds inherent in this view. For Socrates and Plato held that if virtue is realizable, it must be knowable; if knowable, it must be definable; and if definable, it must be some *one thing*. Its essence must be specifiable without reference to any particular facts about its possessor, and must remain the same throughout various different instantiations and contexts.

This view of the nature of virtue, perhaps traceable to the historical Socrates but developed by Plato in other dialogues, is a minority view in classical Greek culture. Far more common is the ethical pluralism of which Meno provides an extreme example. On this view, forms of virtue correspond to gender, social class, and political function. The main philosophical proponent of this widespread ethical pluralism is Aristotle.

In this chapter I will explore the virtues which, in Aristotle's moral system, are said to be appropriate to free women and to slaves, and will locate a theoretical instability or contradiction pertaining to the theory's placement of them in the scheme of human life as a whole. And since Aristotle remains much closer to the traditionally dominant values of the culture he inhabits than, for example, Plato, he is in some ways the spokesperson for the ideology of the classical Greek polis. So in examining his views I am more broadly surveying some central values of that peculiar social and political institution.

Exploring the moral typology of free women and male and female slaves in classical antiquity will be illuminating in two ways. First, it will shed light on the general issue of gender and class in ethics by providing one clear example of an ethical outlook which considers gender and class to be variables in moral philosophy. Secondly, it will enrich the understanding of the ancient Greek views of human nature, especially insofar as these views tend toward polarization of traits along gender and class lines. I will try to show that the gender- and class-differentiated ethics of Aristotle, and of the dominant culture of which he is the philosophical spokesperson, both presuppose and validate a conception of the natures of women and slaves which ranks them as borderline creatures, lacking full humanity in ways importantly analogous to the ways non-human animals lack humanity.[2] For slaves, beasts, and (non-slave) women all are essentially *marginal beings* in the Greek male outlook.[3] I am thus dealing with a powerful ideology defining an ontological-status stratification of gender, race, class, and species. It is important to understand how such an ideology works, how it hangs together, what its motivating assumptions are, and thus how it can most effectively be deconstructed.

Section I: Aristotle on Gender and Class in Ethics

It is Aristotle's view that male and female human beings differ from one another morally in crucial ways. One key text pinpointing a difference appears in the first book of his *Politics,* which presents a three-level moral typology corresponding to men, women, and slaves (the latter being treated as genderless in the context). The topic under discussion is the question whether slaves can be said to possess virtue.

> ... (T)he freeman rules over the slave after another manner from that in which the male rules over the female, or the man over the child; although the parts of the soul are present in all of them, they are present in different degrees. For the slave has no deliberative ability at all; the woman has, but it is without authority (akyron); and the child has, but it is immature. So it must necessarily be supposed to be with the excellences of character also; all should partake of them, but only in such manner and degree as is required by each for the fulfillment of his function.[4]

By contrast to slaves, women, and children, the free man has a deliberative ability (*to bouleutikon*) which possesses the authority requisite to permit his rational choices to govern his behavior. From this critical advantage in practical reasoning-power, it follows that the free man has also the privilege and responsibility of directing the lives of the others: women, children, and slaves. They benefit from his management, because he is doing something for them which they cannot do for themselves.

Aristotle is emphatic in maintaining that this responsibility on the free male's shoulders is a seriously *moral* responsibility. It is not merely everyday how-to advice which he must issue to his charges, but moral guidance as well; for insofar as they are to display virtue, they must do so in relation to the male—their virtue is essentially relative to him.

> The child is imperfect, and therefore obviously his excellence is not relative to himself alone, but to the perfect man and to his teacher, and in like manner the excellence of a slave is relative to

> a master . . . It is manifest, then, that the master ought to be the source of such excellence in the slave, and not a mere possessor of the art of mastership which trains the slave in his functions. That is why they are mistaken who forbid us to converse with slaves and say that we should employ command only, for slaves stand even more in need of admonition than children.[5]

And it is urgently important that the women, children, and slaves be trained for virtue.

> For inasmuch as every family is a part of a state . . . , and the excellence of the part must have regard to the excellence of the whole, women and children must be trained by education with an eye to the constitution, if the excellences of either of them are supposed to make any difference in the excellences of the state. And they must make a difference: for the children grow up to be citizens, and half the free persons in a state are women.[6]

Thus, free women, children, and slaves share a certain moral relatively in Aristotle's view. The well-being of the state depends on their achieving their own specific excellence, but that excellence or virtue is defined in relation to the male who directs them and whose interests they serve. For children (at least male children) this relativity is only temporary; for with the passage of time, they will take over the direction and non-relative moral status at present enjoyed by their male parents. The status of free women and slaves will be the focus of the remainder of this chapter. It is more interesting, because it carries with it a static marginality, an ontologically fixed residence on the fringes of (male) human concerns.[7]

Section II: Women's Virtues

In this section I will argue that Aristotle conceives of women's virtues as being essentially relative and subservient to the larger domain of male-defined human existence. The specific content of women's virtues is supplied by traditional Greek popular morality, and lays heavy emphasis on work. This emphasis pulls in the exact opposite direction from the emphasis in men's ethical lives on freedom from toil, on leisure, on *distancing oneself from slaves as far as possible*. And Aristotle's own interest in leisure as a condition of the good life, an interest shared by many of his articulate predecessors and contemporaries, rules women out of its achievement. Aristotle's great ethical works, the *Nichomachean* and *Eudemian Ethics,* are directed to the free male, whose practical reasoning can be presumed to be at least capable of authoritative conclusions; they therefore have little to say about the virtues of women. The deliberative capacity of the female is not thus authoritative; and moreover, the virtues taken up in these works, and the context in which they are to be actualized, are primarily public and political. The public and the political do not define the context of women's lives in the classical period. Aristotle is not, however, totally silent on the subject of women's virtue.

In the *Rhetoric,* Aristotle describes women's virtues as being two-fold: " . . . in body, beauty and stature; in soul, self-command and an industry that is not sordid".[8] "Philergia", translated "industry" above, really means "love of toil" or "delight in hard work"; it is to be dissociated from sordidness (aneleutherias; literally "unfreedom" or perhaps "servility").

"Sophrosyne" (translated "self-command") is an unsurprising virtue to find here, since it is a basic virtue in much of Greek moral thinking. In the immediately preceding passage, it is also ascribed to men (along with courage). So male and female alike must have this critical virtue which entails moderation, self-control, a certain sober and balanced view of what is important in life, an avoidance of excesses. In addition, females must delight in hard work and males must display courage.

The association of women with work, both in actuality and in ideology, is very old and very deep in the Greek cultural tradition, though it has attracted surprisingly little attention.[9]

Herodotus tells the story of a prodigiously hard-working woman of Paeonia, whose brothers parade her before Darius in order to catch his admiration. Her brothers, Pigres and Mantyes,

> came to Sardis and brought with them their sister, who was tall and beautiful. They waited until Darius had established himself in the outskirts of the Lydian city, and this is what they did: they dressed up their sister as well as ever they could and sent her out to bring water, with a vessel on her head, leading a horse behind her with a bridle on her arm, and spinning flax. As she passed the king, Darius noticed her, for what was done by this woman was not done like the women of the Persians, Lydians, or any of the people of Asia. . . . (W)hen she came to the river, she watered the horse; and after watering him she filled the vessel with water and went back the way she had come, bearing the water on her head and drawing the horse after her . . . , while she constantly turned the

> spindle. (Darius) asked them if all the women in that country were
> as diligent workers (ergatides) as this girl. To which they readily
> answered "Yes" . . . [10]

There is a note of unmistakable Greek chauvinism in the contrast
between this wonder-woman and "the women of the Persians, Lydi-
ans, or any of the people of Asia". "Ergatis" is a term frequently
used of work-animals, and can connote grinding labor. Herodotus
takes a nationalistic pride in this symbol of industrious Greek womanhood, capable of performing three useful jobs simultaneously.

In the Homeric poetry, women are almost invariably presented
at work, and this is true from the top to the bottom of the social
scale. In the *Odyssey,* Nausicaa does laundry, though she is a royal
princess;[11] her mother, a queen, weaves from morning until late at
night.[12] Penelope, also a queen, weaves tirelessly alongside her domestic slaves.[13] The goddesses Calypso and Circe weave, cook, and
garden.[14] By contrast, Odysseus' father Laertes' willingness to tend
his vineyard himself is taken as evidence of mental derangement.[15]
In the *Iliad,* even Helen is at work on a large tapestry in which (of
course) she herself figures prominently. Cassandra lives the ex-
hausting life of a prophetess/priestess, serving at the shrine of
Apollo day and night.

Laziness is a widely deplored female vice. In Semonides' "Catalogue of Women", a lyric poem of the mid-seventh century B.C., four
of the nine undesirable female types are characterized by laziness.
The pig-woman, for example, is a horrendously bad housekeeper:

> In her house everything lies in disorder, smeared with mud, and
> rolls about the floor; and she herself unwashed, in clothes unlaun-
> dered, sits by the dungheap and grows fat.[16]

The earth-woman, highlighted for her stupidity and gluttony, also
fails to delight in toil. "The only work she understands is eating."[17]
The donkey-woman will work, but only when beaten. The horse-
woman "pushes servile work and trouble on the others; she would
never set her hand to a mill, nor pick up a sieve nor throw the dung
out of the house, nor sit over the oven dodging the soot; she makes
her husband acquainted with Necessity". Presumably, if he is not
very wealthy, he has to take on some of these tasks himself. The sig-
nal desirable female type, the bee-woman, is (like her animal name-
sake) a regular workaholic.

> The man who gets her is fortunate, for on her alone blame does not
> settle. She causes his property to grow and increase, and she grows

old with a husband whom she loves and who loves her, the mother
of a handsome and reputable family . . . She takes no pleasure in
sitting among women in places where they tell stories about love.
Women like her are the best and most sensible whom Zeus bestows
on men.[18]

Hardworking and productive of a large number of children, she de-
prives herself of female companionship in order to more efficiently
serve "his property".

Here is what could properly be called a *gender-specific work
ethic*. For it would not be at all virtuous for a free male to display
"philergia". In the classical period, it is perfectly acceptable and
even expected for a free male to express contempt for persons who
work, precisely because they are workers. There are abundant
sources expressing this attitude.

Demosthenes' speech "On the Crown" contains a class-based di-
atribe against a litigant of humble origins. Damaging evidence of
those humble origins consists in the work which the litigant has
done, all his life.

As a child you were brought up in great poverty, helping your father in a school, grinding the ink, wiping the benches, sweeping
the waiting-room, doing the duty of a slave and not a free-born
boy . . . (In adulthood) you hired your services to actors, you played
the third roles . . . Then ask these gentlemen here whose fate each
of them would choose. You taught writing, I went to school; you initiated, I was being initiated; you were a scribe, I took part in the
assembly; you played third roles, I was a spectator; you fell down,
I booed.[19]

The employment history of the unfortunate litigant is a deep strike
against him; he has spent his life laboring to provide the services
which truly free Athenian men enjoy without labor. Demosthenes
stresses the passivity of his client's role in relation to the activities
of his opponent; with the exception of taking part in the assembly
and booing, both rational exercises and therefore permissible to free
males, the concluding passage is a study in the passive voice.

Plutarch's life of Pericles also contains some choice meditations
on work.

We take pleasure in perfumes and purple garments, but we regard
dyers and perfumers as men unworthy to be free and as mean
artisans. Antisthenes was therefore quite right in saying, when he
was told that Ismenias was an excellent flute-player, "He is good

for nothing, for he would not otherwise be such a good flute-player." Similarly Philip, when his son was playing the cithara at a banquet with much charm and skill, asked him, "Are you not ashamed to play so well?" . . . No young man of good birth having seen the Zeus of Pisa or the Hera of Argos desired to become Pheidias or Polycleitus, nor Anacreon, Philemon, or Archilochus for having been delighted with their poems. A work may delight us with its charm, but there is no need to regard its creator with admiration.[20]

Well-born Athenian males will take all the pleasure they like in the productions of others, but will shrink from producing anything themselves.

Aristotle shares Demosthenes' high disdain for labor. In Aristotle's ideal state, the citizens (male) will do *no work whatsoever.*

. . . (A) state with an ideal constitution—a state which has for its members men who are absolutely just, and not men who are merely just in relation to some particular standard,—cannot have its citizens living the life of mechanics or shopkeepers, which is ignoble and inimical to goodness. Nor can it have them engaged in farming: leisure is a necessity both for growth in goodness and for the pursuit of political activity.[21]

It can be readily seen that if women are typified morally by a fondness for labor, and if labor is inimical to the good life, then women are excluded from the good life by a well-ordered syllogism. I turn now to the women's near neighbors on the margins of polis life: slaves.

Section III: The Virtues of Slaves

Aristotle is notorious among philosophers for having provided one of the most extended arguments in favor of slavery in the history of western culture. He maintains that some humans are naturally suited for slavery, though not all slaves are natural slaves and not all free people are naturally free. The decisive difference is the aforementioned capacity for rational deliberation, which slaves are said to lack altogether. However, Aristotle says little that is explicit about the virtues of slaves. Apart from the claim that they lack the deliberative capacity, there are only scattered comments and implications concerning the slave's potential for achieving a form of goodness. And even that one claim, clear though it seems, is a vexing one to interpret. What can Aristotle mean by denying to slaves the ability to conduct rational deliberations within themselves? Any answer one supplies must also accommodate the fact that Aristotle *does* allow that slaves should be given reasoned explanations for the commands they are to follow. He maintains, with explicit reference to others who have argued otherwise, that a slave is not merely to be commanded, or spoken to in the imperative mood, but must also be a party to some sort of discussion about the project in hand.

> That is why they are mistaken who forbid us to converse with slaves and say that we should employ command only, for slaves stand even more in need of admonition (noutheteteon) than children.[22]

Though hardly the expression of a liberal sentiment, this passage does complicate Aristotle's case for natural slavery. For the "admonition", or reasoned guidance, if it is to have any point at all, must be intended to form the basis for future decisions, to shape future behavior. 'Nouthetesis' is not punishment but rational reproof, as in "Don't do that because it makes the vines wilt", or the like. It is instructive that, in the passage just quoted, Aristotle compares slaves to *children* in this regard. For the reproofs people offer to children are intended precisely as part of the children's education and development into rational choosers on their own. In what spirit are they to be offered to slaves?

The problem deepens when one reads Aristotle denying than slaves can life a life "based on choice". The context is the assertion that political society has a larger and more comprehensive end than mere survival. It is not for life alone that states are formed, but for the sake of the good life.

> (I)f life only were the object, slaves and brute animals might form a state, but they cannot, for they have no share in happiness or in a life based on choice.[23]

It may be that there are many serious contradictions in Aristotle's views on natural slaves, as some have argued.[24] But there is a contradiction here and it will prove fatal to the entire project of gender and class ideology-construction in which Aristotle is here engaged, and which was broadly based within his culture. Before I turn to that contradiction, however, I would like to try to deepen the description of the virtues of slaves by appealing, as I did in the case of the association of women and work in an earlier section, to the views of the average upper-class free Greek citizen—how were slaves regarded by the dominant culture, as concerned their moral attributes?

Here, too, one comes up against a problem of evidence. Unlike the later Romans, whose bureaucratic proclivities bequeathed a wealth of legal doctrine and jurisprudential speculation about the statues of slaves, the classical Greeks did not devote a large amount of discussion to the issues here involved.[25]

It is known that Athenian law during the classical period decreed mandatory torture for any slave (male or female) who was to testify in court.[26] This obviously presupposes in the slave a deep constitutional disposition toward dishonesty, even an incapacity to be honest without the coercion of considerable pain. It is also known that there were set amounts of restitution which could be recovered by the owners of such slaves as were damaged (i.e., injured or killed) during this process of torture. It was possible to withhold one's slave from torture, but only at risk of appearing to have something to hide.

Another thing that known is that slaves worked alongside the free women of the household in many cases. This co-worker relationship must have been extremely interesting. First of all, it would establish in one obvious sense a parity between slave and free woman; as Aristotle himself remarks repeatedly, shared projects are the very firmest basis for solidarity. One can only speculate whether it would also instill a sense of shared status, with slave-mothers nursing their babies alongside free mothers doing likewise, slaves working wool beside free wool-workers, etc. In middle-to-lower income households, there can have been little outward distinction of dress or ornament to mark the status of freedom. Herodotus writes that, before the institution of slavery took root in Athenian society, the work which slaves would later do was done by women.[27] With respect to political involvement, the free woman and the slave were equally distant (at least if one refuses to accept the theory that free women would have had political influence through their husbands, a theory which I find most implausible). In other words, there are several important ways in which slaves and free women resemble one another, both politically and morally.

And finally, it seems perfectly safe to infer that the slave, like the woman, is essentially typified by work as a continuing activity which represents his/her function. Even more clearly in the slave's case than in that of the (free) woman, work is life. Naturally enough, then, the paramount virtue of a slave is willingness to work long and hard.

In Roman times, the prejudice against taking the subject of slave-management seriously (which Aristotle enunciates in *Politics*) begins to fade, and there are texts such as that of Columella, the *Res Rusticae*, which treats the main vices and virtues of slaves, and how most efficiently to encourage the latter while discouraging the former. Paramount among the vices is a kind of stubborn laziness (*desidia, pigritia*).[28] It is plausible to suppose that this would be the most significant slave "vice" in any society. Also continuous into Roman times is the association of women's virtue with industriousness. The common epitaph for a dead Roman woman of even the upper classes is "Lanam fecit, domum servavit"—"She made wool, she served the household."[29]

I would like to conclude this section by suggesting, somewhat speculatively, that western culture presents, at its classical base, a gender- and class-differentiated *work-ethic*, which set itself the difficult task of ennobling labor only as done by certain sectors of the population (slaves and free women), and maintaining a distaste for work as done by the dominant class (free men).

Section IV: Deliberation, Education, and Emancipation

There is a deep contradiction in Aristotle's moral outlook on women and slaves, however, and it concerns the very skill or capacity which women and slaves lack fully or partially: deliberation. For Aristotle is willing to maintain that the capacity to deliberate successfully is *the kind of capacity which is wholly the result of education.*

In the *Nichomachean Ethics,* one is told that " . . . intellectual virtue in the main owes both its birth and its growth to teaching (for which reason it requires experience and time)".[30] And practical wisdom, and the deliberation which it makes possible, are parts of intellectual virtue, and therefore also the products of education. What slaves and women fail to achieve is entirely within the province of education to train into them. The inability to deliberate, evinced by slaves, and the inability to have one's deliberations carry authority into action, evinced by women, are alike failures of education, on Aristotle's own grounds.[31]

Given that this is so, and it seems undeniable, it is difficult to see how we can explain Aristotle's failure to draw the conclusion of a practical syllogism as follows:

(1) Women and slaves suffer from a deficiency in respect of practical reason:
(2) Practical reasoning is the result of education;
Therefore (3) Women and slaves should be educated.

It would be easy, perhaps too easy, to refer here to the common charge that Aristotle shares unreflectively the prejudices of his day.[32] For there are a number of important prejudices which Aristotle conspicuously does *not* hold. For example, he is willing to inveigh with all his considerable logical resources against contemporary Athenian squeamishness about biological and botanical research.[33] In fact, in carrying out his own research agenda, Aristotle must have come perilously close to offending his principles regarding the indignity of manual labor. The collection of specimens, observation of animal behavior, and dissections can all be fairly arduous activities.

It has been argued that Aristotle denies the deliberative capacity to women and slaves in a biological sense, meaning that women and slaves are intellectually defective in the way they are because of a kind of natural lobotomizing which occurs early in their fetal development.[34] This way of understanding Aristotle comes out of texts such as the following, from his *Generation of Animals:*

> Just as the young of mutilated parents are sometimes born mutilated and sometimes not, so also the young born a female are sometimes female and sometimes male instead. For the female is, as it were, a mutilated male . . . [35]

It is also argued that Aristotle's biological outlook encourages him to analyze gender difference in terms of innate physiological capacities and deficiencies.[36] All this might lead one to suppose that what women and slaves lack in deliberative skill cannot be supplied by education in any quantity; the defect is part of the normal functioning of the biological organism, as it were.

It is undeniably true that Aristotle finds real physiological differences between male and female animals of many species including the human, and that many of these differences are described in language which privileges the male animal and derogates the female. But the question at issue concerns the nature and origin of one very specific human capacity: *phronesis* or practical wisdom, the exercise of which in moral and political deliberation is the mark of complete humanity. A person whose practical reasonings carry authority over his or her decisions and the actions they entail is a potentially valuable contributor to the life of the city-state. And authority is imparted to practical reasoning-power *through education and training*.

It may well be that Aristotle would never have granted that women and slaves could deliberate as authoritatively and skillfully as free men, and that he would have explained this by reference to biological causes. Thus he might have maintained an innate in-principle limitation on their educability. But this leaves open an indeterminately large area for potential improvement, within which women and slaves if properly educated and trained could expand their *phronesis* and thereby increase their participation in the goods which constitute human fulfillment.[37] Given that Aristotle has all of the ingredients for a radical proposal for education and emancipation, why does he not combine them?

I would like to suggest that Aristotle does not conclude his syllogism for a deeper reason, having to do with the virtues of women and slaves in themselves. Women and slaves are marginal to Greek society, politically and morally, because they are untrained in practical reasoning; and they remain untrained in practical reasoning because they are marginal. What stabilizes this vicious circle of exclusionary thinking is the fact that neither women nor slaves are the slightest bit marginal from the economic standpoint. It is their virtuous labor which provides the work-free open space in which democratic political life is lived by citizen males, and free women even provide those citizen males themselves through their reproductive labor.

In Euripides' *Bacchae,* one of the eerier elements of Dionysus' onslaught on Thebes consists in the fact that he has caused the Theban women to abandon their work. The chorus sings,

> Soon all the land will dance . . .
> Dance off to the mountains, to the mountains,
> Where the throng of women await,
> Driven from loom and shuttle
> By the frenzy of Dionysus.

And at the gruesome conclusion of this play, as Agave holds the head of her dismembered son, she cries:

> I have left my shuttle by the loom; I have gone to greater things, to hunting animals with my hands. I bring in my arms, as you see, this prize of my courage, to hang on your walls . . . [38]

Significantly, Agave has appropriated the male virtue of courage, the gender-symmetric partner of the emblem-virtue of "philergia", which she has abandoned (cf. the passage from Aristotle's *Rhetoric* quoted on p. 133 above).

I submit that it is this economic obstacle which blocks the classical Greek mind from promulgating education for women and slaves which would enable them to develop the reasoning skills and strength so crucial to political participation. Aristotle and his contemporaries construct a moral ideology which ratifies what is in essence an economic need—for willing laborers to construct and reproduce the material basis of the culture. Aristotle can do this, in spite of his own views on how practical reasoning comes about in human beings, and in spite of his commitment to state-supported general education for citizen males precisely so that they will be able to function as political deliberators.

> . . . (F)or the exercise of any faculty or art a previous training and habituation are required: clearly therefore for the practice of excellence. And since the whole city has one end, it is manifest that education should be one and the same for all, and that it should be public, not private . . . [39]

From one standpoint, one can applaud Aristotle for bringing together the raw materials for an education proposal which would be deeply radical and emancipatory (the two premises of the practical syllogism on p. 140 above, coupled with the call for state-funded general education). From another standpoint, though, the mysteriously missing conclusion of that syllogism provides sad and sober testimony to the limits of the human imagination. One lesson one can learn from this particular failure concerns the deep pull of economic factors on the belief-structures which they nurture and ground. The relegation of women and slaves to the margins of moral life in classical antiquity in as much a function of the importance of their physical labor as it is a function of beliefs about their incapacity for meaningful moral labor. As a recognition of their importance, it is a bitter accolade. Here as elsewhere, ethics and economics are deeply intertwined, and mutually supportive.

Notes

I am indebted to the Women's Studies Colloquium audience at Purdue University, and to the Philosophy Colloquium at Queen's University, Kingston, for very helpful comments and suggestions about earlier versions of this paper, and to Bat-Ami Bar On for useful advice on a later draft.

1. *Meno* 71e–72. The translation is that of G.M.A. Grube, in *Plato: Five Dialogues;* Hackett, 1981.

2. The expression "women and slaves" will sometimes be used for its brevity, though it will be remembered that the category "slaves" includes women and men, along with children of both sexes.

3. For an illuminating study of this marginality with special attention to the iconography of monuments, see Page duBois, *Centaurs and Amazons: Women and the Prehistory of the Great Chain of Being* (Ann Arbor: University of Michigan Press, 1982).

4. *Politics* 1260a9–16.

5. *Politics* 1260a31–33; 1260b2–8.

6. *Politics* 1260b14–20.

7. But for a very interesting discussion of the importance of the theoretical treatment of children in the formation of the western moral-philosophical tradition, see Judith Hughes, "The Philosopher's Child", in *Feminist Perspectives in Philosophy* edited by Morwenna Griffiths and Margaret Whitford (Indiana University Press, 1988), pp.72–89.

8. *Rhetoric* 1361a8–9.

9. An interesting and controversial study of the iconography of women's work in vase-painting is Eva Keuls, *The Reign of the Phallus: Sexual Politics in Ancient Athens* (Harper & Row, 1985), ch.9, "The Sex Appeal of Female Toil"; pp.229–267.

10. Herodotus, *The History* V.12–13, tr. David Grene (University of Chicago Press, 1987).

11. *Odyssey,* book VI; lines 90–95.

12. *Odyssey,* book VI; lines 51–3 (morning), 305–7 (night).

13. *Odyssey,* book I; lines 355–7.

14. Calypso's weaving: *Odyssey* book V, lines 61–2; her gardening: the same book, lines 68–9; her cooking, the same book, lines 92–3. Circe weaving: *Odyssey* book X, lines 221–3; her rather sinister cooking: the same book, lines 234–6.

15. *Odyssey* book XVI, lines 140–141.

16. Semonides "On Women", tr. H. Lloyd-Jones. Reprinted in Lefkowitz and Fant, *Women's Life in Greece and Rome,* pp.14–15.

17. Ibid., p.15.

18. In Euripides' *Trojan Women,* Andromache also mentions her avoidance of female companionship as something that contributed to her reputation as the ideal wife. "I did not admit inside my doors the smart talk of women" (lines 651–2).

19. Demosthenes, "On the Crown," 257–65. In *Economic and Social History of Ancient Greece,* M. M. Austin and P. Vidal-Naquet (University of California Press, 1977), pp.344–5.

20. Austin and Vidal-Naquet op. cit., p.178.

21. *Politics* 1328b37–1329a2.

22. *Politics* 1260b5–7.

23. *Politics* 1280a31–34.

24. See Nicholas Smith, "Aristotle's Theory of Natural Slavery" (*Phoenix* 37, 1983, pp.109–122), especially pp. 110–111 which list the apparent contradictions.22

25. On Roman slavery, see K. R. Bradley, *Slaves and Masters in the Roman Empire:* A Study in Social Control (Oxford University Press 1987); and Jane F. Gardner, *Women in Roman Law and Society* (Indiana University Press, 1986), chapter 10, "Slaves and Freedwomen" (pp.205–233).

26. See Yvon Garlan, *Slavery in Ancient Greece* (tr. Janet Lloyd; Cornell University Press, 1988), pp.42–45, for a discussion of the mandatory torture of slaves, and the value of testimony extracted under such conditions.

27. Herodotus VI 137; quoted in Austin and Vidal-Naquet op.cit., pp.184–185. See also the quote from Pherecrates on p.185: "In those days no one had any slaves . . . but the women had to do themselves all the housework. What is more, they had to grind the corn at dawn, so that the village rang with the noise of their mills."

28. On Columella's treatise, see K. R. Bradley op.cit., chapter 1, "Loyalty and Obedience".

29. See Eva Cantarella, *Pandora's Daughters: The Role and Status of Women in Greek and Roman Antiquity* (Johns Hopkins Univeristy Press, 1987), ch.9.

30. Aristotle, *Nichomachean Ethics* 1130a14–15; tr. W. D. Ross, *The Complete Works of Aristotle,* ed. Jonathan Barnes (Princeton, 1985), volume 2.

31. Here it might be objected that there is a qualification in the *NE* passage; intellectual virtue is only said to originate and grow by means of education *for the most part* (*to pleion*). This could be read, and indeed has most commonly been read, as limiting the scope of such virtue to free men. But the subsequent line actually emphasizes the fact that intellectual virtue *comes to be in the first place* because of education; it owes both its *genesis* and its *auxesis* to education (the *kai..kai* construction makes this precise). Aristotle here insists, perhaps polemically, on the essential importance of education in moral development.

32. The prejudice explanation of Aristotle's general outlook on women and slaves is offered by Jean Bethke Elshtain, *Public Man, Private Woman* (Princeton University Press, 1981), p.51.

33. *Parts of Animals* I.5.

34. See, for example, W. W. Fortenbaugh, "Aristotle on Slaves and Women", in *Articles on Aristotle* vol. II, Ethics & Politics; St. Martin's Press, 1977, pp. 135–139. Fortenbaugh argues that women and "natural slaves" (of whom he believes there are none) are deprived of a portion of the mind, specifically that portion which F. designates "the logical part of the reasoning half" of the soul. But the texts he cites in support of this convey only Aristotle's denial of certain intellectual operations, not of a section of mind which could perform their operations.

35. Aristotle, *Generation of Animals* 2.3 737a26–7. Oxford translation. An illuminating discussion of this passage and other similar ones is given by Gareth Matthews, "Gender and Essence in Aristotle"; *Australasian Journal of Philosophy* (Supplement to Vol.64; June 1986), pp.16–25.

36. Dorothea Wender, in "Plato: Misogynist, Paedophile, and Feminist", *Arethusa* 6 (1973) pp.75–91, links Aristotle with other biologically-oriented thinkers, among them Freud and Dr. Spock, who track the construction of gender dimorphic human behavior to biological difference. She maintains that it is Plato's *non*-biological outlook which enables him to advance arguments for equal-opportunity guardianship in his *Republic,* while still holding views about women which are deeply sexist.

More recently Diana H. Coole, in *Women in Political Theory* (Wheatsheaf/Lynne Rienner, 1988), tracks Aristotle's views of the status of women to his theories about the relative contributions of male and female animals to reproduction, designating the latter theories "symptomatic of his whole approach" (p.41).

37. Aristotle comes perilously close to admitting that slaves *can* in fact be educated to a degree that would enable them to direct their own lives, thus removing the rationale for their enslavement, when he argues that slaves must be given "reasoned admonition" rather than simple commands (*Politics* 1260b5–7). "Reasoned admonition" is a key ingredient in moral education. See Nicholas Smith, "Aristotle's Theory of Natural Slavery", referred to in note ( ) above, especially pp. 115 and 121, for a discussion of this point about slave education.

38. Euripides, *The Bacchants;* in *Euripides: Ten Plays,* ed. Moses Hadas (Bantam Classics, 1960).

39. *Politics* 1337a20–23.

Nourishing Speculation:
A Feminist Reading of Aristotelian Science

Cynthia A. Freeland

> *To go back inside the philosopher's house requires, too, that one be able to fulfill the role of* matter—*mother or sister. That is, what always begins anew to nourish speculation, what functions as the* resource *of reflection. . .*
>
> —*Luce Irigaray*[1]

A Personal Preface

I wrote my dissertation on the topic of "Aristotle's Theory of Actuality and Potentiality." Most of my research has focused on Aristotle's metaphysics and philosophy of science, while including some attention to his ethics and theory of the soul. I have occasionally been asked by feminist philosophers (in more or less friendly ways) about why I chose to devote myself to this philosophical patriarch. The question has caused me both some discomfort and some defensiveness: *Of course* women philosophers can study, and even love, chauvinist thinkers!

But recently I have also come to feel more uneasy in teaching Aristotle. I've had a harder time trying to decide what to say to students about his notorious claims about women. It seems superficial to isolate and detach just these from Aristotle's other views, criticizing and discounting them as the product of "ancient cultural attitudes." As Alison Jaggar has observed, feminist scholars at times " . . . suspect that the misogyny of most major philosophers may . . . have given a hitherto undetected bias to other parts of their work."[2]

Anyone interested in feminist philosophy will already be well aware of Aristotle's many problematic claims about women. He stands, along with Schopenhauer, Nietzsche, and select others, as paradigmatic of Western Philosophical Sexism. Aristotle says that while the courage of a man lies in commanding, a woman's lies in obeying[3];.that "matter yearns for form, as the female for the male and the ugly for the beautiful"[4]; that women have fewer teeth than men[5]; that a female is an incomplete male[6] or "as it were, a deformity" which contributes only matter, and not form, to the generation of offspring[7]; that in general "a woman is perhaps an inferior being" and that female characters in a tragedy will be inappropriate if they are too brave or too clever.[8]

Feminist philosophers have already written serious critical studies of many of these claims. For example, three of the sixteen articles in the 1983 feminist philosophy collection *Discovering Reality* concerned Aristotle.[9] His name routinely turns up in feminist critiques of patriarchal aspects of logic, science, metaphysics, and epistemology in the western philosophical tradition. But, as Jaggar has explained, it need not be true that "feminists who have revived these texts [are] primarily interested in muckraking."[10] Instead, feminists take up seminal texts of our tradition in an attempt to correct imbalances and to address topics heretofore suppressed.

It is of course important for feminists to understand the tradition; as Bat-Ami Bar On has explained:

> ... [A]n understanding of the power and promise of feminist-motivated scholarship, as well as being able to be critical of it, presupposes an understanding of the disciplinary canonical texts, problems, and methods.[11]

Or again, Lynda Lange writes in her essay in *Discovering Reality* that "there is a presumption that knowing the history of an idea is always useful in attaining full command of it, or, effectively opposing it."[12]

But how far can I ever depart from the model of interpretive and respectful scholarship I have learned? Discussing the parallel problem, of critically recognizing the interpretive models learned within her own field of literary criticism, Annette Kolodny has commented that . . .

> Graduate schools, at their best, are training grounds for competing interpretive paradigms or reading techniques. . . . The delight we learn to take in the mastery of these interpretive strategies is often mistakenly construed as our delight in reading specific texts, especially in the case of works that would otherwise be unavailable or even offensive to us . . . [13]

In contributing to Engendering Origins: *Critical Feminist Essays in Plato and Aristotle,* there's a presumption that I'll be critical *of* the history of Western philosophy, specifically of my particular assigned figure—Aristotle. Perhaps I can help illuminate his role in the patriarchal tradition. Or perhaps instead I can explain why those things that Aristotle said that sounded strange, extreme, and false weren't so wrong—explain why they are "interestingly" false. I would like to maintain that women, too, can claim their heritage from the great male Greek thinkers. This is rather like being a good daughter. As Irigaray writes,

> To put it another way: the option left to me was to have a fling with the philosophers, which is easier said than done . . . for what path can one take to get back inside their ever so coherent systems?[14]

"Having a fling" with Aristotle doesn't seem quite the right thing, though, if I'm supposed to be "critical." So I must begin from my own ambivalence toward my philosopher. I find a related ambivalence, or a certain paradox, in feminist readings of Aristotle. While his views in metaphysics, epistemology, philosophy of science, or logic are often the target of feminist attacks, in the contexts of ethics and metaethics he is often championed by feminist philosophers. There seem to be two key aspects of Aristotle's approach in ethics that feminists wish to appropriate. First, he emphasizes the cognitive value of emotions, that is, their role in aiding people to assess moral situations. He advocates contextual seeing of concrete situations from the standpoint of a particular subject, rather than the impartial, universalizing application of rules; he emphasizes character and virtues rather than rights and duties. In other words, Aristotle's approach in ethics resembles that described as "feminine" by psychologist Carol Gilligan in her well-known book *In A Different Voice*.[15]

Second, Aristotle discusses the notion of the "wise person" (he speaks of the *phronimos,* the wise man) as someone who has acquired the ability reliably to reach such contextual judgements. This means he supposes that there can be a sort of acknowledged expertise or standard of knowledge—at least in certain fields—despite the fact that it would be difficult to provide a formal account of exactly in what such expertise or knowledge consists. An appreciation of this feature of Aristotle's view of moral knowledge is evinced, for example, in a recent article by Lorraine Code which cites it as a paradigm of what she is advocating in "feminist epistemology."

> There is no transcendent vantage point from which, and no absolute standards by which, such judgments can be made. But, as

with Aristotelian judgments of virtuous conduct, there are touchstones, exemplars, points of reference: hence knowledge is possible.[16]

But—to highlight the sort of paradox I have in mind—in the very issue of the APA *Feminism and Philosophy Newsletter* in which Code's article appeared, one could also find several critical references to Aristotle's role within the patriarchal tradition valorizing male dominance, aggression, etc. through his models of knowledge and logic. That is, we could read forward from Code's remarks on p. 28 to find on pages 31 and 35 a blistering attack on Aristotle's role as foremost sexist in logic and epistemology.[17]

I will not try to explain away this paradox. In fact, I wish to deepen it, for I believe that it will show up again in an unexpected way when we seek a feminist reading of Aristotle's views in the philosophy of science and in philosophy of biology, in particular. Part of what draws historians of philosophy to work on Aristotle is the difficulty of providing a satisfactory and coherent account of his views on any one topic. As against the scholars' delight in tinkering with this challenge of surface contradiction, it strikes me that feminist readings of Aristotle often seem simple and joyless, remaining too close to the surface and resisting complexity. Yet some would claim that a feminist reading of a text is precisely one which refuses to draw simple conclusions from its surface—one which eschews desires for dominance, mastery, or the possibility of final interpretations. Feminist readers search instead for what has been repressed in a text, teasing out an author's ambiguities and exploring contradictions. Irigaray explains,

> . . . [W]e need to pay attention to the way the unconscious works in each philosophy, and perhaps in philosophy in general. . . . What is called for . . . is an examination of the *operation of the "grammar"* of each figure of discourse, its syntactic laws or requirements, its imaginary configurations, its metaphoric networks, and also, of course, what it does not articulate at the level of utterance: its *silences*.[18]

In trying to provide such a feminist reading of Aristotle here, I will concentrate on aspects of my own scholarly interests in his philosophy of science. Recent years have seen major new publications modifying our understanding of Aristotle's aims and methods in science; the implications of these studies have yet to be explored by feminists.[19] I will begin, in Section I, by making some introductory observations about Aristotelian science in relation to feminist discussions critical of the "western scientific tradition." Next I sketch two broad features of Aristotelian science which I take to be of some interest to feminists: first, his imagery of the scientist's relation to nature (Section II); then, his conception of science as a practical activity related to specific human interests and contexts (Section III). The following two sections, which constitute the heart of my paper, represent my attempt to play out some of the tensions I observe for feminists examining Aristotelian science. In the first of these (Section IV) I argue that, perhaps surprisingly, Aristotelian biology actually meets the criteria for "gender-free" science recently proposed by Evelyn Fox Keller. Nevertheless, certain very important problems remain, associated particularly with Aristotle's teleology and anthropocentrism; I criticize these aspects of his science in Section V, which focuses on the role of logic and hierarchy within his biology. Finally, in an Epilogue, I reflect upon sexual dynamics within Aristotle's dualistic metaphysics of form and matter.

I. Introduction: Science and Feminism

Discussions of "the science questions in feminism" sometimes proceed on the assumption that readers have a fairly clear grasp of what is meant by the science in question. Feminist articles discuss "*science*'s exclusionary practice as regards women" and "*its* method of inquiry."[20] This *science* is vaguely "western"—white, male, empiricist; and the scientist is a paradigmatically male knower who embodies the traditional male virtues of rationality, objectivity, aggressiveness, dominance, etc. "Science" in this problematic tradition, like western philosophy more generally, supposedly sets up a variety of dualisms, valorizing one member of each pair. Ann Garry writes, for example,

> Worse than this neglect of women was the philosophers' tendency to identify women with the less valued half of the major dichotomies in modern philosophy—mind/body, objective/subjective, reason/emotion, the intellect (in the form of science) dominating over nature.[21]

In feminist critiques of "science" Aristotle fairly naturally falls into place as the founder/father of the problematic western tradition—without much acknowledgement of internal complexities within that tradition. Here, for example, is Donna Haraway writing on this subject:

> [T]he analytic tradition, deeply indebted to Aristotle and to the transformative history of "White Capitalist Patriarchy" . . . turns everything into a resource for appropriation, in which an object of knowledge is finally itself only matter for the seminal power, the act, of the knower. Here, the object both guarantees and refreshes the power of the knower, but any status as agent in the productions of knowledge must be denied the object. It—the world—must, in short, be objectified as a thing, not as an agent . . . [22]

Notice that although Haraway does not call Aristotle either a capitalist or an analytic philosopher, he certainly suffers guilt by association. There are important links between Aristotle's approach to male/female issues and these other approaches (for example, the associations between maleness/rationality and femaleness/irrationality), but Haraway does not trace them here. Instead, she offers a somewhat reductive assimilation which produces a mistaken view of the nature of science and knowing in Aristotle. Aristotelian *episteme* is quite different from various notions of science that succeeded it. For example, prediction, experimentation, and control are entirely foreign to the Aristotelian scientific enterprise. Unlike capitalist scientists, the Aristotelian scientist aims to reflect upon and even love nature.[23] Domination of a certain sort does typify the Aristotelian scientist's attitude, and yet it would be alien to him to imagine one could exploit, utilize, or consume nature as raw material for human production.

Again, although Aristotle is an empiricist, he resembles neither the strict Baconian nor the reconstructed positivist version of a scientist. Aristotle's empiricism requires dialectical attention both to "*endoxa*" (received opinion, accumulated tradition, and linguistic evidence) and "*phainomena*" (empirical facts). In seeking these facts the scientist is *passive* before the *agency* of nature which is seen as complexly purposive and efficiently organized. It is extremely important to keep in mind that for Aristotle the paradigm science—in terms of both his own activity and his metaphysical schemata—is biology, rather than what post-Newtonian scientists and analytic philosophers have typically regarded as the paradigm, physics. Obviously it will have a significant impact on his conception of scientific inquiry and explanation that the objects of his inquiry are living beings manifesting complex abilities, structures, purposes, and interrelationships. Teleology is *the* facet of Aristotelian science most often deplored by the subsequent tradition; what significance does this fact have for feminist reflection on his science?

I find it surprising that, on the whole, the scientific methodology and outlook of Aristotelian biology have been neglected by feminists. Of course, feminists have described Aristotle's role in arguing for biological essentialism: he assigned women an inferior essence and subordinate role in his biology, as in his politics. This topic was the subject of Lynda Lange's critique in her essay on Aristotle in *Discovering Reality,* "Woman Is Not a Rational Animal."[24] It is also a theme stressed in Ruth Bleier's book *Science and Gender: A Critique of Biology and Its Theories on Women.* Bleier refers to

> . . . the 20-centuries long concept and tradition, stemming from Aristotle, that women, as totally passive beings, contribute nothing but an incubator-womb to the developing fetus that springs full-blown, so to speak, from the head of the sperm.[25]

But feminists seem not to have looked beyond what Aristotle actually says about females in his biology to examine what he implies (as Irigaray would put it) in his metaphors, syntax, grammar, and in his silences.

By contrast, one could say that the subtle textures of Plato's views on form and matter, the knower and the object of knowledge, have preoccupied feminist writers. Irigaray herself, for example, devoted much of her book *Speculum of the Other Woman*[26] to a discussion of Plato ("Plato's Hystera"), tracing implications of his imagery of the cave in the *Republic* in great detail and with ingenuity. By comparison, Aristotle received a far more minimal (if suggestive) treatment. Similarly, Evelyn Fox Keller's *Reflections on Gender and Science*[27] (1985) includes only three cursory citations of Aristotle, but devotes an entire chapter to Plato's views on the erotics of knowledge ("Love and Sex in Plato's Epistemology"). Since her book pays special attention to biology, it seems all the stranger that Fox Keller chose to study Plato, who was not a practicing scientist and had no real interest in biology, rather than Aristotle, who was by general admission a great biologist.[28]

Why this asymmetrical attention and attraction? Plato perhaps fascinates readers more because of his obvious ambivalences and paradoxes. From the gynophobia so evident in his descriptions of matter as mere "receptacle" in the *Timaeus,* he can shift dazzlingly to depictions of the educated and independent female philosophers in the ideal *Republic*.[29] Besides, Plato is a more literary writer than Aristotle (at least, in the material we possess), and both Irigaray and Fox Keller are clearly intrigued by the stirring imagery he uses to describe acquisition of knowledge and philosophical partnerships. Fox Keller claims that Plato's account of the "erotics of knowledge" is "informed . . . by the sexual mores of Athenian culture." Furthermore,

> . . . its analysis reveals a parsing of sexuality into eros and aggression in Platonic epistemology that has continued to reverberate throughout Western intellectual history.[30]

There are serious problems, however, with Fox Keller's claim that Plato's view represents "Athenian sexual mores." Even though, as Foucault has recently shown,[31] formalized pederastic relationships played a significant role within a certain stratum of aristocratic/intellectual Athenian culture, they were far from being the whole story on "Athenian sexual mores." Thus, commenting on the fact that all of Plato's descriptions of beauty and erotic attraction concern male objects of desire, Gregory Vlastos has written:

> This is perhaps all that could be expected of a one-track pedophile deficient in that instinctual attraction which women would have had for him if he had been one of those regular Athenians for whom Aristophanes cracked his bisexual jokes.[32]

While not a native Athenian, Aristotle may afford a better picture of the typical Greek male's notions of marriage and erotic attraction.

Furthermore, though Fox Keller is right to mention Plato's effect on Western epistemology, there is little doubt that Aristotle's epistemology and philosophy of science had a far greater impact on the subsequent tradition—not least in prompting the mechanistic/ materialist critique and backlash of the scientific revolution. For these reasons I believe it is important to begin looking not just at what Aristotle says about *women* in his ethics, politics, and biological works, but to examine his epistemology and philosophy of science for its *gender metaphors* and implications. Does he share with Plato (as Fox Keller characterizes him) an ideal vision of the chaste sexuality of the scientist? Does he envisage nature as an irrational unruly woman waiting to be organized and dominated? How does he picture the scientist's relationship to the object of inquiry, nature?

II. Aristotle's Imagery of Nature

As Fox Keller has shown using the examples of Plato and Francis Bacon, a philosopher's picture of the relationship between the knowing scientist and his object, nature, may reflect his basic personal or cultural conceptions of erotic and/or marital relations. She concludes that, to some extent, modern science follows what she describes as Plato's "script":

> In this script it appears inevitable that intercourse with material nature evokes the domination and aggression appropriate to women and slaves.[33]

Bacon offers an equally influential but distinct view of science as "a chaste and lawful marriage between Mind and Nature," emphasizing the need for male scientists to "conquer and subdue" nature. Often in Bacon's imagery this amounts to a form of seduction, sometimes even rape.

Does Aristotle's picture of the relationship between the scientist and nature reflect any of this fundamental pattern? Ultimately, I believe, the answer is no. To begin seeing this it is useful first to recall Aristotle's conception of erotic relations, and male/female relations in general. A clear idea of these is conveyed in Aristotle's notorious discussion of marriage in Book I, chapter 13 of his *Politics*. Here Aristotle mentions the wife's lesser rationality and need for husbandly guidance (slaves are said to possess even *less* rationality, hence presumably requiring firmer, more masterful guidance). Aristotle's view here is often represented as the simple denial that women are rational.[34] But Jaggar comes closer to getting it right when she refers to

> ... women's allegedly defective capacity to reason, a defect that was elaborated with virulence and imagination by major philosophers such as Aristotle, Aquinas, Kant and Hegel.[35]

Women *do* have a kind of rationality, according to Aristotle, "but it is without authority." Presumably he means by this that women are less able than men to attain theoretical wisdom and to formulate fully adequate conceptions of *eudaimonia* (happiness or flourishing) on which to ground their practical decision-making. They are, however, said to have a characteristic virtue which does include some practical/managerial rationality.[36] (And he emphasizes that "half the free persons in a state are women."[37]) By contrast to the view of women Fox Keller wants to emphasize in her account of Athenian society, Aristotle's discussion here is probably more accurate about the actual role of upper-class Athenian women, who, despite living in a restricted environment with limitations on their ability to inherit and own property, retained some economic power, functioning as practical domestic managers within their households.[38] We may look back to Penelope in the *Odyssey* as the model for such a woman whose practical wisdom about preserving household goods (not to mention her own independence) provides a complement for Odysseus' own resourceful intelligence.

In the *Ethics* Aristotle discusses marriage not within the context of erotic relationships, but rather as one of several possible types of *friendship* (*philia*) surveyed in Books VIII and IX. There are "friendly" relations among members of a state, business partners, or pleasure-seekers, and also ones with stronger feelings of love (*stergein*), as between siblings, parents and children, or partners in a marriage. The highest form of friendship described by Aristotle, or "character-friendship" is based on each partner's possessing and respecting the other's fundamentally good character.[39] These friendships are both most stable and most fulfilling. Aristotle explicitly notes that a marriage may be such a friendship, "provided that each partner is good in the appropriate way."[40] Undoubtedly he supposes that a woman's goodness will involve certain skills and manifested abilities that are different from those of a man, including, as one would expect from the *Politics*, skills at domestic management. Thus even if Aristotle imagines the relationship between a scientist and nature as a sort of marriage, it could be a partnership involving some degree of mutual love and respect.

Much of Book II of the *Physics* is devoted to describing and defining nature. Aristotle characterizes things which exist by nature as those having within themselves a principle of motion or stationariness.[41] These are things that act on themselves by virtue of what they really are. He has in mind, for example, an acorn's having some internal principle directing it to take in material which will then be transformed into the developing form of an oak. In this sense nature involves a range of beings exhibiting behavior that is purposive and intelligible. Nature is contrasted to a wide variety of other forms of directed processes, including those that are necessary, merely material, "spontaneous" (accidental), or lucky. Nature is *not* seen as perfect or as serving our limited human purposes. Just as at times a doctor pours out the wrong ingredients, so too can nature make mistakes; this occurs when freaks or monstrosities result.[42]

Of course, it is also part of the *Physics'* view of nature that any nature involves a combination of two factors, form and matter. Within this pair, form (inevitably associated with the masculine) is seen as the active, directive agency, while matter (the feminine) is passive and acted upon. (For example, within the acorn some formal aspect is at work directing the material to grow as it must to become a mature oak.) I will return in the Epilogue to consider this dualism, along with the claim from the *Physics* I quoted at the start, that matter "yearns for form as the female for the male and the ugly the beautiful. . . ." However, for now I wish to note that nature—and anything natural, from the elements to plants, from bodily parts to whole philosophers—combines form and matter inextricably. All natural things act purposively, even if at times, for most minimal levels of form, the purpose may be hard to discern.[43] This teleological outlook will facilitate a view of the scientist as being *like* the objects of his study.

The *Parts of Animals* emphasizes this commonality toward the very start in a memorable passage recommending potential biologists not to feel squeamish about the animals they study:

> . . . [W]e must not betake ourselves to the consideration of the meaner animals with a bad grace, as though we were children; since in all natural things there is somewhat of the marvellous. . . . In like manner, we ought not to hesitate or to be abashed, but boldly to enter upon our researches concerning animals of every sort and kind, knowing that in not one of them is Nature or Beauty lacking. . . . If however there is anyone who holds that the study of the animals is an unworthy pursuit, he ought to go further and hold the same opinion about the study of himself. . . . [44]

As in the *Physics,* so also here nature is understood to be a composite of form and matter; form's inclusion directs the matter toward a purpose, an end-state of full realization of potentials. Nature is often contrasted to mere inert matter.[45] In this book Aristotle consistently presents metaphors of nature as an efficient craftsman.

The *Generation of Animals* presents an even wider range of metaphors for nature, but again, most of them reflect the Aristotelian conception of nature as an artisan. This text does once explicitly compare nature to a good housekeeper.[46] But more frequently nature is compared to a craftsman: a carpenter, a clay-modeller, a cook, a painter, or an artist.[47] Nature does nothing idly or in vain.[48] In another, distinct, metaphor, he says that nature is like a runner covering a double course and retracing her steps.[49] It is especially noteworthy that there are simply no images or metaphors here describing nature as passive; every metaphor is an attempt to represent nature's *activity*. Nature plans and produces results that are both useful and aesthetically pleasing.

Does Aristotle's imagery of nature as it emerges in his physical and biological works reflect an association with women? Does his notion of scientific inquiry presuppose that it resembles a healthy marriage? To a small extent he does envision nature as being like a good wife, that is, a skilled planner who is efficient and wastes no economic resources. There are important limitations to this analogy, however. Whereas a good Aristotelian husband remains in charge of and advises his wife, there are no indications that Aristotle believes that the scientist can in any sense be "in charge of" managing nature, making it more rational, etc. Furthermore, nature is never gynomorphized to the extent of being seen as a person responsive to/participating in a mutual partnership. Nor is nature seen as caring or beneficent (as "Mother Nature"). English translations which capitalize "Nature" (such as A. L. Peck's Loeb translations) bear connations not present in Aristotle's Greek. The Greek word for nature, "*phusis.*" is a feminine noun (so, I might point out, is the word for "science" (*episteme*)). But Aristotle explicitly avoids all talk that would recall the anthropomorphizations of earlier Greek Olympian mythology. David Balme explains,

> In nature it is as though the ship-building were within the timber (*Phys.* II, 199b28). There is no deliberating in nature, just as there is none in the craft. . . . Since it is the craftsman who deliberates, this last statement shows that the analogy lies between nature and craft rather than between nature and craftsman. In all such statements Aristotle seems to be consciously guarding against one false feature of the craft analogy—that it suggests a dualism between constructive force and material. Thus he denies any support that the analogy might give to his personification of Nature who 'does nothing in vain', who 'fashions' things and acts like a householder. Such language maybe due to popular habit, but it is also convenient.[50]

In other words, Aristotle's conception of nature is different from some significant ones feminists have criticized in the western tradition. For example, in a recent survey article Karen Warren has written about two dominant metaphors connecting women with nature (drawn from Carolyn Merchant's book *The Death of Nature*): "nature as kindly, benevolent, nurturing female ("Mother Nature") and nature as disorder or chaos to be controlled by "the man of science."[51] But these are not the relevant Aristotelian conceptions.

If anything, Aristotle's metaphors for nature convey not so much a *sexist* attitude as a *class* bias. Nature may achieve the level of perfection appropriate either to a practically wise wife and helpmeet *or* to an efficient and excellent craftsman. But either sort of person is regarded by Aristotle as having a status inferior to that of the philosopher, whose speculative activity is more leisurely and divine (cf. *N.E.* X). Philosophical activity is highly valued by Aristotle because it fulfills the criteria for an *"energeia"*—it is an *activity* realizing its end within itself, rather than outside itself. By contrast, he regards crafts and practical activities as subordinate to the artifacts and goals they aim at producing. Since he regards species as fixed and permanent,[52] Aristotle does not maintain that a *species* as a whole aims at some goal outside itself. All natural processes aim at maintaining the *status quo*—the continuous production of similar processes. It makes no sense to say that spiders, for instance, are striving to evolve or climb any ontological ladder; in reproducing spiders they perfectly and perpetually fulfill their natural goal. It makes a bit more sense within his system to describe an individual natural being as aiming at an end outside itself, namely the production of an offspring, when it reproduces—but, contrary to what at least one feminist has asserted, this is equally true of male *and* female creatures.[53]

III. Science and Human Interests

I have just been suggesting that Aristotle does not regard nature as an object in the sense of being a mere passive body (feminine or slave) to be consumed, used, or acted upon. Below (in Section IV) I will provide further evidence that Aristotle regards nature as active, purposeful, and crucially *like* the investigating scientist. For now I would like to pursue further his vision of the scientist/ inquirer. In particular I wish to show that Aristotle does not regard the scientist as a hypothetically pure and disembodied observer occupying a privileged position outside human culture. Recent years have seen some major developments in the scholarly understanding of Aristotle's view of the scientific enterprise. There have been critical studies of his treatise on the scientific method, *The Posterior Analytics,* of such supplementary works as the *Topics,* and of his actual scientific texts (in particular, his biological writings). Here I will sketch what I see as two areas of investigation in this recent research which have significance for any feminist assessment of Aristotelian science. First, scholars have discussed the role of dialectic and rhetoric in Aristotle's model of the scientific enterprise; his empiricism is tempered by a heavy emphasis on the role played by received opinions, or *endoxa,* as starting points of scientific inquiry. Second, some scholars and philosophers of science have interpreted Aristotle's well-known theory of the four causes as an account of the "pragmatics of explanation." By attending to a variety of types of possible scientific explanation, Aristotle reveals some sensitivity to the pragmatic concerns of actual human inquirers. Let me discuss each of these two topics in turn.

A. The role of received opinions in scientific inquiry

Aristotle maintains that science must begin from premises that are self-evidently true and certain. This appears to require that the scientist be a sort of perfect knower, directly intuiting universal and necessary truths. Feminists sometimes criticize such conceptions of the autonomous and impersonal scientific inquirer.[54] But in fact Aristotle believes that dialectic and rhetoric play an important role in getting the community of scientists to such starting-points.[55] Because he holds that humans have a natural propensity toward the truth, Aristotle believes it is methodologically sound to begin any inquiry, even within an empirical science such as biology or meteorology, by examining the *endoxa*—either commonly held views or the opinions of acknowledged experts. (He himself almost invariably surveys such *endoxa* before advancing his own explanations within a science.)[56] Recent debates have advanced our understanding of the relations between *endoxa* and *phainomena* (empirical facts) within Aristotelian science, tempering earlier pictures of his crude empiricism.[57]

One point that has been at issue is whether Aristotle regards *endoxa* themselves as empirical data. Perhaps the most extreme position that has been advanced in this debate is Martha Nussbaum's; she contends that Aristotle understands empirical data to include whatever "appears" to people, even to observers *via* their own language:

There is, in fact, no case for crediting Aristotle with anything like the Baconian picture of science based on theory-neutral observation. He was not concerned, in his talk of experience or how the world 'appears,' to separate off one privileged group of observations and to call them the 'uninterpreted' or 'hard' data. Such a bounding-off of a part of the data of experience as 'hard' or 'theory-free' was, in fact, unknown to any early Greek scientist. Instead of the sharp Baconian distinction between perception-data and communal belief, we find in Aristotle, as in his predecessors, a loose and inclusive notion of 'experience', or the way(s) a human observer sees or 'takes' the world, using his cognitive faculties (all of which Aristotle calls 'kritika', 'concerned with making distinctions' [footnote omitted].[58]

Nussbaum's view is controversial.[59] What scholars can agree on is that, despite his emphasis on an idealized scientific knower, Aristotle recognized in practice that science is a communal enterprise relying upon accumulated human experience, in particular that of "experts." Who are these experts? Almost invariably they are men—the great men, the wise, powerful, and famous ones. Aristotle's empiricism thus explicitly incorporates a conservative deference to tradition—of course in his case a patriarchal tradition:

Some of these views have been held by many people and from ancient times, others by a few distinguished men, and neither class is likely to be altogether mistaken; the probability is that their beliefs are at least partly, or indeed mainly, correct.[60]

In one sense, then, Aristotle's scientific enterprise could seem more conservative than a pure Baconian empiricism. But in another sense his position is interesting, in that it explicitly acknowledges the scientist's indebtedness to a tradition and a community. Thus the scientist is discouraged from pretending to begin *de novo* as lone heroic inquirer forcing pristine nature to reveal her secrets. Some arguments advanced for a feminist philosophy of science emphasize that scientists should recognize their own ties to the human community and the accumulated wisdom of lived experience. Aristotle frequently uses language as a guide to inquiry because he recognizes that it is a culturally encoded repository of experience; and many feminists would agree—provided we supply the important qualification that the experience in question has heretofore been predominantly *male* experience.[61]

B. The pragmatics of explanation

I turn now to a second main feature discussed in recent studies of Aristotle's philosophy of science. Aristotle maintained that there are four patterns or types of causal explanation. Interpreted in a fairly minimal way, his view is that processes occur in the world in four different ways that may arouse human curiosity. Further, because the world itself causes people to discover concepts, according to Aristotle, they may be satisfied in these four different sorts of areas of curiosity. So a scientific question will at least need to be specified in relation to one of these areas. Furthermore, a proposed scientific account of something—in Aristotelian science this would take the form of a definition—could be useful for persons who wish to answer any of these four types of questions. For instance, I might ask why an armadillo has such an odd appearance. Perhaps I am wondering about the *purpose* served by its armored skin; does it help cool the animal in its hot environment, or is it a protection against predators? Or perhaps I just wonder about the *material* the skin is made of: is it really like skin, or more like an insect's hard casing? Or yet again, I could be wondering about what *"form"* or family the armadillo belongs to—is it a sort of lizard, a mammal, or what? A fully adequate Aristotelian definition of armadillo ought to satisfy my curiosity on all of these points.[62]

Scholars have argued that Aristotle's Greek term *"aitia"* is better translated and understood as "explanation" rather than as "cause."[63] Explanations, unlike causes, are relative to the interests, questions, and concerns of questioners. So some scholars (myself included) suggest that Aristotelian science takes into account "the pragmatics of explanation."[64] In discussing this notion Bas Van Fraassen has remarked that it concerns the application of science, or the use of scientific analyses/definitions to answer human questions. Feminists sometimes criticize "science" for refusing to acknowledge the importance of actual human interests, in other words, for supposing that an ideal knower is impersonal, "objective" and neutral with regard to the outcome of his research.[65] Because he emphasizes the role of human interests in scientific inquiry, I do not think that Aristotle holds just such a picture of science. He does acknowledge that scientific definitions play useful roles in contexts of actual human inquiry. However, he appears to believe that human's theoretical interests are universal. That is, he takes it as evident that the types of questions people wonder about are generally common to groups of people. He uses language as a guide in reaching this conclusion, but does not entertain the thoughts that language may function differently for distinct groups, or that various people may have differential modes of access to and empowerment via their own language.

IV. Biology

I turn now from my general discussion of Aristotle's logic and scientific method to a more specific examination of his philosophy of biology in particular. It is helpful to approach this topic by considering what might characterize a nonsexist and nontraditional approach within the science of biology. One proposal has been advanced in Evelyn Fox Keller's discussion of Nobel Prize winner Barbara McClintock, in chapter Nine of *Reflections on Gender and Science*. In this chapter, "A World of Difference," Fox Keller describes McClintock as a scientist "[k]nown to her colleagues as a maverick and a visionary."[66] She argues that "at the heart of [McClintock's] world view lies . . . respect for difference."[67] According to her, McClintock's gender is in some way crucial to this "respect for difference." It is tempting to

> . . . call McClintock's vision of science 'a feminist science.' Its emphasis on intuition, on feeling, on connection and relatedness, all seem to confirm our most familiar stereotypes of women.[68]

However, this assessment would be too simple, and actually wrong. First, McClintock herself rejects all notions of her approach as gender-specific. Furthermore, her views are shared by at least some of her colleagues (otherwise she would not have received the recognition she did, belatedly at least). So Fox Keller concludes that McClintock represents instead the commitment to gender-free science, and that this commitment has played a role in the actual social construction of science in her case. She reflected critically upon a tradition which sees the scientist as the male naming/knowing the passive female object, nature:

> Nature must be renamed as not female, or, at least, as not an alienated object. By the same token, the mind, if the female scientist is to have one, must be renamed as not necessarily male, and accordingly recast with a more inclusive subjectivity.[69]

What does Fox Keller have in mind in speaking of the *"respect for difference"* that so peculiarly characterized McClintock's approach? First, one distinctive aspect is McClintock's *holism*. Structure and function must be seen as integrally related; she wanted to understand not just how genes work in relation to the rest of the cell, but in relation to the organism as a whole.

Second, McClintock emphatically believes that the complexity of nature *exceeds our ability to categorize*. The scientist must approach nature in humility, must "listen to the material":

> 'Exceptions' are not there to 'prove the rule'; they have meaning in and of themselves. In this respect, difference constitutes a principle for ordering the world radically unlike the principle of division of dichotomization (subject-object, mind-matter, feeling-reason, disorder-law).[70]

And third, Fox Keller describes McClintock's *feeling of intimacy*, identification with, and even love for the objects of her study as another facet of her "respect for difference." In other words, she has a sense of connectedness with, rather than dominance over or alienation from, the natural realm. This attitude results in a distinct approach to the *naming* of nature:

> Similarly, explanations that satisfy us about a natural world that is seen as 'blind, simple and dumb,' ontologically inferior, may seem less self-evidently satisfying for a natural world seen as complex and, itself, resourceful.[71]

What interests me are the suggestive links between the approach Fox Keller describes as somehow "feminist" and approaches that have been described by Gilligan and others as characteristic of women in assessing and diagnosing moral situations. In both contexts feminists emphasize respect for concreteness and complexity, as well as a feeling of intimacy and identification. Now let me return to Aristotle. Recall that at the start of the chapter I noted that feminists often admire his approach to ethical decision-making and practical wisdom in the *Nicomachean Ethics*. Here, once again, the very features that Keller assigns to McClintock and a feminist approach show up as well in Aristotelian biology.

I will briefly supply evidence to show that Aristotle expresses the same attitudes Fox Keller regards as characteristic of a gender-free and supposedly "nontraditional" approach to nature—holism, respect for difference as shown by a sense of love for and and identification with natural objects, and humility in naming or categorizing objects in nature. *Holism* quite clearly characterizes Aristotelian biology, since he asserts that no individual body part (down to the simplest so-called *homoiomerous* or uniform parts like blood and skin) can be defined outside of the living being to which it belongs. Aristotle emphasizes in the *Parts of Animals* that animal parts may only possess their functions, hence their identities, when they are within a live organism; as he puts it, then, a hand or eye which merely painted or removed from a body would not truly deserve their names.[72]

The clearest passage demonstrating Aristotle's recommendation that a biologist proceed to study nature with *love and empathy* is the text I quoted above from the opening of his *Parts of Animals,* in which Aristotle writes that scientists who scorn animals must also scorn themselves. Furthermore, even though natural objects in the superlunary sphere are divine and of highest worth,

> We have better means of information, however, concerning the things that perish, that is to say, plants and animals, because we live among them; and anyone who will but take enough trouble can learn much concerning every one of their kinds. . . . [B]ecause they are nearer to us and more akin to our Nature, they are able to make up some of their leeway as against the philosophy which contemplates the things that are divine.
>
> . . . So far as in us lies, we will not leave out any one of them, be it never so mean; for though there are animals which have no attractiveness for the senses, yet for the eye of science, for the student who is naturally of a philosophic spirit and can discern the causes of things, Nature which fashioned them provides joys which cannot be measured.[73]

Finally, Fox Keller suggests that respect for difference involves recognition of nature's extraordinary complexity. By comparison, the urge to categorize and define may reflect a form of aggression, or the desire to dominate nature by imposing one's categories upon it. Now, Aristotle could hardly be more willing to acknowledge that our categories apply only very inadequately to delineate the full range of natural beings. He emphasizes continuities in which class divisions may be impossible to fix:

> Nature proceeds little by little from inanimate things to living creatures, in such a way that we are unable, in the continuous sequence to determine the boundary line between them or to say on which side an intermediate kind falls. Next, after inanimate

things come the plants: and among the plants there are differences between one kind and another in the extent to which they seem to share in life, and the whole genus of plants appears to be alive when compared with other objects, but seems lifeless when compared with animals. The transition from them to animals is a continuous one, as remarked before. For with some kinds of things found in the sea one would be at a loss to tell whether they are animals or plants.[74]

This acknowledgement of the difficulty in establishing clear demarcations between types of living things reappears within Aristotle's more specific schemata delineating animal species. That is, he repeatedly emphasizes that there are types of animals which do *not* fit neatly into his classificatory sketches. Whales, for example, don't fit into ready categories—they seem to be like land animals in some ways (having lungs, nursing their young, etc.), and like water animals in other ways (with respect to their environment and locomotion). Such animal species are called "dualizers" by the Loeb translator A. L. Peck, though David Balme has more recently suggested the expression that they "tend to both sides." Balme's translation is better because it shows that the animals in question have diverse sorts of characteristics, rather than actually belonging to two categories.

Aristotle's biology is full of mention of these exceptions to the categorial rules. As Balme has commented,

> Aristotle gives many examples of 'tending to both sides', and seems even to go out of his way to emphasize the difficulty of precise grouping [here Balme provides a list of 14 passages illustrating this from Aristotle's biological works]. These cases are not dismissed as exceptions that prove a rule; nor are they assigned to both sides of a division . . . ; since they seem to have some characteristics of each side, they compel a 'more precise definition.' . . . But their proper grouping is rarely decided, and they seem to be brought into the discussion not in order to be classified, but in order to bring out sharper distinctions in the differentiae concerned, or more precise statements of the ways in which the differentiae can be combined.[75]

An Aristotelian biologist aims to grasp the distinctions nature itself supplies. In his recent book *Aristotle's Classification of Animals,* Pierre Pellegrin has argued that Aristotle's goal was never to produce a master taxonomic scheme.[76] On Pellegrin's reading,

Aristotle examines natural groupings to identify a range of possibilities within individual categories—e.g., possible kinds of feet, possible kinds of skin-covering, possible kinds of lungs or breathing-organs, possible modes of reproduction, etc. He does so to *emphasize difference* rather than to produce controlling and reductionistic categorizations. As Pellegrin sees it, it is actually because of his devotion to examining the concrete sort of being (*ousia*) manifested by an animal that Aristotle *failed* to produce a coherent and complete taxonomy:

> At first glance, modern taxonomists, too, seem to condemn immediateness, in that they try to construct an objective classification of animals, a classification free of the subjectivity of the individual taxonomist. But as a matter of historical fact, it was only by the elimination of the ousiological goal that taxonomy came into being. Its development depended upon a renunciation of the desire to grasp the intimate nature of the living thing. Instead, taxonomy reduces the living thing to a collection of characteristics.[77]

As a matter of fact, Aristotle frustrated successors who wished to ascribe a taxonomic project to him by frequently noting cases in which there is "overlapping of groups" (*epallaxis*). A wide range of examples of this phenomenon are listed in *Generation of Animals* II, 1:[78] "Bipeds are not all viviparous . . . nor all oviparous . . . ; quadrupeds are not all oviparous . . . nor all vivparous . . . (etc.)." Examples of *epallaxis* mentioned in *P.A.* 4.13 include cetaceans (which are in a way both terrestrial and aquatic), seals (which fall between or share in both the aquatic and terrestrial realms) and bats (which are both winged and terrestrial). Aristotle writes of these, "[T]hey belong to both groups as well as to neither." Pellegrin remarks about Aristotelian *epallaxis* that "A taxonomist obviously could not have left this problem alone after having noticed it."[79]

I have tried briefly here to show that Aristotle's biology includes explicit acknowledgment of the complexity of nature and of nature's recalcitrance to neat categorization. This fact, coupled with the advice to aspiring scientists to love and empathize with nature, and to pursue holistic explanations, should establish clearly that indeed Aristotelian biology contains some key features which could be regarded as either feminist or gender-free according to Fox Keller's proposed criteria. Though this conclusion may seem surprising, we can reflect that perhaps it is less so, because in his respect for knowing nature as it really is Aristotle shows the same recognition of intricate details in real-life contexts that feminists have admired in his ethics. Further, that his biology should share features with a view Fox Keller dubs "non-traditional" makes sense when placed in appropriate historical perspective. That is, views that Fox Keller can call nontraditional no doubt are so because they involve a critical stance toward the received western scientific tradition. I have already tried to show that feminists often do not recognize the complexity of this tradition; after all, this tradition only became emphatically ateleological, reductionist and mechanistic through a critical rejection of various theses which were central to Aristotelian science.

V. Hierarchy and Values in Natural Classifications

Although Aristotelian biology may share certain features recently extolled as gender-free, I can hardly stop here, leaving an impression that all is well within this arena. After all, Aristotle did adopt essentialist and derogatory judgments about women such as those cited at the start of the chapter—that they are deformed beings, incomplete males, inferior creatures, and so on. So now I must turn from noting the valuable aspects which his philosophy of biology shares with his ethics to examine the more objectionable claims that have made him the target of feminist critiques. A particularly problematic aspect of Aristotelian biology which I did not highlight in the previous section is his view that there are natural hierarchies. That is, even if he has no master taxonomic plan, certain value judgments do emerge from time to time within his natural classifications. Feminists have suggested that these hierarchies, which involve both anthropocentrism and androcentrism, are intertwined with certain apparently more neutral aspects of Aristotle's logic, epistemology, and psychology.[80] A recent and virulent example of such a critique was advanced by Vance Cope-Kasten in his article, "A Portrait of Dominating Rationality"; Cope-Kasten described patriarchal elements in western conceptions of rationality as stemming in large part from Aristotelian logic.[81] Again, it strikes me that feminist authors such as Cope-Kasten have written in ignorance of an interesting and rich debate on these topics within the contemporary scholarly literature, and so my own feminist reading of Aristotle will challenge what I regard as the extreme and unsoundly based critiques in Cope-Kasten's article.

I do not dispute the thesis that particular conceptions of rationality or logic may reflect patriarchy and empower men more than women. Nor can I undertake here a comprehensive feminist examination of Aristotelian logic.[82] Cope-Kasten bases much of his own critique on two other studies which have discussed ways in which Aristotelian "hierarchical thinking" is related to aspects of his abstract and formal approach to the rules of logical thought. First, he cites Jean-Pierre Vernant's argument that reason is itself political.[83] Vernant claimed that because Aristotle's logic is a logic of class *inclusion,* it is also a logic of class *exclusion.*[84] Cope-Kasten argues that a political implication lurks just beneath the surface:

> ... [W]ith the basic structure of one's rationality requiring that everything (and everyone) be either "in" or "outside of" the group, the preconditions for "rational" aggression are established (as in "us" vs. "them.") Sharp dichotomies with rigid boundaries go hand-in-glove with this way of thinking. At the very least, then, any existing motivations for dominating others acquire enhanced legitimacy.[85]

Vernant's reasoning as represented here involves some extreme and impressionistic leaps. Aristotelian logic, the logic of syllogisms, is built out of propositions only *some* of which are universal. Aristotle takes great care to sort out a variety of valid syllogisms involving particular premises; i.e., premises of the form "Some S's are P's," "Not all S's are P's," etc. It makes no sense to say that *this* logic structures one's rationality by "requiring that everything (and everyone) be either 'in' or 'outside of' a group." One is perfectly free to say that some things may either be or not be in a group, and that these relations may vary over time. Aristotle was himself a living example of the slipperiness of "us *vs.* them" categorizations. Are Macedonians imperialistic aggressors? Some [Alexander] are; some [Aristotle] are not. Are they welcome as participants in civilized Athenian intellectual life? Some are [Aristotle, before Alexander's rise to power]; some are not [after his death]. Do they help to form the Athenian outlook on the world? Some do [if they reside in Athens and run important schools there]; some do not [when forced into exile]. All of these propositions are readily formulable in Aristotelian terms.

Of course, Aristotle did especially prize first-figure syllogisms using universal affirmative premises (i.e., ones having the form "All

A's are B's."). He believed that syllogisms of this form (subsequently designated "Barbara") were the most perfect vehicle of scientific rationality, having supposedly the most evident validity. But in his own treatise on scientific method Aristotle regularly supplies non-Barbara syllogisms. More notoriously and importantly, for our purposes, he supplies few syllogisms of any sort within his actual scientific writings. This is a problem that has elicited much commentary in recent years; Jonathan Barnes, for example, writes,

> Here too it may seem as though the *Analytics* is a sterile work: it offers a philosophy of science which its inventor tacitly ignores in his own scientific enquiries; it suggests a mode of presenting scientific knowledge which Aristotle's own scientific treatises do not adopt.[86]

Faced with this difficulty, Barnes has argued that the *Posterior Analytics'* theory of demonstrative knowledge was intended as a model of *pedagogy* rather than a representation of actual scientific inquiry. Other scholars have challenged this claim, or have instead suggested ways of "finding" syllogistic structures within Aristotle's actual scientific treatises.[87]

If the implications of the syllogistic/demonstrative model of Aristotelian logic for this actual science are so unclear, can one at least accept Cope-Kasten's description of syllogistic logic as a vehicle for articulating thought with "sharp dichotomies and rigid boundaries?" It should be kept in mind that there are significant gaps between Aristotle's logic and his scientific practice. (Aristotle's refusal to impose rigid boundaries on nature have already been discussed.) It is worth remembering that Aristotle advanced previous studies of dichotomous thinking in his logic by setting out the famous square of opposition, which carefully notes differences between *contraries* and *contradictories*. This distinction is exactly the sort of logical move that allows for *not* drawing "sharp dichotomies" when we assert that "S is not P." One might mean merely that the predicate P does not apply to S, or might mean instead that a particular contrary predicate not-P does apply to S. This has some important ramifications within Aristotelian biology, for example, where contraries may only be specified *relative to some context*. Thus to describe something as "nonoviparous" may imply that it is "viviparous," or equally, in other contexts, that it is "ovoviviparous." Such context-dependent classifications do not seem to me to exemplify "sharp and rigid dichotomous thinking."

Cope-Kasten also criticizes another implication of Aristotelian dichotomous thinking, this time following up on an assertion made by Page duBois in her book *Centaurs and Amazons*.[88] DuBois discusses the "rationalization of hierarchy" in Plato and Aristotle, focusing on Aristotle's critique of Plato's view that definition best proceeds by *diaresis*, or dichotomous division:

> [O]nce Plato's project of *diaresis*, of division and categorization, was explicitly acknowledged, the focus of discourse shifted away from reasoning through analogy, from the Greek/barbarian distinction, to internal divisions, towards a hierarchization which rationalized differences inside the troubled city. Plato . . . turned his attention to the male/female difference, but concentrated finally on reasoning based on subordination and domination.[89]

Cope-Kasten argues, following duBois, that in advancing beyond Plato (by moving from twofold dualistic *diaresis* to relationships of three terms) Aristotelian syllogistic logic facilitated hierarchical modes of evaluation:

> The logic of the syllogism is also wonderfully fitted to hierarchical modes of thinking. Since each syllogistic argument has three terms . . . it can be used to get beyond the unworkably simplistic dualisms that Page duBois . . . notes characterized Greek thought before the Greek men went to war with each other.[90]

These passages misrepresent the scientific implications of both Platonic *diaresis* and Aristotelian logic. It is worth considering, for example, that Aristotle's ideal of scientific knowledge involves syllogisms whose premises are necessarily and essentially or *kath'hauto* true. This crucial requirement is difficult to understand, but certain passages suggest he believes that ideally, the terms within scientific syllogisms must be *convertible*.[91] In other words, when listing the premises of such ideal syllogisms *it makes no difference* whether we write "All A's and B's" or "All B's are A's," because the A's and B's in question are such that anything with one property necessarily has the other (thus, for example, all animals with hearts have kidneys, and vice versa). This requirement of convertibility makes it obvious nonsense to argue that syllogistic structure in Aristotle's ideal vehicle of scientific knowledge has hierarchical ramifications, because the classes discussed by the syllogism are *coextensive*. In fact, I have a difficult time supplying any examples from my reading of the texts that would illustrate hierarchical thinking encouraged or structured by the use of syllogistic alone.

Further, Aristotle's critique of Platonic *diaresis* has nothing to do with his development of syllogistic. It is true that Aristotle criticizes Platonic *diaresis* because it is in some sense not properly hierarchical. But this critique is unrelated to his view that syllogisms involve three terms and three propositions. The critique, as most effectively stated, may be found in the *Parts of Animals,* I, 2–3. It is stated there as a part of his methodology for biological definition, and is not set out as a general matter in his logical works. In his biology Aristotle criticizes Platonic *diaresis* not so much because it divides things into dichotomous classes as because it proceeds without any particular order, randomly shifting both the subject and the nature of the division at each level. This results in the arbitrary (for convenience) splitting up of natural groups. Things get grouped together that don't belong together (two-footed includes both man and bird), and vice versa (ants may be both winged and walkers, and goats may be both wild and tame). In Aristotle's own recommended procedure, division need not be dichotomous, but it must be somehow a continuous, logically related process, and above all it must aim at capturing the groups *the way they exist in nature.* To recognize natural groups requires the use of multiple differentiae rather than single dichotomous divisions: "Each of these groups [birds, fishes] is marked off by many differentiae, not by means of dichotomy."[92]

For example, suppose scientists are trying to describe birds' legs in an orderly way. If at one stage they note that birds' legs can be either long or short, then at the next stage, when proceeding to subdivide the category of short-legged birds, they should do so by focusing on some aspect of these birds' short-leggedness, for example, short legs with webbed feet *vs.* short legs with spurs. In addition, the short-legged/web-footed birds will also have sets of related characteristics—since they're probably water-dwellers, they will possess distinct sorts of oily feathers, broad bills, and so on.

It would not make any sense in Aristotle's framework to ask whether short legs or long legs are "best" for birds. This question must be relativized: best *for what?* For scratching in the dust, for hovering over hibiscus blossoms, for wading through swamp water, or for perching on branches? It would be equally nonsensical for an Aristotelian to claim that an entity at either the "top" of a chain of definitional divisions (e.g., bird) was somehow superior to one at the "bottom" (e.g., hummingbird). In fact, as I noted above, Pierre Pellegrin has argued persuasively in his recent book that Aristotle *did not have a taxonomical aim at all* in his biological works. That is, he did not intend to define *species* or *kinds* of animals in his *Parts of Animals;* instead he sought to characterize the various possibilities concerning their *parts:* legs, beaks, feathers, etc. This is a very important point, because if Aristotle had no master taxonomic plan placing all animals in one "flow chart," so to speak, then he had no master hierarchical ordering ranking certain animals over or below certain other ones.[93]

Even so, it would be wrong simply to dismiss the complaint that Aristotle adopts a hierarchical view of nature in which biological niches carry "political implications". In the *Politics* Aristotle does adopt a version of universal teleology which is anthropocentric, arguing that other animals (and, ultimately, slaves and women) exist for the sake of men. Though the thesis of universal teleology is not so explicitly asserted within his biological works themselves, Aristotle does seem to regard certain animal parts as poor relations to human parts, or as nature's inferior effort to accomplish what is better done in the human. These sorts of remarks were collected and criticized in Geoffrey Lloyd's recent book, *Science, Folklore, and Ideology.*[94]

Lloyd, in a section of his book titled "Man as Model in Aristotle's Zoology", collects a variety of texts in which Aristotle slides readily from descriptive to evaluative language. For example, he ranks types of offspring of different animals according to their "perfection"—according to how perfectly formed they are at birth. From this, a classificational scheme that Lloyd regards as "intelligible", however, he proceeds to grade the mature creatures as well on a similar scale of perfectness. "Nor is this by any means the only context in which Aristotle suggests degrees of perfection in the animal kingdom," Lloyd writes.[95]

Pellegrin too acknowledges that Aristotle regards certain animals as being, as it were, "badly drawn sketches for man."[96] However, he notes that there is a tension between Aristotle's theory in such instances and *his actual practice.* That is, in his empirical observations, when he functions as an active scientist. Aristotle sees beyond this limiting anthropocentric approach:

> . . . [A]s is often the case in Aristotle, especially in the biological realm, the metaphysical point of view (here, the anthropocentric

doctrine of the differential perfection of living things), although it continues to be determining, *is, as it were, overcome by observation*. Thus, Aristotle notes the approximate character of this zoology that looks at the human as its goal: human traits still not developed are found, "so to speak," in all the animals. Aristotle recognizes, in the first place, that some living things are so distant from man that it would be illusory to look for real correspondences between the organs and functions of those entities and those of man. Second, preferring observation to finalistic speculation, Aristotle notes that on some points man is outclassed by other animals, as the *History of Animals* remarks (1.15.494ab17) on the senses other than touch. Finally, there is in Aristotle a theory of the adaptation of living things in their environment, *which in fact falsifies the comparison between man and the other animals, since nature does not demand the same performances from all thus making them incomparable.*[97]

Presumed theoretical norms also play a role in Aristotle's often- and justly-criticized claim that nature aims to produce not merely a *human animal* but, more precisely, a *male* human animal. Discussing this assumption in her essay in *Discovering Reality*, Lynda Lange argues that

The alleged inferiority of the female, therefore, is for Aristotle one of the 'starting points' of science, based on a feature of experience which it is the task of natural philosophy to make intelligible, and not the outcome of rational discourse.[98]

A bit more can be done to contextualize and enrich an understanding of Aristotle's claim that the female is "as it were" a defective male. Lange, for example, quotes Aristotle as saying:

The woman is as it were an impotent male, for it is through a certain incapacity that the female is female, being incapable of concocting the nutriment in its last stage into semen. (G.A. 728a18),

and she construes this as follows:

The female is therefore *quite literally* a privation of the male.[99]

But, without giving him too much of the benefit of the doubt, what should one think of Aristotle's qualification that the woman *as it were* is an impotent male? It is possible to gain more insight into this strange-sounding claim by realizing that it is not just females alone that Aristotle describes as natural beings which are, on the whole or *en masse,* defective. As philosopher of biology Eliot Sober has observed,

> A further, fascinating, aspect of Aristotle's position . . . is that he seems to have thought that there are entire species, such as seals and lobsters, that count as monstrosities. The concept of monsters (*terata*) was evidently not limited to an intraspecific standard of normalcy.[100]

Monsters are creatures such as whales, bats, or seals, that is, animals whose natures fall in between the normal categories which appear to characterize nature itself. Once again, Lloyd cites such creatures, in his chapter on "Dualisers" as illustrating the fact that Aristotle's biological science was far from value-neutral. Allan Gotthelf has tried to place Aristotle's biological treatment of females in the context of his views on these other natural "monsters."[101] He explains that in each case Aristotle invokes some standard of comparison involving the broader genus to which the being in question belongs: For example, lobsters are said to be deformed because they use their claws for walking rather than grasping.[102] But, judging from their other features, lobsters belong to a class of animals that more typically use claws for grasping.

Gotthelf writes:

> . . . [T]he biological point is that we have organs that cannot perform (as well) the functions they are most-suited for, and developed for . . . by the standards of the performance of the version of that organ in the other members of that wider class. (Where the organs perform another function sufficiently well, as the flippers do in seals, Aristotle will say, it seems, that they are only *hosper* deformed . . .)[103]

In other words, it is possible to argue that Aristotle regards creatures like lobsters or seals as biological monstrosities because they appear to violate nature's *own* more regular and orderly categories and plans. Aristotle deserves some credit for acknowledging that nature does not conform to our standards of rationality, that it constantly slips outside categorization. But he seems unable to avoid imposing certain standards of rationality on nature by calling such violations "monsters." Though the term itself seems value-laden, Aristotle usually believes that the creature in question is perfectly well-designed to carry out its specific biological aims. This allows him to describe it as only *"hosper"* defective, "as-if" defective. This is precisely how he proceeds in describing females. Again, Gotthelf has commented:

> . . . the female, who has a natural and necessary function, which she performs perfectly well, thank you, has her "deformity" doubly qualified, and perhaps triply, if *anaperia* is weaker than *peroma,* . . . Aristotle does claim that "femaleness we should look on as *hosper anaperian ten phusin"*—G.A. IV.3. 775a17).[104]

Perhaps one could give Aristotle the benefit of the doubt: by admitting that some natural beings are "monsters," he recognizes limits in the adequacy of his own theory. I think that this is too generous. Even beyond this, there is a significant, irreconcilable tension specifically present in his views on females as monsters. He argues, in *Gen. An.* IV, 3, for the view that females are defective and in every case accidental by-products of a natural process whose normal aim is male offspring. Yet this does not sit well with the thesis, argued for earlier, in 11, 1, at 731b24–732a12, that sexual reproduction and division of the sexes are themselves teleologically ordained. What is the good end subserved by the existence of sexual differentiation and reproduction? He answers as follows:

> . . . [I]t will surely be for the sake of generation that "the male" and "the female" are present in the individuals which are male and female. And as the proximate motive cause, to which belong the logos and the form, is better and more divine in its nature than the matter, it is better also that the superior one should be separate from the inferior one. That is why wherever possible and so far as possible the male is separate from the female, since it is something better and more divine in that it is the principle of movement for generated things, while the female serves as their matter. The male, however, comes together with the female and mingles with it for the business of generation, because this is something that concerns both of them.[105]

In other words, nature includes such sexual differentiations because this is in itself a good end-result. This is the only case I know of in which Aristotle holds that something is both a good end-result in and of itself (rather than simply a "making-do" with limited material resources) and a mere accident or by-product.

My representation of Aristotelian biology as gender-free, in part IV above, must now be qualified by recognition that he does sometimes apply androcentric or anthropocentric criteria to justify claims about the superiority of beings he regards as best—male humans. What I wish to insist on are the ambivalence and tensions in his thought on these topics. Thus on the one hand, Aristotle devises a theory which is meant to accord to each being its own independence and stature; he relativizes and contextualizes his observations and definitions, convinced that each being has beauty and value within its own natural niche. On the other hand, he regards certain natural niches as somewhat less than natural—as "monstrous," in fact. Again, on the one hand he regards the existence of females as part of a design that is overall good and beautiful, while on the other hand he regards them as somehow frequently recurring, less-than-perfect by-products of normal teleological processes. I do not believe that any simple or neat resolution of these tensions can be found.

Epilogue

There is a curious circularity in the argument I have just quoted from the *Generation of Animals,* which perhaps can now be seen as containing its own absurd humor. Aristotle's argument goes as follows: In nature, sexes are differentiated into the male and the female. Define the male as that which contains the form and principle of reproduction, and the female as that which supplies matter. These are differentiated because it's better for the superior and inferior to exist separately. Which is the superior? It's the one which contains the form—in other words, the one just defined as male. Why is it superior? Because of the way it was defined, as the principle supplying form. Why was it defined in that way? So that it would be superior, silly!

I claimed at the start that many scholars are intrigued by the paradoxes and contradictions in Aristotle. Think of the years and pages of scholarly commentary spent on deciding whether or not Aristotle *really* believes in prime matter, whether he believes essences or individuals are primary, whether the best life is philosophically detached or concretely virtuous, whether "active intellect" might be the one part of soul which somehow transcends the body it "informs" to survive in humans after death, and so on. Why keep studying Aristotle, if not for the tantalizing promise of reasonable, consistent, and persuasive answers to these questions and others like them?

I also noted at the start that feminist readings of historical texts should attend to paradox, contradiction, and what has been repressed. So far I have focused on certain implications of Aristotle's logic, philosophy of science, and biology. But now I face, in Irigaray's words,

> ... the necessity of "reopening" the figures of philosophical discourse—idea, substance, subject, transcendental subjectivity, absolute knowledge—in order to pry out of them what they have borrowed that is feminine, from the feminine, to make them "render up" and give back what they owe the feminine. This may be cone in various ways, along various "paths"; moreover, at minimum several of these must be pursued.[106]

Irigaray uses terms of surprising aggression here, "reopening," "prying out," "rendering." In delving "deeper" into Aristotle's text (dare I "penetrate" my philosopher?), feminists come to the "heart" of his metaphysics. And in this heart is found (naturally enough) the force of love: "Matter yearns for form, as the ugly for the beautiful and the female for the male ... " And what of form, the metaphysical male principle? For what does it yearn? Independence, pure actuality—an impossible existence unbound to matter. Though "such a life would be more than human," the philosopher yearns for it—a life with no acknowledgment of a body or of actual human birth, a life of pure speculation with no need for nourishing.

This amounts to a yearning for escape from the fixed conditions of Aristotelian reality, for within his metaphysics, form and matter are *always and only interdependently definable*. Form is the form *of* some matter, without which it cannot exist; matter cannot be, be defined, or be known without form. Within Aristotle's biological universe, all natural beings are complexly multi-layered. What's form at one level is always matter for the next level up. Soul is the actuality *of* a naturally organized body; the body is what is potentially alive. An actuality is always the actualization *of* some potential, which in turn is the potential for that actuality. In short, form and matter, soul and body, actuality and potentiality, are perfect self-deconstructing pairs. Their referents constantly shift and slide, eluding fixity. Neither member of these pairs makes any sense or finds any application without the other.[107]

To be sure, Aristotle does flirt with the idea of "prime matter," the purely potential. He argues that this purely and primitively female sort of being can exist only in concept (imagination); in fact, due to restrictions on the faculty of imagination, neither Aristotle nor we can even really imagine prime matter as something real. Yet for some reason Aristotle is convinced that he can go beyond imagination to possess actual knowledge of the complementary abstraction, of a force that is purely actual and which exists as necessary prop for the entire universe. This purely male principle incessantly spews out its fullness: its life is continuously pleasant, a permanently flowing actualization (of what? of no potentials; it has none). Aristotle longs to be a similar being who is self-creating, self-fulfilling, self-absorbed, self-delighting—a holy God unnourished and unborn of woman. This is an extraordinary, and in some way ultimate, construct of the male metaphysicians' mind.

Aristotle seeks to study nature with love and respect. He admonishes the scientist to see himself as a natural being with close affinities to all the objects of his study—as equally a material and changing creature bent on fulfilling its limited nature. But he longs to escape natural processes of embodiment, of flux and destruction, to assume a position of God-like superiority—someone who, though he does not physically dominate and consume nature, takes himself to be its better, a master who intellectually relishes its beauty and patterns from a position of detached serenity. Meanwhile, back in nature, the female continues to nourish the world of flowing and changing physical processes, and along with it, real philosophers in their material lives and speculations.[108]

Notes

1. Luce Irigaray, "Questions," in *This Sex Which Is Not One.* trans. Catherine Porter (Ithaca, N.Y.: Cornell University Press, 1985), p. 151. Originally published in French under the title *Ce Sexe Qui n'en est Pas Un,* 1974.

2. Alison Jaggar, "How Can Philosophy Be Feminist?", *APA Newsletter on Feminism and Philosophy,* April 1988, p. 5.

3. *Politics* 1,13, 1260a23. In citations from Aristotle, Roman numerals refer to books within his works, Arabic numerals to chapters. Unless otherwise indicated, English translations of Aristotle are those of the revised Oxford translation, ed. Jonathan Barnes (Princeton: Bollingen Press, 1985).

4. *Physics* 1, 9, 192a22–3.

5. *H.A.* 501b19ff.

6. *Gen. An.* 765b9–10.

7. 775a15; *Gen. An.* 1, 22.

8. *Poetics* 15, 1454a21, 23–4.

9. *Discovering Reality: Feminist Perspectives on Epistemology, Metaphysics, Methodology, and Philosophy of Science,* eds. Sandra Harding and Merrill B. Hintikka (Dordrecht: D. Reidel, 1983).

10. Jaggar, p. 5

11. Bat-Ami Bar On, "Balancing Feminism and the Philosophical Canon," *APA Newsletter on Feminism and Philosophy,* April 1988, p. 24.

12. Lynda Lange, "Woman Is Not a Rational Animal," in *Discovering Reality* (note 9 above).

13. Annette Kolodny, "Dancing Through the Minefield: Some Observations on the Theory, Practice, and Politics of a Feminist Literary Criticism," *Feminist Studies 6* (spring 1980); reprinted in *Women and Values: Readings in Recent Feminist Philosophy,* ed. Marilyn Pearsall (Belmont, California: Wadsworth, 1986), p. 248.

14. Irigaray, p. 150.

15. Carol Gilligan, *In A Different Voice: Psychological Theory and Women's Development* (Cambridge, Massachusetts: Harvard University Press, 1982). See also Annette Baier, "What Do Women Want in a Moral Theory?" *Nous* 19 (1985), pp. 53–63. Martha Nussbaum, in her recent book, *The Fragility of Goodness* (Cambridge: Cambridge University Press, 1986) and related writings, has presented an Aristotelian-inspired defense of the importance of complex moral perceptions of concrete situations.

16. Lorraine Code, "The Impact of Feminism on Epistemology," *APA Newsletter on Feminism and Philosophy,* March 1989 (88:2), p. 28. Similarly, writing on feminist epistemology, Hilary Rose does not, but might as well, cite the view of knowledge derivable from Aristotle's *Ethics:*

> Unlike the alienated abstract knowledge of science, feminist methodology seeks to bring together subjective and objective ways of knowing the world. It begins with and constantly returns to the subjective shared experience of oppression.

Hilary Rose, "Hand, Brain, and Heart: A Feminist Epistemology for the Natural Sciences," *Signs:* 1983, vol. 9, no. 1, pp. 87–88.

17. Vance Cope-Kasten. "A Portrait of Dominating Rationality." *APA Newsletter on Feminism and Philosophy,* March 1989 (88:2), pp. 29–34.

18. Luce Irigaray, "The Power of Discourse," in *This Sex Which Is Not One* (note 1 above), p. 75. Author's emphasis.

19. Some relevant readings include Pierre Pellegrin, *Aristotle's Classification of Animals: Biology and the Conceptual Unity of the Aristotelian Corpus,* trans. Anthony Preus (Berkeley: University of California Press, 1986; originally published in French under the title *La Classification des Animaux chez Aristote: Statut de la biologie et unite de l'aristotelisme,* 1982; Pierre Pellegrin and Daniel T. Devereux, eds., *Proceedings of the La Rochelle Conference on Aristotle's Metaphysics and Philosophy of Science* (Paris, 1990); Martha Nussbaum, "Saving Aristotle's Appearances," pp. 267–293 in Malcolm Schofield and Martha Nussbaum, eds., *Language and Logos: Studies in Ancient Greek Philosophy* (Cambridge: Cambridge University Press, 1982); Marja-Liisa Kakkuri-Knuuttila, "Dialogue Games in Aristotle," in M. Kusch and H. Schroder (Eds.), *Text-Interpretation-Argumentation* (Hamburg: Buske, 1989), pp. 221–288; Terence Irwin, "Ways to First Principles: Aristotle's Methods of Discovery," *Philosophical Topics* XV, 1987, pp. 109–34; Allan Gotthelf and James G. Lennox, eds., *Philosophical Issues in Aristotle's Biology* (Cambridge: Cambridge University Press, 1987); Allan Gotthelf, "First Principles in Aristotle's *Parts of Animals,*" in Gotthelf and Lennox, eds., 1987, pp. 167–198; Allan Gotthelf, ed., *Aristotle on Nature and Living Things; philosophical and historical studies presented to David M. Balme on his seventieth birthday.* (Pittsburgh, Pennsylvania and Bristol, England, 1985); Jacques Brunschwig, tr., *Aristote. Topiques,* Livres I-IV (Paris: 1967); Jacques Brunschwig, "Quelques commentaires sur la communication de Robert Bolton," in Devereux and Pellegrin, eds., 1990; Robert Bolton, "The Epistemological Basis of Aristotelian Dialectic," in Pellegrin and Devereux, eds., 1990. It is noteworthy how many of those I proceed to discuss here have been published even more recently than Lynda Lange's 1983 publication, which made use fairly restrictedly of articles by Randall and Hintikka from the secondary literature on Aristotle's philosophy of science.

20. Jacqueline Zita, "The Feminist Question of the Science Question in Feminism," *Hypatia,* vol. 3, no. 1 (spring 1988), pp. 157–168 (emphasis mine).

21. Ann Garry, "Integrating Feminist Philosophy into Traditional Philosophy Courses: Rethinking a Philosophy Syllabus," *APA Newsletter on Feminism and Philosophy,* April 1988, pp. 17. See also Susan Bordo, "Feminist Skepticism and the 'Maleness' of Philosophy," *Journal of Philosophy,* pp. 622–3.

22. Donna Haraway, "Situated Knowledges: The Science Question in Feminism and the Privilege of Partial Perspective," *Feminist Studies* 14: no.

3 (fall 1988), p. 592. See also by Haraway "A Manifesto for Cyborgs: Science, Technology, and Socialist Feminism in the 1980s," *Socialist Review,* no. 80 (March–April 1985), pp. 65–107.

23. For a discussion of the links between science and capitalism, see Hilary Rose's paper "Hand, Brain, and Heart: A Feminist Epistemology for the Natural Sciences" (note 16 above).

24. In *Discovering Reality* (note 9 above). Such hierarchization is also the topic of Page duBois' book *Centaurs and Amazons* (Ann Arbor, Michigan: The University of Michigan Press, 1982), which I discuss further in section III below.

25. Ruth Bleier, *Science and Gender: A Critique of Biology and Its Theories on Women* (New York: Pergamon Press, 1984), p. 3.

26. Luce Irigaray, *Speculum of the Other Woman,* trans. by Gillian C. Gill (Ithaca, N.Y.: Cornell University Press, 1985); originally published in French under the title *Speculum de l'autre femme,* 1974.

27. Evelyn Fox Keller, *Reflections on Science and Gender* (New Haven: Yale University Press, 1985).

28. Lange, for example, cites Darwin's often-quoted remark: "Linnaeus and Cuvier have been my two gods, though in very different ways, but they were mere schoolboys to old Aristotle" (p. 14, n. 9).

29. For discussion of the question of feminism in Plato, see Julia Annas, "Plato's Republic and Feminism," *Philosophy* 51 (1976), pp. 307–21; Gregory Vlastos, "Was Plato a Feminist?" [London] *Times Literary Supplement,* March 17–23, 1989, pp. 276ff; and Dorothea Wender, "Plato: Misogynist, Paedophile and Feminist, *Arethusa* 6 (1973), pp. 75–80.

30. Fox Keller, p. 19.

31. Michel Foucault, *The History of Sexuality,* Volume II, *The Use of Pleasure,* trans. by Robert Hurley (New York: Vintage Books, 1986).

32. Vlastos, p. 289. The reader may find Vlastos' verdict harsh; it is worth noting that he draws important distinctions between the attitudes of Socrates and Plato. Also, readers may be interested in considering Vlastos' more detailed (and somewhat more measured) critique of Platonic love relations in his article "The Individual as an Object of Love," in Gregory Vlastos, *Platonic Studies* (Princeton: Princeton University Press, 1973; originally published in 1969).

33. Fox Keller, p. 31.

34. For a recent example, see Vance Cope-Kasten, "What Vernant does not mention is that Greek women were excluded from this space and its life, and that their equality consisted in being excluded from the class of citizens

and, therefore, somehow or other, from the class of the rational," p. 31. Also recall Lange's title, "Woman is not a Rational Animal." Elizabeth Spelman's article in *Discovering Reality* (note 9 above), "Aristotle and the Politicization of the Soul," presents a more accurate, and I believe more effectively critical, view of this aspect of Aristotle's picture of male/female relations.

35. Jaggar, p. 5.

36. I, 12, 1260a14–16; 20ff.

37. 1260b18–19.

38. Moses Finley's book *Economy and Society in Ancient Greece* (New York: Viking Press, 1981) is a useful source of information concerning social and sex-role stratification in ancient Greek cities (Athens among others). See also Mary R. Lefkowitz and Maureen B. Fant, eds., *Women's Life in Greece & Rome* (Baltimore: Johns Hopkins, 1982), for a selection of writings from ancient sources by and about women which provide information about their roles and occupations. This anthology includes a listing of a variety of occupations of lower-class women in Athens, including seed seller, wet-nurse, woolworker, groceress, and horsetender (p. 29), as well as a rather remarkable conversation of Socrates' reported in Xenophon's *Oeconomicus,* which concerns training a good wife in skills of domestic economy (pp. 100–104).

Also, recall the entertaining exchange in Aristophanes' *Lysistrata,* in which the Police Commissioner evinces skepticism about the women's plans to run the city treasure after taking control of the Acropolis:

"You will superintend the treasure, you!?
"And why should it strike you so funny?
when we manage our houses in everything
and it's we who look after your money." (p. 19, tr. Sutherland)

39. VIII, 3. I borrow this term from the account of Aristotle's view of friendship in John Cooper, "Aristotle on Friendship," in *Essays on Aristotle's Ethics,* ed. Amelie Rorty (Berkeley: University of California, 1980), pp. 301–340.

40. VIII, 12; 1162a25–27.

41. 192b15.

42. 199a34–b8.

43. See *Meteorology* IV, 12.

44. 645a15–28, *passim:* translations from this work are those of A. L. Peck in the Loeb edition.

45. 642a15.

46. 644b15, *hosper gar oikonomos agathos.*

47. 630b15, 643a25, 630b25, 676a1f, 643b20, 634b20, 635a1, 662a15, 675a20.

48. 639b20, 641b1, 644a35, 688b20f.

49. 641b20.

50. David Balme, *Aristotle's De Partibus Animalium I and De Genera-tione Animalium I*, translated with notes (Oxford: Clarendon Aristotle Series, 1972).

51. Karen Warren, "Male-Gender Bias and Western Conceptions of Reason and Rationality," *APA Newsletter on Feminism and Philosophy* 88:2 (March 1989), p. 49.

52. Herbert Granger disputes this claim and considers evidence on both sides in his article "Deformed Kinds and the Fixity of Species," *Clasical Quarterly* 37 (1987), pp. 110–116; but even if he is right, the general implication I am trying to draw here still holds.

53. Lange writes in her essay in *Discovering Reality* (note 9 above) as though the case for men were different: "Final causes he found operant only in relation to the whole species, male and female, or in relation to the male alone. The final cause of the female individual, qua deficient human, was quite literally outside herself . . . " (p. 12). But this is equally true for *all* sublunary creatures, male and female alike. (And of course, supralunary creatures have no gender.)

54. See, for example, Elizabeth Fee, "Critiques of Modern Science: The Relationship of Feminism to Other Radical Epistemologies, in Ruth Bleier, ed., *Feminist Approaches to Science* (New York: Pergamon Press, 1986), pp. 42–56, and Hilary Rose, "Hand, Brain, and Heart: A Feminist Episte-mology for the Natural Sciences" (note 16 above).

55. On this topic, see Bolton, Brunschwig, and Kakkuri-Knuuttila (n. 19 above).

56. For examples and some analysis, see my paper, "Scientific Method and Empirical Data in Aristotle's *Meteorology*," in Pellegrin and Devereux, eds. 1990, and also in *Oxford Studies in Ancient Philosophy*, 1990.

57. See Bolton and Irwin (n. 19 above), and also John Cleary *"Phain-omena* in Aristotle's Methodology," Ms. 1989, pp. 1–40; and G. E. L. Owen, *"Tithenai ta phainomena,"* in S. Mansion, ed., *Aristote et les problemes de methode* (Louvain: Publications Universitaires de Louvain, 1961), pp. 83–103; reprinted in Julius Moravcsik, ed., *Aristotle* (Garden City, N.Y.: Doubleday, 1967), pp. 167–190.

58. Martha Nussbaum, "Saving Aristotle's Appearances," argues against Owen's view, which suggests a clearer separation between *endoxa* and *phainomena*. Owen also argues that some sciences appear to place

greater emphasis on the empirical data (e.g., astronomy), while others emphasize the conceptual presuppositions that are built into the tradition. As Kakkuri-Knuuttila explains, " . . . concept-formation in Aristotle is principally based on linguistic analysis, which reveals implicit assumptions in our use of language." (p. 277).

59. It is criticized in Bolton and Cleary's articles, among others. Based on my own study of a full-length scientific treatise, his *Meteorology* (see note 56 above), I believe that Aristotle instead recommends the use of *endoxa* to help scientists discover empirical facts or *phainomena* relevant to their inquiry by focusing their questions.

60. *Nicomachean Ethics*, 1098b27–9.

61. Interestingly, the "experts" need not always be representatives of the higher, "educated" classes. Aristotle takes his information from fishermen, camel drivers, dog trainers, hunters, beekeepers, etc. One of the strange things about Nussbaum's treatment of this issue is her total neglect of feminist issues in considering whose wisdom gets included in the collection of *endoxa*. She describes a methodological point made in *Politics* I as follows:

> . . . [H]e tells us that the ethical concepts with which his study deals grow out of, and get their sense only in connection with, ways of life that 'bestial beings' and beings without any needs do not share. It seems to follow, if we generalise this principle, that data for an inquiry into our conception of F can come only from peoples whose ways of life are similar to ours with respect to those conditions that gave rise to our use of the term 'F.' Other groups and species not so related to us could not have 'F' (or a term closely enough related to our 'F') in their language, and we do not, therefore, need to ask them what they think about it. (Nussbaum, pp. 275–6)

This seems to assume that gender makes no difference in groups' assumptions of who is relevantly similar.

62. Of course I could also inquire about the efficient cause of armadillos—where do little armadillos come from (are they born alive? from eggs? etc.). A more tentative, but I think more interesting, reading of Aristotle's notion of explanation would assert that all scientific inquiry in fact (though not perhaps ideally or even ultimately) is guided by actual human concerns. I have argued, for example, that in such a science as his meteorology Aristotle surveys previous opinions or *endoxa* not merely to consider proposed accounts of hail, comets, or earthquakes, but to learn about the things that various people have wondered about, or noted in connection with, these things. It turns out that people think that altitude is connected with hail, or dry windy seasons with comets, or certain cloud and wave patterns with

earthquakes. Now obviously people have made such observations about these phenomena because of their interest in the weather, and in potentially dangerous weather events.

63. See, for example, Julia Annas, "Aristotle on Inefficient Causes," *Philosophical Quarterly* (1982), pp. 311–326; and Julius Moravcsik, "Aristotle on Adequate Explanations," *Synthese* 28 (1974), pp. 3–17.

64. See, for example, my paper on the *Meteorology* (note 56 above) and "Accidental Causes and Real Explanations," in Lindsay Judson, ed., *Essays on Aristotle's Physics* (Oxford: Oxford University Press, 1992). See also Bas van Fraassen, "A Re-Examination of Aristotle's Philosophy of Science." *Dialogue* (Canadian) XIX (1980): pp. 20–45; and "The Pragmatics of Explanation," *American Philosophical Quarterly* 14: pp. 143–50.

65. See the citations listed in note 54 above.

66. Fox Keller, p. 158

67. Fox Keller, p. 161.

68. Fox Keller, p. 173.

69. Fox Keller, p. 175.

70. Fox Keller, p. 163.

71. Fox Keller, p. 167.

72. *P. A.* I, 1, 640b36–41a3

73. 644b28–45a11, *passim.*

74. *H. A.* 588b4ff; quoted in Elliot Sober, *The Nature of Selection: Evolutionary Theory in Philosophical Focus* (Cambridge, Massachusetts: MIT Press, 1984), pp. 162–3, n. 27. For further discussion of Aristotle's views on hierarchy and continuity, in relation to the subsequent tradition of the "Great Chain of Being," see also Page duBois (note 24 above).

75. David Balme, "Aristotle's Use of Division and Differentiae," in Gotthelf and Lennox, eds., 1987, pp. 85–6.

76. Pierre Pellegrin, *Aristotle's Classification of Animals.*

77. Pellegrin, p. 45.

78. 732b15ff.

79. Pellegrin, p. 119.

80. For a clear presentation of these intricate interconnections, see Elizabeth Spelman's article in *Discovering Reality* (note 9 above).

81. Cope-Kasten (note 17 above).

82. To do that, I would have to begin from his well-known system of categories, considering Aristotle's rationale for articulating reality in just the way he did, asking if and how his categories reflect aspects of patriarchy and of his own lived experience. A feminist assessment of Aristotelian logic should also explore Aristotle's contributions to informal logic—his treatment of rhetoric and dialectic, as well as in his discussion of inductive arguments. Moreover, a critical account of Aristotelian epistemology would discuss the possible anthropocentrism of his response to ancient skeptical arguments emphasizing diversity among various animals' sensory modalities. These implications have been discussed by Geoffrey Lloyd in Part I of his book *Science, Folklore, and Ideology* (Cambridge: Cambridge University Press, 1983). See also my paper, "Aristotle on the Sense of Touch," in Martha Nussbaum and Amelie Rorty, eds., *Essays on Aristotle's De Anima* (Oxford: Oxford University Press, 1992). I discuss the fact, for instance, that although Aristotle claims that certain men with soft skin may have a superior sense of touch, and hence be more intelligent than others who have skin roughened from manual labor, he does not consider implications of this point for females, whose skin he believes to be on the whole softer than males'!

83. Jean-Pierre Vernant, *The Origins of Greek Thought* (Ithaca: Cornell University Press, 1982).

84. Cope-Kasten, p. 31.

85. Cope-Kasten, p. 31.

86. Jonathan Barnes, "Proof and the Syllogism," in Enrico Berti, ed., *Aristotle on Science: The Posterior Analytics,* Proceedings of the Eighth Symposium Aristotelicum (Padua: Editrice Antenore, 1981), p. 20.

87. For a challenge, see Myles Burnyeat, "Aristotle on Understanding Knowledge," in Enrico Berti, ed. (see note 86 above), pp. 97–139. For sketches of syllogistic structure within diverse sciences, see previously mentioned articles by Bolton, Gotthelf, and Lennox, in Gotthelf and Lennox, eds., 1987 (n. 19 above), as well as Freeland in Pellegrin and Devereux, ed., 1990 (n. 56 above).

88. Page duBois, *Centaurs and Amazons* (n. 24 above).

89. DuBois, p. 132.

90. Cope-Kasten, p. 31.

91. See the elaborate discussion of *Posterior Analytics* I, 4 in Jonathan Barnes, *Aristotle's Posterior Analytics,* translated with notes (Oxford: Clarendon Aristotle Series, 1975), pp. 112–121. See also James G. Lennox, "Divide and Explain: The *Posterior Analytics* in Practice," in Gotthelf and Lennox, eds., 1987, pp. 90–119.

92. 643b12–13.

93. Aristotle suggests such a master hierarchy in a passage in his *Politics* (I, 5, 1254b10ff.), but not in his biological works. Even when he does describe nature as falling into hierarchies of value, he does not rely on syllogistic or class-exclusive reasoning to do so, but concentrates on what he sees as the relative ontological weight (so to speak) of the relevant entities and activities. I will discuss implications on this sort of evaluation, to some extent, in my Epilogue.

94. See note 82 above.

95. Lloyd, p. 36.

96. Pellegrin, p. 92.

97. Pellegrin, pp. 92–3; emphasis mine.

98. Lange (see note 12 above), p. 10. Lloyd (see note 82 above) also pursues a discussion of Aristotle's account of sexual differentiation; see pp. 94–105.

99. Lange, p. 9; emphasis mine. Lange also remarks: "Aristotle regarded the "monstrosity" of the female as an accidental necessity *of the species,* the norm of which species is obviously male. This position is very different from that wherein maleness and femaleness are considered as accidents of individuals. The latter view makes it possible to assign full human ends to all individuals, whereas Aristotle's view does not. Final causes he found operant only in relation to the whole species, male and female, or in relation to the male alone. The final cause of the female individual, *qua* deficient human, was quite literally outside herself, and was that of being instrumental to the reproduction of male humans. Given the function of the female, and the sense in which Aristotle thought of the organs of the body as "instruments" of the unified person, the female has been defined as virtually an organ of the male body. . . . These organs, or parts, are "material causes" of animals, and it may be noted that the female is no more than a material cause of the animal. Reading 'male' for 'person,' what else are women but "matter set in motion by and for the soul of the unified male, for the ends of the (male) species?" (p. 12). This is one example showing how more recent work published since the articles Lange relies by Randall and Hintikka might affect feminist interpretation of Aristotle's science.

100. Elliott Sober, p. 158.

101. Allan Gotthelf, "Notes Toward a Study of Substance and Essence in Aristotle's *Parts of Animals* II–IV, in Gotthelf, ed., *Aristotle on Nature and Living Things.*

102. IV, 8, 684a32–b2.

103. Gotthelf, ed., 1985, p. 40.

104. Gotthelf, ed., 1985, p. 39–40.

105. *Gen. An.* 732a2–12

106. Luce Irigaray, "The Power of Discourse," in *This Sex Which Is Not One,* p. 74.

107. See my paper, "Aristotle on Bodies, Matter, and Potentiality," in Gotthelf and Lennox, eds., 1987, pp. 392–407.

108. I am grateful to William Austin and Charlotte Witt for helpful comments on an earlier version.

Aristotle and the Politics of Reproduction*

Nancy Tuana

The physiology of reproduction provides a foundation for seeing differences between women and men. Women gestate the fetus within them; men cannot. Women give birth; men cannot. Women lactate; men cannot.[1] Women menstruate; men cannot.

The lesson that has been painfully inscribed upon the lives of women, as well as disenfranchised men, is that "difference" is open to many interpretations. One of the insights of contemporary feminist theory is the realization that "difference," in the Western metaphysical tradition, has too often been understood to entail "lack."[2] Woman is different from man because she is lacking in certain qualities: she is less rational, less moral, less evolved. In the words of Aristotle, woman is a misbegotten man. "Difference," when defined in terms of omission, is a term of derision.

But notice my characterization of woman and man's reproductive differences. Inscribed in this fashion, it is man who lacks, not woman. It seems to fly in the face of reason to say that man, who neither gestates, bears, nor lactates, possesses reproductive capacities superior to those of woman. Yet this is exactly what Aristotle did. In his embryological theories, Aristotle ascribed generative superiority to man. For Aristotle, the male is the true parent. Furthermore, he argued that woman's role in reproduction—her gestations, labors, and lactations—are the cause of her intellectual inferiority to man.

In this chapter I will investigate the logic of Aristotle's ascription of lack to woman. I begin with a discussion of the metaphors used to depict generation in ancient and classical Greece in order to locate Aristotle's place in this descriptive practice. It is my contention that this historical period involved a gradual process of degradation of the female generative powers during which the female principle, initially envisioned as the primordial creative source, comes first to be seen as secondary to the male principle, and ultimately, in the biology of Aristotle, is viewed as lacking and defective. I argue that Aristotle's appropriation of female reproductive potency is not a deviation, but arises out of the metaphysical framework of his time.

Flowering Fields

Gaia now first gave birth to starry Ouranos,
her match in size, to encompass all of her,
and be the firm seat of all the blessed gods.
She gave birth to the tall mountains, enchanting haunts
of the divine nymphs who dwell in the woodlands;
and then she bore Pontos, the barren sea with its raging swell.
All these she bore without mating in sweet love. But then
she did couple with Ouranos to bear deep-eddying Okeanos,
Koios and Kreios, Hyperion and Iapetos,
Theia and Rheia, Themis and Mnemosyne,
as well as gold-wreathed Phoibe and lovely Tethys.[3]

The burgeoning fertility of the female principle of creation is a metaphor woven throughout Greek cosmogony. When the Greeks looked back to the earliest periods of creation, to the genesis of the earth and of the gods, they envisioned a powerful female creative force. Gaia, Earth, "the broad-breasted," gives birth parthenogenetically. The sky, the mountains, and the sea flowered from her body. During the initial generations of the gods, the male principle is an addition, neither primordial nor primary. Chaos, giving birth initially to Erebos and Night, never takes on a male consort, but remains virginal—independent from the male—in all her creations.[4]

Metaphors of earth as the fertile source of life perhaps hearken back to a preagrarian society, if not in reality, at least in myth and ritual. We can find images of the earth as an "Eden" in which men were nourished by its plentiful fruits.[5] Hesiod, in his *Works and Days,* describes a time, prior to the evils carried by Pandora, when "human tribes lived on this earth / without suffering and toilsome hardship / and without painful illnesses that bring death to men."[6] During this time, the earth's harvest was so plentiful that "a day's labor could bring a man enough / to last a whole year with no more work."[7]

Similar images of the earth can be found throughout Homer's *Illiad.* In numerous passages he characterizes the earth as "bountiful" and "prospering."[8] Similarly when Homer refers to the grief of

Althaia over the death of her brother he depicts her as "many times beating with her hands on the earth abundant."[9] Homer also connects the fertility of the earth to the sexual conduct of the gods. When Hera lay with Zeus,

> underneath them the divine earth broke into young, fresh
> grass, and into dewy clover, crocus and hyacinth
> so thick and soft it held the hard ground deep away from them.
> There they lay together and drew about them a golden
> wonderful cloud, and from it the glimmering dew descended.[10]

Given the association of woman and nature, it is reasonable to expect that during a period when the earth is envisioned as a fertile field, the female principle in creation would be emphasized and woman's role in reproduction would be acknowledged, if not revered. Women's bodies, like the fecund earth, would be seen as the fertile ground from which children blossom.

With the shift to an agrarian culture, the metaphors for creation, both divine and human, shift to ones of cultivation. Creation comes to be seen not as a spontaneous flowering of the earth, but rather of plowing, planting, and harvesting.[11] The land, no longer envisioned as the autonomous body of the goddess, is now property of man, who must work by plowing and sowing the fields in order to harvest its fruits, which are in turn his property. Like the land, the body of woman comes to be seen as property, and children as crops, products of man's labor, and owned by him.

Metaphors of the sowing and planting of the male seed become the prevalent expression of creation, replacing the image of the spontaneous flowering forth of the earth. Hesiod explains that "The ninth of midmonth is better toward evening, / and the least harm for men is found in the first ninth; / this is a good day for men and women both to plant offspring / and to be born themselves."[12] Aeschylus employs a similar metaphor to refer to

> the father-slaying son,
> King Oedipus, who sowed
> his outrageous agony
> in the inviolate field
> of his mother, the same womb
> that bore and cherished him;
> and planted there in blood
> the wrath-bearing root.[13]

And Sophocles, in the *Antigone,* depicts Creon as responding to Is-
mene's question of how could he kill Antigone, his own son's bride,
that "others have furrows that can be ploughed."[14]

This change in metaphor provides the foundation for a shift in
perception of the potency of the female creative principle. Far from
the image of the freely flowering earth, woman must now be culti-
vated and planted with man's seed. But this leaves open the question of woman's contribution. Man provides seed. Does woman too
provide seed or only the soil in which man's seed is planted?

The Primacy of Male Generative Powers

The woman you call the mother of the child
is not the parent, just a nurse to the seed,
the new-sown seed that grows and swells inside her.
The *man* is the source of life.[15]

The true parent, the source of life, argues Apollo, is the man.
Woman is wet-nurse, oven, the soil in which man plants his seed.
This image of woman as incubator, expressed by Aeschylus to vin-
dicate Orestes, murderer of his mother Clytemnestra, is given the
scientific credibility of systematization in Aristotle's *History of Animals* and *Generation of Animals.*[16] Rejecting the prevalent Hippocratic view that women as well as men produce seed, albeit
weaker seed, Aristotle argued that the man alone contributes seed
to generation.

While denying woman's seed, Aristotle acknowledged both female and male principles in generation. The male contains "the efficient cause of generation" while the female contains "the material
of it."[17] But a close examination of the female role in generation, reveals that woman provides the least important part of generation.
Aristotle posited four factors involved in creation:

first, the final cause, that for the sake of which; secondly, the definition of essence (and these two we may regard pretty much as
one and the same); thirdly, the material; and fourthly, that from
which the source of movement comes.[18]

Woman contributes nothing to the form or function of the created
being. She merely supplies the matter that provides nourishment

to the seed of man. "What the male contributes to generation is the form and the efficient cause, while the female contributes the material."[19]

How does one read this image of woman? Clearly, woman's role in the Aristotelian schema is inferior to that of man's, but there remains an ambiguity in how to interpret the notion of a material cause. By adopting an image like that of Aeschylus, seeing woman as the soil in which man plants his seed, one can still attribute to woman a richness and fertility. Such an image contains glimpses of the earlier view of the earth, Gaia, and her soil bursting forth in plenty. Although now the soil of woman must be planted to be fertile, still she continues to actively contribute to the growth of the seed planted within her. Her fertility passes into the seed and nourishes it. Gone is the earlier image of the female principle as self-directing; she no longer provides the form or end of that which generates within her. Yet, in the image provided by Aeschlyus, woman remains a living, organic force in the production of life. She has a role, a weaker role, perhaps, in not herself providing seed. Nevertheless, she is perceived as an active force in reproduction.

Aristotle selected a very different metaphor to illustrate woman's role in reproduction. Rather than the fertile earth, woman is likened to the wood out of which a carpenter carves a bed. Aristotle reinforced his claim that the female role in generation is passive while the male role is active by arguing that "the one thing which is produced [the fetus] comes from them only in the sense in which a bed comes into being from the carpenter and the wood."[20] Elaborating upon this metaphor, Aristotle explained that

> . . . in the female is the material from which is made the resulting product . . . the male does not emit semen at all in some animals, and where he does this is no part of the resulting embryo; just so no material part comes from the carpenter to the material, i.e. the wood in which he works, nor does any part of the carpenter's art exist within what he makes, but the shape and the form are imparted from him to the material by means of the motion he sets up. It is his hands that move his tools, his tools that move the material; it is his knowledge of his art, and his soul, in which is the form, that move his hands.[21]

The male, like a craftsperson, imparts form and function. In this image the matter of woman is wholly passive, adding nothing to the seed of man. Woman merely provides the workplace and the inert material from which man crafts a human life. Far from the fertile, flowering, burgeoning earth, the female principle is seen as inert wood. The matter of woman is not the living, nourishing soil, but the severed, lifeless limb of a tree—that which although was once living is now dead.

Aristotle's image of conception relegates woman to a very insignificant role in generation. Woman merely provides the material out of which man forms the fetus. The female role is passive and is limited to the least perfect of all the causes:

> ... the first efficient or moving cause, to which belong the definition and the form, is better and more divine in its nature than the material on which it works ... for the first principle of movement, whereby that which comes into being is male, is better and more divine, and the female is matter.[22]

Aristotle attempted to reinforce his thesis of the excellence of the male contribution to generation by arguing that it, unlike the female contribution, involves nothing material. The assumption implicit here, of course, is that nonmaterial substance is superior to, that is, has a higher degree of perfection than, material substance. Using his analogy of the carpenter, Aristotle represents the male semen as a tool that moves upon the material within the womb, imparting both form and motion, but which does not become a part of the material of the fetus. According to Aristotle, when a male ejaculates that "which is emitted [is] the principle of soul." The matter that is ejaculated with it dissolves and evaporates and is not a part of the generation process. Aristotle associated the male contribution with "something divine." "While the body is from the female, it is the soul that is from the male, for the soul is the substance of a particular body."[23]

The role of the female in generation in the Aristotelian framework is greatly diminished from the preagrarian images of potent fertility. The female actually has little to do with generation. Woman is that "out of which comes into being the offspring previously existing in the generator," where the generator is man.[24] From active creative principle, woman becomes the passive material upon which the male artist works. "[T]he female, as female, is passive, and the male, as male, is active, and the principle of movement comes from him."[25] Thus, the true creative act in generation arises from the actions of the male. In this respect, Aristotle is in full agreement with Aeschylus—the male is the true parent.

A World Without Women

Aristotle's shift in metaphor, from field to inert wood, is in turn founded upon the bias that the "proper form" of a human is male. Aristotle insisted that nature always aims at the production of the male form. An embryo becomes female only "when the first principle does not bear sway and cannot concoct the nourishment through lack of heat nor bring it into its proper form."[26] The belief that the original or proper form of humans is male was not unique to Aristotle. It was a metaphor prevalent in the religion, literature, and philosophy of classical Greece.

The belief in the primacy of the male form is reflected in the image of a world without women. Euripides' Hippolytos provides one of the numerous literary expressions of this image.

> Zeus, let me set you straight about women.
> Men chase their glitter, but it's all fake.
> You were mistaken to flood our lives with them—
> because if your purpose was to ensure
> perpetuation of the human race
> you could have by-passed women completely.
> A better idea would be this—
> to let prospective fathers
> come to your temples and pay you
> in bronze, iron, or solid gold
> for seeds which will flourish into men,
> each father paying for his sons
> in proportion to his wealth and status.[27]

Hippolytos' plea for a world without women mirrors Hesiod's account of the creation of humans in which the creation of woman is represented as secondary, both temporally and metaphysically, to the creation of man. Just as Hippolytos wishes for seeds, bought with bronze, iron, or gold, from which to grow sons, Hesiod tells of the five races of man—gold, silver, bronze, the heroes, and iron.

The first generation were a golden race who

> . . . lived like the gods, carefree in their hearts, shielded from pain and misery. Helpless old age did not exist, and with limbs of unsagging vigor they enjoyed the delights of feasts, out of evils' reach. A sleeplike death subdued them, and every good thing was theirs; the barley-given earth asked for no toil to bring forth a rich and plentiful harvest.[28]

The second race, a race of silver, was much worse than the first. They lived a short life of foolishness and reckless violence. The third race of bronze was "dreadful and mighty / and bent on the harsh deeds of war and violence."[29] The fourth race was the divine race of heroes, the demigods. The fifth race of men, the final generation, is the race of iron. "Neither day nor night / will give them rest as they waste away with toil / and pain."[30]

In the *Theogony*, Hesiod depicts mankind as existing prior to the creation of women. Putting the two accounts together, one can conclude that the original race, the golden race, was a race of men only, for, as I will illustrate, it is only with the creation of women that man lived a life of suffering, illness, and toilsome hardship.

In the *Theogony*, Hesiod's account of the creation of woman is preceded by the story of Prometheus. While preparing the ritual sacrifice for the gods, Prometheus devised a plan to deceive Zeus. Prometheus took an ox, carved it, and divided the parts into two piles. In one pile he placed the meat, entrails, and some of the fat within a hide, and covered it over with the ox's stomach to render it unappealing. In the other pile he put only the bones of the ox, but covered this with fat so that it would like the more desirable of the two. When Zeus, seeing the two piles, accused Prometheus of being selfish and trying to keep only the best for man, Prometheus slyly replied that Zeus could have his pick of the two piles. Zeus reached down and picked up the pile covered with fat and carried it to Mt. Olympos. Uncovering the bones, Zeus knew he had been deceived, and anger rushed through him. Taking fire and keeping it with him, Zeus declared that mankind would no longer know its benefit. But Prometheus deceived Zeus yet again and, by hiding an ember within a hollowed fennel stalk, stole the fire from Zeus and returned it to man.

When Zeus saw the flash of fire among mortal men, his heart filled with anger and he devised terrible punishments for Prometheus and for mankind. Because of his disobedience, Zeus chained Prometheus to a pillar where a long-winged eagle continually tore at his liver by day, but where there was no end to the pain for by night his liver grew whole again. Mankind he punished by contriving an evil. Zeus created a being destined to live among men and cause them great suffering—woman. Zeus called upon the gods to create a being with the external appearance of a goddess, to be a "tempting snare / from which men cannot escape."[31] In creating woman, Zeus employed the same trick that Prometheus used with the ox. He made her external appearance desirable in order to trick man into embracing the wickedness within. In the *Works and Days,* Hesiod explains that Zeus has Hermes place "in her breast / lies, coaxing words, and a thievish nature."[32] Although woman has the appearance of a goddess, this external covering, like Prometheus' fat, merely disguises and masks reality. Once man embraces her the deception is quickly uncovered and woman's true nature is revealed—"a scourge for toiling man."[33] Woman is a nagging burden, the cause of man's suffering and toil. Hesiod, like Aristotle after him, views woman as a deviation from the original or "true" form.

Plato similarly depicted woman as a secondary creation. Given that Aristotle was a student of Plato, it is reasonable to conjecture that he would have been influenced by the Platonic view of the creation of woman.

The *Timaeus* contains Plato's account of the creation of mankind. Having created the universe, Plato explained that the divine being made a mixture of the four elements, earth, air, fire, and water. "And having made it he divided the whole mixture into souls equal in number to the stars and assigned each soul to a star."[34] After dividing the mixture into souls, god implanted each one in a body and gave each being the faculty of sensation and the emotions. Each was equal in perfection to all the others, and all were male.

As in the *Theogony,* Plato posited an original world without women. The primordial form of humans was male. However, each man had to choose how to live his life and use his faculties. According to Plato, men's destinies were determined by how they dealt with their feelings and sensations. "If they conquered these they would live righteously, and if they were conquered by them, unrighteously."[35] The soul of a man who retained control over his emotions and who used his intellect to govern his sensations would, upon the death of his body, return to his appointed star, whereupon he would have a "blessed" existence. However, the man who failed to rein in his appetites or emotions would be reincarnated as a woman. "[A]t the second birth he would pass into a woman, and if, when in that state of being, he did not desist from evil, he would continually be changed into some brute who resembled him in the evil nature which he had acquired."[36] Man then is the true form; woman is the result of a defect.

Aristotle grafted this belief in the cosmogonical primacy of man onto his biology. Rather than positing an eden-like world without woman, Aristotle viewed women as a necessary mutation, engendered from a deficiency, but required for the reproduction of the species.

The Primacy of the Male Form

Aristotle's biology is based on the central premise that heat is the fundamental principle in the perfection of animals. Heat serves to "concoct" matter, that is, to enable it to develop. The more heat an animal is able to generate, the more developed it will be. "[T]hat which has by nature a smaller portion of heat is weaker."[37] Given this premise, an animal's degree of perfection is determined by the amount of heat it can generate. Thus, his acceptance of the belief that the male form is more perfect than the female required that Aristotle demonstrate that women generate less heat than men.

Aristotle's proof of woman's defect in heat is tied to his view that the male is the true parent. His argument is based on a comparison of female and male semen. Aristotle deviated from the prevalent scientific view in arguing that only male semen contained seed. The Hippocratic position held that women contributed seed to the production of the fetus, although female seed was seen as weaker than male seed.[38] Aristotle rejected this view and replaced it with the position that women's semen is impotent.

Aristotle believed that semen is derived from blood. He labeled the male ejaculate "semen" and noted that it did not resemble blood, but was white in color. He used heat as the mechanism to explain the color of male semen, arguing that a substance is transformed by being concocted through the infusion of heat. On the basis of this he concluded that the whiteness of male semen had to be the result of an infusion of blood that concentrated the potency of the blood and changed its appearance.

But what of woman's semen? Aristotle equated menses with male semen. Menstrual fluids are "analogous in females to semen in males."[39] His justification for this equation was that "semen begins to appear in males and to be emitted at the same time of life that the menstrual flow begins in females" and that "in the decline of life the generative power fails in the one sex and the menstrual discharge in the other."[40] Since the menstrual flow, like the ability to emit semen, commences at puberty and ceases (or declines) with old age, Aristotle correctly concluded that it had to be associated with reproduction. However, Aristotle incorrectly assumed that female semen, like male semen, would be visibly emitted.

Aristotle's proof of woman's defect in heat should now be obvious. Female semen, on Aristotle's account, is abundant and resembles blood. Male semen is scarce and is quite unlike blood. Aristotle claimed that these differences are accounted for by the fact that

women are unable to "cook" their semen to the point of purity—
thus "proof" of their relative coldness. Lacking heat in comparison
to man, woman's semen is not transformed and looks like blood. It
is also more abundant than man's because a woman is unable to reduce it through the infusion of heat. Aristotle then claimed that
woman's defect in heat is what causes her lack of seed. "[I]t is plain
that the female does not contribute semen to the generation of the
offspring. For if she had semen she would not have the menstrual
fluid; but as it is, because she has the latter she has not the
former."[41] In other words, woman's menstrual fluid is the blood that
would be turned into potent semen if she had sufficient heat to concoct it.

The untenability of Aristotle's account obviously rests upon his
equation of menses with semen. Although men have nothing that
corresponds to menstrual fluids, there are striking differences between menses and semen. The most obvious being that menses occur only once a month and are not associated with intercourse or
genital stimulation, while male seminal fluid is generally emitted
whenever there is sufficient stimulation for ejaculation. Given this,
it would have been logical for Aristotle to have considered whether
females have a fluid emitted during intercourse or other genital
stimulation that was the analogue to male semen. In fact, such a
view was popular enough that Aristotle thought it was important to
refute it. "Some think that the female contributes semen in coition
because the pleasure she experiences is sometimes similar to that
of the male, and also is attended by a liquid discharge."[42]

Aristotle offered three arguments designed to prove this view
false. What these arguments actually illustrate is the power of
Aristotle's bias. In the first, he insisted that this discharge does
not occur in all women. It appears only "in those who are fair-
skinned and of a feminine type generally, but not in those who are
dark and of a masculine appearance."[43] Aristotle offered no explanation of how he arrived at this obviously contrived observation.
Given his belief that some women do not have this discharge, yet all
can conceive, Aristotle concluded that it cannot constitute woman's
seminal fluid.[44]

The second argument against labeling these emissions seminal
was that "the pleasure of intercourse is caused by touch in the same
region of the female as of the male; and yet it is not from thence that
this flow proceeds."[45] Aristotle appears to be arguing that it would
be incorrect to associate this discharge with male semen for it is unlike semen in that it does not issue from the place of stimulation.

Aristotle is clearly straining against observation to support his theory. All women have lubricating fluids. These fluids can be produced by stimulating the vulva or vagina, thus causing the fluids to issue from the place touched. Furthermore, a man can ejaculate from stimulation of areas other than his penis, in which case the flow proceeds from a region other than that touched.

The third argument is less contrived, but still contains an unanswered dilemma. Aristotle argued that the association of woman's lubricating fluids with semen is incorrect because women often conceive without the sensation of pleasure in intercourse.[46] In other words, since a woman can conceive without emitting such fluids, the fluids cannot be seminal. While acknowledging the strength of this piece of reasoning, one cannot help but notice that Aristotle does not deal with the anomaly that men frequently ejaculate during intercourse without this resulting in pregnancy. This fact gives us good reason to believe that male ejaculate alone is not sufficient for conception, otherwise one would expect a pregnancy everytime a man ejaculated into a woman's vagina. Aristotle failed to mention this anomaly. Had he dealt with it, he might have been led to speculate about the existence of a female seed which is only periodically emitted.

Although Aristotle used his position concerning the condition of woman's "seminal" fluids to support his claim that women possess less heat than men, to complete his theory he needed an explanation of the mechanism of this incapacity. That is, what is the cause of woman's defect in heat? Aristotle's response is simply that "the first principle does not bear sway and cannot concoct the nourishment through lack of heat nor bring it to its proper form."[47] This is not an explanation, but merely an assertion of the bias that the "proper form" of a human is male. Given this assumption, Aristotle concluded that a female embryo is a deviation from nature, a "monstrosity." Aristotle defined a monstrosity as a "departure from type" and claimed that the "first departure [from type] indeed is that the offspring should become female instead of male."[48] Holding that nature always aims to create the most perfectly formed being and accepting the Greek belief in the primacy of the male form, Aristotle simply inferred from the conjunction of these beliefs that a female must be the result of some lack of generative heat or some adversity. On this account, woman is a misbegotten man, resulting from some defect in the heat of the generative process.

The evidence that Aristotle offered in support of his position that the female form was the result of a defect in heat, demonstrates the extent to which his biases affected his science. He claimed that

> [o]bserved facts confirm what we have said. For more females are produced by the young and by those verging on old age than by those in the prime of life; in the former the heat is not yet perfect, in the latter it is failing. And those of a moister and more feminine state of body are more wont to beget females, and a liquid semen causes this more than a thicker; now all these characteristics come of a deficiency in natural heat.[49]

Given his theory, the claim that individuals not in prime condition would be more likely to give birth to females is a logical conclusion. Such individuals are least able to provide the heat necessary for concoction of a fetus into its "proper form." However, careful observations would have disconfirmed this hypothesis since there is no correlation between the age of the pregnant woman and the sex of her offspring. Furthermore, the circularity of Aristotle's position is obvious in his claim that a "feminine" state of body results from a defect in natural heat.

Another contention that would not have withstood careful testing was that the greater heat of the male fetus causes it to develop more quickly than the female. Aristotle claimed that the male fetus first moves in the womb about the fortieth day while the female does not move until the ninetieth day.[50] This is a reasonable inference from his theory, but one that could be easily disconfirmed by carefully recording fetal movements in women.

Furthermore, there are a number of points at which Aristotle's arguments are strained. He insisted that a defect in heat resulted in woman being born a "mutilated male."[51] Yet he noted that males are more often born defective than females. It would seem logical here to conclude that such higher rates of mutations in males were due to a defect in heat, thus an argument against the premise of male physiological superiority. Aristotle, however, managed to turn the higher preponderance of birth defects in males into a mark of perfection. He insisted that deformities in male babies were caused not by a defect in heat, but rather by the male's superior heat. He explained that due to the greater heat involved in the production of a male fetus, it "moves about more than the female, and on account of moving is more liable to injury."[52]

One sees the power of Aristotle's biases once again as he attempted to account for the fact that females reach puberty more

quickly than do males. Aristotle had earlier claimed that acceler-
ated development was a mark of superior heat, the reason, for example, that male fetuses move more quickly than do female. By
making an unsupported distinction between pre- and postnatal development, Aristotle pointed to puberty rates as additional proof of
woman's imperfection.

> For females are weaker and colder in nature, and we must look
> upon the female character as being a sort of natural deficiency. Ac-
> cordingly while it is within the mother it develops slowly because
> of its coldness (for development is concoction, and it is heat that
> concocts, and what is hotter is easily concocted); but after birth it
> quickly arrives at maturity and old age on account of its weakness,
> for all inferior things come sooner to their perfection, and as this is
> true of works of art so it is of what is formed by nature.[53]

It should be clear that Aristotle's premise of the superiority of
the male form was an unsupported tenet. In fact, it was a belief so
obvious to Aristotle, that he was willing to bend logic and even observation to hold fast to it.

The Misbegotten Man

Viewing woman as a deviation from the "true form" obviously
has significant consequences. On this premise, woman's difference
from man will be defined in terms of lack. For Aristotle, woman is
like a man, only less developed, less perfect, and ultimately less human. Aristotle attributed woman's reproductive differences to her
inferiority. Only an individual who was unable to fully concoct matter would be capable of nourishing a fetus. The male, capable of concocting all of his matter, would have no residue with which to feed a
growing fetus. Aristotle concluded that although "the female is, as it
were, a mutilated male" it is a mutilation necessary for the perpet-
uation of the race.[54] Woman is less perfect than man, but her imperfection is a "natural" one.

Aristotle consistently defines woman's "natural defects" in
terms of lack. Because woman is incapable of fully concocting her
matter, she is, in many important ways, less developed than man.
Because woman has less heat, she will be smaller and weaker
than man.[55] Woman's defect of heat results in her brain being
smaller and less developed, and her inferior brain size in turn
accounts for much of her defective nature. Woman's less concocted

brain renders her deliberative faculty too ineffective to rule over her emotions. Her deliberative faculty is, at best, without authority, for it is easily overcome by the irrational part of her soul.[56] This defect similarly causes woman to be mischievous and impulsive.[57] She is "more jealous, more querulous, more apt to scold and to strike . . . more prone to despondency and less hopeful than the man, more void of shame, more false of speech, more deceptive, and of more retentive memory."[58]

Aristotle's degradation of the female principle in creation thus ties to his general degradation of woman's abilities. The replacement of the potent image of fertile fields with that of inert wood passively fashioned by the male, carries with it a view of woman as lacking: lacking in potency, lacking in heat, lacking in the highest of the human qualities. Aristotle's reproductive theories arise out of and in turn reinforce an interpretation of woman's differences as defects.[59]

Notes

*The initial research on this topic was supported by a grant from the American Association of University Women. My thanks to Bat-Ami Bar On and William Cowling for their helpful comments on an earlier draft of this essay.

1. In acknowledgment of the fact that men can lactate if given hormonal injections, this statement should be read "men cannot lactate without artificial modification of their hormonal levels."

2. For an excellent collection of feminist explorations of the concept of difference, see The Future of Difference, ed. Hester Eisenstein and Alice Jardine (New Brunswick, NJ: Rutgers University Press, 1985).

3. Hesiod, Theogony, trans. Apostolos N. Athanassakis. (Baltimore: Johns Hopkins University Press, 1983) 126–136.

4. Hesiod, Theogony 123ff.

5. I use the gender specific "men" here intentionally. As I will show, this eden-like period was also envisioned as a time prior to the creation of women.

6. Hesiod, Works and Days, trans. Apostolos N. Athanassakis. (Baltimore: Johns Hopkins University Press, 1983), 91–93.

7. Hesiod, Works and Days, 43–44. Actually, Hesiod believed that the earth retained such fertility, but that the gods hid its fruits from humans because of the sins of Prometheus.

8. Homer, *Illiad,* trans. Richmond Lattimore (Chicago: University of Chicago Press, 1970). References to the bountiful earth include 3.89, 8.277, 12.193, and 16.481. The earth as prospering is mentioned on 3.265 and 6.213.

9. Homer 9.568.

10. Homer 14.347–51.

11. An excellent analysis of ancient metaphors for the female body to which I am indebted can be found in Page duBois' *Sowing the Body: Psychoanalysis and Ancient Representations of Women* (Chicago: University of Chicago Press, 1988).

12. Hesiod, *Works and Days* 810–813.

13. Aeschylus, *Seven Against Thebes,* trans. Anthony Hecht and Helen H. Bacon (London: Oxford University Press, 1974), 955–962 (English translation lines).

14. Sophocles, *Antigone,* trans. Andrew Brown (Wiltshire, England: Aris and Phillips, 1987), 569.

15. Aeschylus, *The Oresteia,* "The Eumenides," trans. Robert Fagles (New York: Viking Press, 1975), 666–669.

16. All citations are from *The Complete Works of Aristotle,* ed. J. Barnes (Princeton: Princeton University Press, 1984): *Generation of Animals,* trans. A. Platt; *History of Animals,* trans. d'A. W. Thompson.

17. Aristotle, Generation of Animals 716.a.5.

18. Ibid., 715.a.5.

19. Ibid., 729.a.10.

20. Ibid., 729.b.15.

21. Ibid., 730.b.1–20.

22. Ibid., 732.a.1–10.

23. Ibid., 738.b.25.

24. Ibid., 716.a.20.

25. Ibid., 729.b.10.

26. Ibid., 766.a.18–20.

27. Euripides, *Hippolytos,* trans. Robert Bagg (New York: Oxford University Press, 1973), 940–952 (English translation lines).

28. Hesiod, *Works and Days* 113–119.

29. Ibid., 146–147.

30. Ibid., 176–177.

31. Hesiod, *Theogony* 589–60.

32. Hesiod, *Works and Days* 79–80.

33. Ibid., 83.

34. Plato, *Timaeus*, trans. Benjamin Jowett, *The Collected Dialogues of Plato*, eds. Edith Hamilton and Huntington Cairns (Princeton: Princeton University Press, 1961), 41d.

35. Plato, *Timaeus* 42b.

36. Ibid., 42b–c.

37. Aristotle, *Generation of Animals* 726.b.33.

38. Hippocrates, *Regimen*, XXVIII & XXIX, trans. W. H. S. Jones (Cambridge: Harvard University Press, 1943).

39. Aristotle, *Generation of Animals* 727.a.3–4.

40. Ibid., 727.a.5–10.

41. Ibid., 727.a.25–30.

42. Ibid., 727.b.35.

43. Ibid., 728.a.1.

44. I reject the view that Aristotle was an "armchair" biologist who merely speculated about living forms and did not base his conclusions on observational data (see, e.g., Igemar Duering, "Aristotle's Method in Biology," *Aristote et les problems de methode*, Louvain, 1961). Many of Aristotle's tenets involved biological investigations and were not simply the result of accepting common opinion. For a detailed argument in support of this view, see Michael Boylan, *Method and Practice in Aristotle's Biology* (Lanham, MD: University Press of America, 1983). If this example, and the following, represent lapses in Aristotle's critical empiricism, such a lapse would be significant, and would point to his bias of female biological inferiority.

45. Aristotle, *Generation of Animals* 728.a.30.

46. Ibid., 727.b.5–10.

47. Ibid., 766.a.18–20.

48. Ibid., 767.b.8–9.

49. Ibid., 766.b.28–33.

50. Aristotle, *History of Animals* 583.b.3–5.

51. Aristotle, *Generation of Animals* 737.a.27–28.

52. Ibid., 775.a.6–7.

53. Ibid., 775.a.14–21.

54. Ibid., 737.a.27–28.

55. Aristotle, *History of Animals* 538.a.23–b.8.

56. On Aristotle's account, the free woman's deliberative faculty is without authority, while the slave woman is without the capacity to deliberate. For an excellent discussion of Aristotle's views concerning free and slave women, see Elizabeth Spelman's *Inessential Woman: Problems of Exclusion in Feminist Thought* (Boston: Beacon Press, 1988).

57. Aristotle, *History of Animals* 608.a.32.

58. Ibid., 608.b.10–12.

59. For a discussion of the influence of Aristotelian embryology upon subsequent biological theories, see my essay "The Weaker Seed: The Sexist Bias of Reproductive Theory," *Hypatia: A Journal of Feminist Philosophy,* 1988, 3(1):35–59.

Aristotle: Women, Deliberation, and Nature

Deborah K. W. Modrak

The free-man rules over the slave after another manner from that in which the male rules over the female . . . for the slave has no deliberative faculty at all; the woman has, but it is without authority.[1]

These words from the mouth of a philosopher who holds that all human beings are the same in essence are truly baffling.[2] Humans are rational animals, the possession of reason is the distinctive feature of such an animal. If the deliberative faculty is the rational faculty, then women are defective human beings and (natural) slaves are sub-humans.[3]

Although there are passages in the Aristotelian corpus that seem to support this reading, it would, especially in the case of women, be highly problematic.[4] The human species is by nature sexually dimorphic. Nature, according to Aristotle, always acts to the good; its claim to universal good would be seriously undermined, should it turn out that as a result of natural processes as many defective creatures were produced as excellent ones.[5] Without a doubt, an explanation is required and at least two suggest themselves: (1) Aristotle believes that women are defective humans and is blind to the threat this view poses to his teleological conception of nature; or (2) Aristotle believes that women are full-fledged humans and thus he intends to pick out a moral rather than a rational defect when he attributes a weak deliberative faculty to them.

In the case of a thinker who is as systematic as Aristotle, it is impossible to understand the full import of a position asserted in one passage without putting it in the context of related discussions elsewhere in the corpus. Accordingly, I plan to look at the two most plausible readings of the *Politics* passage; namely, (a) women are defective rational beings or (b) they are defective moral beings, within the context provided by Aristotle's conception of rationality and his conception of moral action. Having arrived at an interpretation of the *Politics* claim, I shall consider whether gender difference for Aristotle is due to culture or nature and whether his view of women commits him to positions that are inconsistent with other parts of his philosophy. Finally, since, even if Aristotle's doctrine is internally consistent, from a modern moral perspective something seems to have gone wrong in his thinking about women, I shall look for the genesis of that error.

I

Suppose Aristotle thinks that just in virtue of being female one has a tenuous hold on rationality, that one's faculty of reason is weak. If this is the case and Aristotle is consistent, then there must be something about the account of the way in which rationality is realized in a female body that explains this defect. We should expect to find the theoretical underpinnings of the *Politics* passage in Aristotle's characterization of reason in the *De Anima* and in his account of the transmission of human characteristics across generations in the *Generation of Animals*.

The *De Anima* is of no help in this regard. Nowhere in that work does Aristotle differentiate between the rational capacities of the sexes. The entire discussion is gender-neutral. Aristotle is concerned to explain why human beings are able to think. This ability is based in part on the ability to perceive and to store perceptual information for future use and in part on the ability to generalize on the basis of this information.[6] Unlike the objects presented in perceptual experience, the objects of thought are universals. For instance, humans see and touch bodies of water, as do other animals, but humans alone also grasp the essence of water, what it is to be water.[7] The ability to apprehend and manipulate universals is constitutive of human thinking and this power supervenes on perceptual capacities.

Perceptual capacities are realized through bodily organs; sight, for instance, is exercised through the eyes. The capacity to think, however, has no bodily organ, Aristotle argues, because if it did, then the range of the objects one could think about would be limited by the organ's physical make-up.[8] Since reason's grasp is unrestricted, the power to think must be unembodied. This in turn seems to limit the potentiality that sexual differences would possess to affect the rational capacity of individual human beings because sexual difference is, on Aristotle's account, physiological.[9] This feature of rationality together with the *De Anima*'s gender-neutral description of human cognitive capacities forces us to look elsewhere for an explanation of the alleged difference between the rational faculty of the male and the female.

Turning to Aristotle's biological writings, one soon discovers that the support to be found there for a negative assessment of the rational capacity of women is slight at best. With respect to internal physical structures, the differences between male and female anatomy are solely due to differences in sexual organs.[10] Insofar as human rationality is dependent on the body, more specifically on the perceptual system, there would appear to be no obvious difference between the sexes.[11] Insofar as an individual's rational capacity is a direct consequence of the successful replication of the human form in that person, Aristotle's theory of reproduction may leave some room for systematically generated differences between the sexes.

According to Aristotle's summary description of reproduction, the male parent provides the form or essence and the female parent the matter.[12] More precisely, conception takes place when the sperm of a male works up the *catamenia* (the residue in the uterus) of the female. The vehicle of the form is *pneuma* (hot vapor) in the semen; its role is simply to cause the changes in the material supplied by the female that transform that material into an embryo, a composite of form and matter.[13] If all goes well, the embryo develops into a viable animal which belongs to the same species as its parents and also exhibits, besides species-specific characteristics, other more distinctive features inherited from one or both of its parents or their ancestors. In the best case, Aristotle believes, the male parent generates another male resembling himself in the material supplied by the mother.[14] If, however, the motions in the male's sperm are weak, they may be overpowered by the motions in the *catamenia;* in this case, a female offspring is produced.[15] Weaker movements in the semen also account for the birth of offspring resembling the mother instead of the father, or resembling the father's ancestors or the mother's ancestors.[16] In all these cases, the male has failed in varying degrees to replicate himself fully in his offspring.

What is needed to fill out Aristotle's story in the *Politics* is evidence that weakness in the movements of the semen correspond to the defective replication of the human form such that female humans have poorer ratiocinative powers. Such evidence, however, is hard to come by. Aristotle holds that gender differentiation is not a proper part of the essence or form of a living creature.[17] This suggests that insofar as the capacity for thought is transmitted through sperm, this capacity is not sex-linked.[18] Moreover, as we have seen, reason as possessed by an existing individual is without a bodily organ. As a result, when Aristotle describes human reproduction, he is hard pressed to explain how rationality is transmitted. All other psychological powers come into being when the matter of the embryo is shaped into the appropriate organ. The power to see, for instance, is acquired when the eyes develop. In the development of a bodily organ, the movements natural to the matter supplied by the female parent may interfere with the movements due to the sperm and hence an imperfect organ may be formed. The power of thought, however, enters from "outside," Aristotle says,

> ... mind (*nous*) alone comes besides from outside and it alone is divine, because bodily activity has no part in its activity.[19]

Apparently, the rational faculty comes into being in the embryo not as a direct consequence of the body or matter undergoing some change, and it is acquired at a relatively late stage of development. Granted, this is a very baffling doctrine; fortunately, for our purposes, it is not necessary to solve all the puzzles.[20] It is enough to notice that if the material substrate of the embryo has no part in the process by which the rational capacity is acquired, then one should not look to biology for an explanation of the weakness of the deliberative faculty in women.[21] For, as Aristotle says in the *Metaphysics*, differences between male and female are not differences in the form but in the composite of form and matter.[22]

II

The other strategy open to an interpreter of *Politics* I.13 is to look at Aristotle's ethics and see if Aristotle has good theoretical reasons for supposing that women are defective moral agents. On this reading, the claim that women possess a weak deliberative faculty (*bouleutikon*) is not construed as a sweeping condemnation of female rationality but as a narrower claim about a specific kind of reasoning, practical deliberation.

A survey of Aristotle's employment of the adjective βουλευτικός (*bouleutikos*, capable of deliberation) in the *Nicomachean Ethics* supports the present line of interpretation.[23] He describes the practically wise individual as *bouleutikos* (capable of deliberation) whereas the person who impetuously acts against his or her best judgment is said to be not-*bouleutikos* (not capable of deliberation).[24] The legislative art is also described as *bouleutike* (capable of deliberation).[25] As used in the *Ethics, bouleutikos* is narrower in meaning than 'capacity for rationality'; it is the ability to arrive at correct judgments about what should be done. Such judgments involve the application of general principles to particular cases.

Practical wisdom consists in the ability to recognize what action should be performed in a particular case. Such judgments have two components, (a) the morally correct general principle(s) and (b) the application of the principle to a particular case. A practically wise person not only has the right principles but also knows when and how to apply a particular principle. Moral principles, according to Aristotle, give agents general directives for action, for instance, 'be courageous'. Such a principle does not tell an agent what she or he should do on any particular occasion. Even if the agent accepts Aristotle's analysis of courage, she or he knows only that she or he should seek the mean relative to her or his situation between fear of death and reckless indifference to death.[26] To reach the decision that today she or he should risk her or his life for her or his city requires an understanding of what constitutes the mean in her or his particular circumstances. Since the circumstances in which human agents find themselves are infinitely variable, Aristotle believes that it is impossible to formulate moral principles with such precision that an agent can simply read the right action off the principle.[27] To be consistently moral, an agent, in addition to having the right values, must have an art that Aristotle compares to perception and to cleverness—this is the ability to "see" which one of a number of prospective actions satisfies the applicable moral principle.[28] This art is practical wisdom. The practically wise person is good at a particular kind of means-end reasoning, deliberation, where the starting point (the end) is a moral principle and the conclusion is a decision about what should be done here and now.

It begins to seem that what women lack is the ability to recognize the connection between general principles and particular cases so that women frequently fail to act in accordance with their moral principles. If this is the force of Aristotle's statement that the deliberative faculty of a woman is without authority, then it is not surprising that he also describes the morally weak person as not-*bouleutikos* (not capable of deliberation).

Aristotle describes two types of morally weak persons—one fails to act in accordance with his or her deliberations, the other is impulsive and not capable of deliberation.[29] Since neither type of morally weak agent is capable both of reasoning from his or her moral principles to the correct decision about what ought to be done and then performing that action, both would seem to possess a deliberative faculty that is without authority. *Akrasia* (moral weakness) on Aristotle's analysis, consists of a failure to recognize which actions follow from the moral principles one accepts.[30] One may, for instance, believe that temperance is good and that temperance proscribes the eating of sweets, and thus one should recognize on a particular occasion when a sweet is presented that one should not eat that sweet. The temperate individual makes the right choice and abstains; the morally weak person eats the sweet while still holding onto the general principle that sweets should not be eaten.

Aristotle explains this failure of character as a cognitive failure which in several respects is similar to a mistaken perceptual judgment. When one perceives a particular object, one not only perceives its sensible characteristics, for example, its color and shape, but one also apprehends the object as a certain sort of thing having certain properties. These more complex perceptions are dependent upon the percipient's general beliefs about the world. She or he sees an animal grazing in the field, she or he recognizes that it is a mule and typically, since she or he has the general belief that mules are sterile, she or he also perceives that the animal is sterile. Occasionally, however, she or he makes a mistake; perhaps because the animal has a large belly, she or he also "sees" that it is pregnant.[31] For some reason the percipient has failed to bring her or his correct general belief to bear on the case at hand.

Moral weakness is the same sort of failure; there too the agent subscribes to the correct general principle but fails to recognize its implications for the case at hand. Sometimes the akratic agent has no conscious awareness of the applicable principle at the moment of action and knows the principle only in a dispositional sense. Sometimes the agent is dimly aware of the principle and its implications for his or her current behavior but does not have a firm grip on this information. This person, Aristotle says, is like a drunk reciting the verses of Empedocles; the drunk says the right words but does not understand what he is saying.[32] In either case, the morally weak agent acts contrary to his or her moral beliefs, and this is explained by appeal to perceptual error.

> . . . for it is not in the presence of what is thought to be knowledge proper that the affection ⟨*akrasia*, moral weakness⟩ arises (nor is it this that is dragged about as a result of passion) but in that of perceptual knowledge.[33]

Aristotle may believe that women are in a condition similar to that of the akratic agent. That women are more lascivious than men is claimed in the *Ethics* and the *Politics*. This Aristotle thinks is clear from empirical evidence. The Spartan women who have many more legal and political rights and greater freedom than Athenian women are to Aristotle's mind much less disciplined and given to wanton behavior. This is not only bad for them but also for the state.

> The licence of the Lacedaemonian women defeats the intention of the Spartan constitution, and is adverse to the happiness of the state. For a husband and a wife being each a part of every family, the state may be considered as about equally divided into men and women; and, therefore, in those states in which the condition of the women is bad, half the city may be regarded as having no laws.[34]

If by 'deliberative faculty' in *Politics* I.13 Aristotle does not mean rationality *simpliciter* but the capacity for practical rationality, then he can cite the lascivious nature of women as evidence of their weaker hold on practical rationality. In short, in a woman, reason does not control passion.[35] Women possess a weak *bouleutikon* (deliberative faculty) in precisely the same way that the morally weak agent does. Further evidence that the present interpretation is on the right track is provided by Aristotle's discussion of the relation between softness of character and moral weakness in *Nicomachean Ethics* VII.7. There Aristotle describes *akrasia* (moral weakness) as a kind of softness and then associates being soft with being like a woman.[36]

The recognition that Aristotle thinks that women are constitutionally akratic explains why he thinks women should be ruled by their husbands (or fathers before marriage) and why this difference between men and women is not reflected in a difference in essence or form. What a morally weak person needs to enable him or her to be virtuous is some way to make the morally correct, general principle that *ex hypothesi* is accepted by the agent sufficiently vivid in the context of action so that he or she will recognize its implications for his or her behavior. This would be achieved were a practically wise individual present to remind the akratic person of the principle and its implications. Understanding marriage as a relation between a person who is capable of deliberation and one who is much less adept at it, Aristotle might be led to conclude that the way to avoid failures of moral judgment for the latter is to put the former in charge.

III

Is this feminine proneness to making mistakes of practical judgment due to culture or to nature? Women might, with the right education and life experiences, be able to develop a deliberative faculty that holds its own against the forces of passion.[37] In this respect Athenian women might resemble non-Greeks who, even if well behaved, lack the virtues proper to Athenian citizens. There is no evidence that Aristotle thinks that people living in more primitive societies fail to be human.[38] They too possess all the essential properties of human beings but their cultural stage limits the range of activities in which their humanity can be exhibited.[39] If the cultural development of women has been arrested, then there may be some justification for attributing different roles to men and women in the family and the state. Moreover, were it the case that society functions best where the social and cultural institutions are such that women remain at a less developed stage than males, then one might argue that a greater good is served by preserving these institutions. That is, Aristotle might agree with Plato that the acculturation of women in existing societies is not conducive to their realizing their full potential as moral agents and citizens and yet reject Plato's inference to the advisibility of changing these conditions.[40] As Aristotle puts it, the virtue of the part must have regard to the virtue of the whole, and he believes that the whole is best served by maintaining male dominance.[41]

An appeal to acculturation would also resolve the apparent conflict between attributing a weaker deliberative faculty to women and the teleological conception of nature, because this defect would be produced not by nature but by the education and socialization of women. Nor is there any difficulty in assigning socialization such an important role, for Aristotle holds that humans are born with a capacity for being virtuous or vicious; this capacity becomes a disposition for performing either virtuous actions or vicious ones as a result of training and practice.[42]

Unfortunately, there is no textual evidence for this suggestive line of interpretation and some against it. In the *Politics,* briefly alluding to Plato's proposal in the *Republic* that young women be given the same education and opportunities as young men, Aristotle dismisses this proposal on the grounds that the analogy with other species, which Plato appeals to in support of his position, is specious because only humans manage households.[43] This objection alone, even if granted, does not justify Aristotle in assigning women the subordinate role in household management. Perhaps, women and men should alternate domestic roles in the same way that the citizens and rulers alternate roles in Aristotle's constitutional state; Aristotle, however, rejects this arrangement out-of-hand.[44] This argumentative ploy would not be immediately available to Aristotle if he granted Plato's intuition that many, if not all, the differences in the observed behavior of actual men and women were the outcome of education and experience. Were the relevant difference between the sexes culturally engendered, then the practices producing that difference would need to be defended on independent grounds before the difference could be used to justify the subordination of wives. An appeal to natural inferiority, however, would secure Aristotle's position. When Aristotle turns to the subject of education in the last two books of the *Politics,* he is exclusively concerned with the education of the citizen, and the good citizen is repeatedly identified with the good man.[45] Women are mentioned only in connection with eugenics.[46] This too suggests that the moral limitations of women originate in natural differences between the sexes and are not liable to improvement through education. In short, Aristotle never backs away from the claim he makes early in the *Politics:*

> Further the male is by nature superior and the female inferior; and the one rules and other is ruled.[47]

Thus explaining why women naturally possess weaker deliberative powers than men remains an urgent matter. At the end of the last section, I was stymied because any difference between individuals in the same species must be a difference at the level of the concrete individual and not a difference in the form or essence, and yet a difference in basic rationality seemed to require a difference in form. The analogy with moral weakness provides a way out of this dilemma. The ultimate explanation for moral weakness is, Aristotle claims, physiological.[48] Some state of the agent's body, e.g., sexual arousal, interferes with his or her recognizing that a moral principle he or she accepts prescribes a different action than the one he or she is about to perform. Since this failure occurs at the interface of the rational and perceptual faculties, appealing to a bodily condition to explain it is unproblematic on Aristotle's psychology. Similarly, the state of the material substrate in the uterus that causes the production of a female child might also issue in a bodily condition that interferes in some way with the application of accepted moral principles to particular cases. This condition might, for instance, simply be the susceptibility to sensuous desire such that desires frequently override judgments based on principle. Were this the case, it would explain why women who are not restrained by laws or husbands are lascivious. In short, Aristotle can tell a story that is consistent with his biology and metaphysics which makes having a weak deliberative faculty a natural characteristic of women and a story that is consistent with his observations of women and justifies the subordination of women to men under the law in a well-designed state.

Moreover, insofar as the state, according to Aristotle, benefits from assigning differential roles to males and females, and human beings by nature live in political groups, it may be possible to meet the objection based on teleology. It is better for people to live in states than in isolation.[49] States are built out of smaller, family units and these units function best, Aristotle believes, when hierarchially organized.[50] If the foundations of family and state are secured by a difference in character between men and women, then this difference, like sexual differentiation, is in the interest of the species as a whole and thus compatible with the providence of nature.

Nor does this difference make it impossible for women to possess virtue or excellence of character. Unlike the morally weak agent who, *ex hypothesi,* is not virtuous, a woman may be virtuous. While her virtue is not the virtue proper to a man, it is virtue nonetheless. Rejecting Socrates' view that virtue is the same in all people, Aristotle posits virtues that differ according to social role and ability.

> For those who say generally that virtue consists in a good disposition of the soul, or in doing rightly, or the like, only deceive themselves. Far better than such definitions is their mode of speaking, who like Gorgias, enumerate the virtues. All classes must be deemed to have their special attributes; as the poet says of women, 'Silence is a woman's glory', but this is not equally the glory of man.[51]

A courageous woman is not nearly as bold as a courageous man, and a temperate woman is more modest than a temperate man.[52] Aristotle does not believe he has to defend these claims because they, like much else he says about the virtues, reflect the popular understanding of what constitutes courage and temperance for each sex.

Not only are women capable of virtue, but a woman and a man are also capable of a friendship based on the virtue of each, although typical friendships between men and women are based on utility or pleasure rather than virtue—the last is the best type of friendship.[53] This concession on Aristotle's part suggests that feminine virtue, although distinct from masculine virtue, must have much in common with it. All of which indicates that a weak deliberative faculty is not one that is unable to reach the right conclusions about what should be done but one that is unable to insure that these decisions will issue in action. Backed up by various social constraints, the weak deliberative faculty is adequate for virtuous living.

Further support for this finding is provided by the simplified psychological model that Aristotle appeals to in the *Ethics* and the *Politics*.[54] This model divides the human soul into a rational and an irrational part and then divides the rational part again into a faculty that obeys reason and another which exercises reason.[55] In the *Politics*, Aristotle likens the obedient part of reason to the subject and the executive part to the ruler;[56] he also claims that the natural slave is capable only of obeying reason and is wholly incapable of exercising reason.[57] Since a (free) woman's capacity for virtue falls somewhere between a free man's and a natural slave's, she would presumably also share in the highest type of reason but to a lesser degree than a man. Her ability to exercise practical reason would be limited by her inability to realize her moral judgments in concrete actions. Her faculty for practical reasoning is weak, *akuron*. Aristotle's choice of the term, *akuron* (without authority), to describe this condition is instructive. This word is used to describe laws that have been annulled. Left to her own devices, a woman's practical judgments all too often will be overriden by other psychological forces.[58] However, a constitution and mores that take this feature of feminine psychology into account enable her to act in accordance with practical reason and hence to be genuinely virtuous.

IV

At first it looked as if Aristotle's descriptive and prescriptive statements about women in the *Politics* not only conflicted with modern moral intuitions but also were inconsistent with other parts of his philosophy. On closer examination, it turned out that Aristotle's claims about women can be construed in a way that makes them compatible with his conception of human essence and its replication in the next generation, with his account of rationality, and with his teleological picture of nature. The uncomfortable fact remains, however, that from a modern perspective, Aristotle's views on women and natural slaves are morally repugnant. What went wrong in his thinking about these matters? The problem lies in his empiricism. With the exception of mathematics Aristotle believes all areas of science, theoretical as well as practical, should be based on observation and experience, and as an investigator he acts accordingly. Having given a general characterization of the subject to be examined, Aristotle typically canvasses the best thought of his philosophical predecessors; the critical evaluation of these received doctrines (*endoxa*) generates a framework in which Aristotle formulates the questions he will pose and ultimately answer as he develops his position on subjects as diverse as physics, biology, psychology, and politics. This pattern is familiar and displayed in all the extant treatises. In the ethical and political writings, however, since the focus is on understanding in the interests of acting, not on understanding as an end in itself, Aristotle makes the mature person with years of practical experience the expert whose moral intuitions will be appealed to throughout.[59] Even the definition of moral virtue is framed in terms of a normative moral agent: virtue is the disposition to choose the mean in accordance with the right rule, that is, the rule the practically wise individual would employ.[60] Aristotle is committed to articulating ethical principles that have practical import and thus he would not make reference to the practically wise individual in this context were that person an abstract construct, an unrealized ideal; the existence of people actually possessing practical wisdom is a presupposition of the definition.[61]

Aristotle assumes that there are people in his society whose moral intuitions are trustworthy and hence that to appeal to the intuitions of well educated and experienced Athenians is morally sound. This means that the value system of the upper classes in fourth century Athens provides the context in which Aristotle examines ethical positions and develops his own ethical and political analysis. This greatly limits the extent to which his ethics can provide an adequate basis for social criticism.[62] Were a widely held moral belief to prove inconsistent with the rest of popular morality, Aristotle could point the inconsistency out and argue against the aberrant belief. What Aristotle cannot do is reject a coherent set of moral beliefs that are accepted by the best people in his society.

As a result, from today's vantage point, Aristotle appears to have been an apologist for a particular social and gender class. Yet a single, and to this day widely accepted, methodological assumption, namely, that the norms of the society he lives in are for the most part morally sound, is the only theoretical mistake he makes. Therein may lie an important moral.

Notes

1. *Politics* 1260a8–14. Unless otherwise noted, Benjamin Jowett's translation of the *Politica* will be used.

2. *Met.* 1058b29–33.

3. Scholars often take this to be Aristotle's position. See, for example, J. Lear, *Aristotle: The Desire to Understand*, pp. 198–99.

4. *Gen. An.* 775a9–17 suggests that femaleness is as it were a deformity (*hosper anaperian*). Cf. *Gen. An.* 732a6–10. That is why wherever possible and so far as possible the male is separate from the female, since it is something better and more divine in that it is the principle of movement for generated things, while the female serves as their matter. Cf. *Physics* 192a16–25.

5. See, however, *Gen. An.* 728a18–22: a woman is as it were (ὥσπερ, *hosper*) an infertile male and is female on account of an inability . . . ; see also the definition of male and female at 765b9–19.

6. The details of this process are found in the epistemological writings; see especially *Pst. An.* II.19 and *Met.* I.1–2. See also Deborah K. W. Modrak, *Aristotle: The Power of Perception* (Chicago, 1987), chapter 7.

7. Cf. *De An.* 429b10–14.

8. *De An.* 429a18–27. As evidence for this claim, Aristotle notes that each sense which is an embodied power is for that very reason limited to a certain type of object; eyes perceive colors but not flavors whereas tongues perceive flavors but not colors.

9. Cf. *Hist. An.* 497a31: female differs from male internally only with respect to the uterus. In the *Gen. An.* Aristotle makes the functional role in reproduction the basis for defining 'female' and 'male' as that which lacks or has, respectively, the power to concoct semen (716a18–23, 765b9–19).

10. *Hist. An.* 497a31, *Gen. An.* 716a27–34, 766a4–5.

11. For the moment, I shall postpone discussion of this complex issue. It will be treated in greater detail below.

12. This capsule claim appears throughout the corpus. Aristotle works out the details in the *Generation of Animals*. For a synoptic account, see *Gen. An.* IV.1–3.

13. Cf. J. Cooper, 'Metaphysics in Aristotle's Embryology,' *Proceedings of the Cambridge Philological Society,* no. 214, 1988: 14–41.

14. *Gen. An.* 767b21–24.

15. Ibid., 766a17–30.

16. Ibid., 767a36–769a7.

17. *Met.* 1058a29–b3; *Gen. An.* 723a27–b3.

18. Cf. *Gen. An.* 737a8–13.

19. *Gen. An.* 736b26–29.

20. See Modrak, 'Aristotle on How We Think,' *Proceedings of Boston Area Colloquium in Ancient Philosophy,* vol. 2, 1987.

21. The possibility remains open that there exists a cognitive deficit due to differences between the perceptual powers of male and female since unlike reason these powers are housed in bodily organs and hence Aristotle could appeal to the material substrate of the embryo for an explanation. This possibility will be explored in the next section.

22. *Met.* 1058a29–b2, b22–25.

23. *Bouleutikos* is the masculine form of the adjective meaning capable of deliberation. The neuter form with a definite article (*to bouleutikon*) does the work of a noun and means the faculty for deliberation; the latter is the form of *bouleutikos* used in the *Politics* passage.

24. *N.E.* 1152a19.

25. *N.E.* 1142b27, b33, *Pol.* 1316b31.

26. Cf. *N.E.* 1106a26–1107aa26. See *N.E.* III.6–9 for the detailed analysis of courage.

27. Cf. *N.E.* 1109b14–27.

28. *N.E.* 1142a23–31.

29. *N.E.* 1152a16–19.

30. See *N.E.* VII.1–4 for Aristotle's account of *akrasia*.

31. Cf. *Pr. An.* 67b6–12.

32. *N.E.* 1147a10–24, b8–13.

33. *N.E.* 1147b15–17.

34. *Pol.* 1269b13–18; cf. 1260b18, 1314b27, 1361a12–13.

35. Cf. *Hist. An.* 608a32, b10–12.

36. *N.E.* 1150a32–b16.

37. Cf. *Pol.* 1335a24–25: women who marry early are more apt to be wanton (*akolastoterai*).

38. Aristotle uses '*barbaros*' (barbarian) as a term for non-Greek cultures that are at a more primitive stage of development than that of the Greek city state, but he also recognizes that Greek civilization developed out of more primitive states (see *Pol.* I.2; cf. 1268b37–1269a10).

39. Cf. *Pol.* 1253a30–38.

40. See *Republic* V.

41. *Pol.* 1260b14; 1337a27–30.

42. *N.E.* 1103a18–b25.

43. Aristotle presents his objections to the more controversial proposals of the *Republic* at length in *Politics* II.1–5.

44. *Pol.* 1259a39–b10. Aristotle repeatedly claims that the rule of husband over wife is aristocratic (*N.E.* 1160b33, 1161a21–22, *E.E.* 1241b30); in the unusual circumstance that a woman rules over a household, her role is oligarchical because it rests on inherited wealth or power and not on her own excellence (*N.E.* 1160a3–4).

45. Aristotle's favored term for 'man' in these discussions is not the gender-neutral *anthropos* (human) but the gender specific *anar* (man).

46. *Pol.* VII.16.

47. *Pol.* 1254b13–14, translation follows Jowett. Cf. 1259b10.

48. *N.E.* 1147b6–8.

49. *Pol.* 1252a26–32.

50. This conception of the state is presented and defended in *Politics* I.2–7.

51. *Pol.* 1260a25–31.

52. 1277b20–23.

53. 1162a19–27.

54. In the *De Anima,* Aristotle rejects this model as simplistic and provides a much more complex and philosophically interesting account of the human mind. However, in the ethical writings, he is content to appeal to the simple model because it suffices for the task at hand.

55. See *N.E.* I.13 for a lengthy description of the rational and irrational parts of the soul.

56. *Pol.* 1254a33–b9.

57. *Pol.* 1254b20–22.

58. Cf. *N.E.* 1102b19–22: For exactly as paralyzed limbs when we intend to move them to the right turn on the contrary to the left, so is it with the soul; the impulses of morally weak people move in contrary directions.

59. *N.E.* 1094b27–1095a11.

60. *N.E.* 1106b36–1137a2; cf. 1144b21–24.

61. Aristotle rejects Plato's approach to ethics on the grounds that even if the Good-Itself, a transcendent ideal, exists, it would be of no help to actual agents engaged in concrete decision making (*N.E.* 1096b30–34).

62. Aristotle is not a cultural relativist. While he recognizes that different cultures have different mores, he draws a distinction between the good by nature and the good by law (*nomos*). Nevertheless he argues from Athenian moral intuitions to claims about the good by nature and hence implicitly assumes that what is deemed good by right-minded Athenians is good by nature as well as good by *nomos*.

Aristotle on the Woman's Soul

Christine M. Senack

The Approach

There is no doubt that Aristotle's theories on women are wrong. As his views are presented in what follows here, all one needs is general knowledge in areas such as biology, sociology and psychology to offer evidence against and successfully refute Aristotle's ideas about what sort of creatures women are. For example, it is not necessary to have studied gynecology to know that a woman's menstrual discharge is not an impure form of male semen as Aristotle contended. Criticizing Aristotle's views on women, once they have been made known, is an easy task. However, as with the analysis of any author's work (and especially the analysis of an author's work posthumously) it is not completely clear what are Aristotle's theories about women. It is particularly challenging because it involves piecing together sections of a number of his works. Thus the difficult task of the analysis of Aristotle's theories on women is the same task with which this paper is mainly concerned. That is, the development of a complete and coherent theory about women which can be in some manner attributed to Aristotle.

Because he is known to take an "anatomy is destiny" approach to living organisms, it is intuitively logical to begin with Aristotle's theories about the biology of women.[1] But even if this way of proceeding is correct, it might be problematic because Aristotle's "objective" scientific discoveries could be culturally biased. Recently feminist philosophers and philosophers of science have explored the influence exerted by culture and society on scientific study. They have revealed that the objectivity of science is often (if not always) limited by societal biases and that these biases are not acknowledged. The denial of these biases in science are likely not only to have an effect on the conclusions that the scientists defend but also the biases are likely to have an effect on how we interpret scientific results. In her article, "Science, Fact and Feminism,"

Ruth Hubbard explores the alleged objectivity in a number of the sciences, but her discussion of natural sciences is especially relevant to Aristotle's case:

> Natural scientists attain their objectivity by looking upon nature (including other people) in small chunks and as isolated objects. They usually deny, or at least do not acknowledge, their relationship to the "objects" they study ... When I report a discovery, I do not write, "One sunny Monday after a restful weekend, I came into the laboratory, set up my experiment and shortly noticed that ..." No; proper style dictates, "It has been observed that ... " This removes relevance of time and place, and implies that the observation did not originate in the head of a human observer ... [2]

Nowhere in Aristotle's biological treatises or in works thought to be his notebooks is there reference to his position as an observer. Because all science is biased in the way that Hubbard describes, it is fair to assume that somehow Aristotle's scientific discoveries, including those concerning women, are biased. However, it is impossible to determine the depth of bias or the type of bias that is present in Aristotle's theories. Given this, it is best to avoid beginning with Aristotle's biological theories about women.

Where should this discussion begin? The same kind of bias that Aristotle as a natural scientist suffered can be attributed to Aristotle as a sociologist or as a psychologist. Thus if the point of least bias is the correct place to begin, no aspect of his views is any better of a starting line than the other aspects. Aristotle himself tells us where to begin with the analysis of living organisms. In *De Anima* it becomes apparent that he believes that a sound position on living organisms begins with a discussion of the soul:

> The knowledge of the soul admittedly contributes greatly to the advance of truth in general, and, above all, to our understanding of Nature, for the soul is in some sense the principle of animal life.[3]

Thus a sound understanding of the human soul will give one insight to the other aspects of human life. Because women are, of course, human beings, it is sensible to begin the development of his theories on women with an account of his view of the woman's soul. If Aristotle is correct about understanding the soul, once his view of the soul is comprehendible, this should illuminate other areas of his views on women.

One particular area that will be examined here is his argument regarding women's social inferiority. After reviewing the argument and some special Aristotelian concerns, the discussion here will comment on the areas of Aristotelian views on women that are not illuminated by the discussion of the soul, but might become visible from a different perspective.

The Human Soul

For Aristotle, though the soul is not the same in each living creature, everything living has a soul because the soul is that which causes life.[4] Although he pictures the soul as a functioning whole, he notices the different functions of the soul and as a result he divides the soul into parts or faculties which correspond to these different functions. Throughout Aristotle's works the soul is divided on two levels. The first division creates a bipartite soul and the second is a division of one of the two parts of the first division.

The first division is presented in the *Nicomachean Ethics* during a discussion of the necessity of understanding the soul in other disciplines. Aristotle states " . . . one element in the soul is irrational and one has a rational principle."[5] This distinction is reiterated in a similar discussion of the soul in *De Anima*.[6] The rational part of the soul is perhaps the most sophisticated and is found only in humans. This part of the soul is divine and separated from the physical activity of the body, and because of this it is the immortal part of the soul.[7] It is this part of the soul which contains the "thinking power."

The irrational part of the soul is divided into further parts. I am interpreting these to be the locomotive, sentient, nutritive, and the appetitive.[8] The locomotive faculty of the soul is present only in some animals and it is that which causes movement in the animal. It is not discussed when the differences between men and women are addressed. I believe this was because it does not differ between them. The three faculties of the irrational soul which are relevant to the discussion of Aristotle's view of the woman's and man's soul are the sentient, nutritive, and the appetitive.

The sentient faculty is present in all animals. It becomes important in the discussion of the soul of men and woman because it is the faculty of the soul that the male contributes to the generation of a new human. In fact the contribution of the sentient soul by the male is the necessary condition to form a new human being.[9]

The nutritive faculty of the soul is yet another key when comparing and contrasting the souls of women and men. This faculty is contained in all living creatures, both plants and animals. Within the discussion of the woman's and man's soul, Aristotle speaks of it mainly in terms of the woman's soul. The female contributes this faculty of the soul to the embryo:

> Of the rational element one division seem to be widely distributed, and vegetative in its nature, I mean that which causes nutrition and growth; for it is this kind of power of the soul that one must assign to all nurslings and to embryos, and this same power to full grown creatures. . . . [10]

Although Aristotle does not directly speak of it with regard to men, I believe it must exist in men because men grow, need nutrition, and are living creatures, too. However, it is not present to the same extent in man as compared to woman for it is in the woman's fetation but not in the man's sperm.[11]

The final faculty of the irrational soul is the appetitive. This is present in all animals. It is perhaps the most important aspect of the irrational part of the soul with regard to the discussion of man and woman, yet it is also the most unusual aspect of the irrational part of the soul. I classify it as belonging under the irrational part of the soul here because I am following Aristotle's classification of it.[12] However, it is actually a combination of the irrational and the rational parts of the soul. Unlike the nutritive faculty of the irrational part of the soul, the appetitive faculty "shares" in the rational part of the soul. This faculty is classified as irrational because it does not do the deliberation or reasoning, but it is responsive to reason. It is the faculty of the irrational part of the soul which is normally persuaded by the rational part of the soul.

Woman's vs. Man's Soul

The distinction between the rational and the irrational parts of the soul serves as a premise in an Aristotelian argument designed to prove that the scientific differences between woman and man are significant enough to support different attitudes toward the two sexes. The argument links physical and natural differences between the sexes to social ones in an effort to prove that physical sex polarity is socially relevant.

The clearest formulation of this argument is in the *Politics* 1260a where the argument appears in the context of a discussion of household management. Aristotle says:

> Here the very constitution of the soul has shown us the way; in it one part naturally rules, and the other is subject, and the virtue of the ruler we maintain to be different from that of the subject;—the one being the virtue of the rational and the other of the irrational part. Now, it is obvious that the same principle applies generally, and therefore almost all things rule and are ruled according to nature. But the kind of rule differs;—the freeman rules over the slave after another manner from that in which the male rules over the female, or the man over the child; although the parts of the soul are present in all of them, they are present in different degrees. For the slave has no deliberative faculty at all; the woman has, but it is without authority, and the child has, but it is immature.[13]

In this passage it becomes clear that Aristotle believes that the social relationships are determined by natural constraints. Nature not only determines certain dispositions people have and which ones of these are better than others, but nature, through these dispositions, also determines the place of people with certain dispositions in society. It should be made clear here that Aristotle is not completely condemning women, children and slaves as subject to the domination of men because he concludes that all can be virtuous in their own ways and that "half of the free persons in a state are women."[14] What Aristotle's formal argument here accomplishes is proving that there are important sociological differences between man and woman.

The argument can be represented as follows:

Premise 1)	In every set of opposites there is one natural ruler.
Premise 2)	Man and woman are opposites.
Conclusion 1)	Therefore, in the relationship between man and woman, there must be a natural ruler.
Premise 3)	By nature man has a fully rational soul and woman has a rational soul without authority (*akuron*).
Premise 4)	The rational soul rules the irrational in the soul by nature.
Conclusion 2)	The fully rational male is naturally suited to rule over the female.[15]

The argument here has two parts. The first is a biological argument with a conclusion that states that of man and woman, one of them must be a "born ruler." The second argument adds a psychological basis for the conclusion about the social status of women. However, the argument is not without its problems. The investigation of concerns about premise two and premise three will present a clearer interpretation of the argument and perhaps a better understanding of Aristotle's views of women.

Opposition and Privation

There is little doubt that man and woman differ, but to call them opposites in Aristotle's terms means much more than what is currently meant when one uses the word. This renders the second premise ambiguous. For Aristotle, the concept of opposites is inherently intertwined with the concept of privation discussed in the *Metaphysics:*

> Privation has several senses; for it means (1) that which has not a certain quality and (2) that which might naturally have it but has not it, either (a) in general or (b) when it might naturally have it, and either (α) in some particular way, e.g., when it has not completely, or (β) when it has not it at all.[16]

For Aristotle privation is the inability of one opposite to become its other because of its lacking qualities. Aristotle uses the Greek word *steresis* for "privation." This word is the root word for "sterility" which implies emptiness, infertility and the like. In other words, when woman is termed as the privation of man, she is described in terms of what she is lacking to be a man, not in terms of what she has or lacks independently of man.[17]

This concept of opposition as privation is of particular importance in Aristotle's theory because woman lacks those characteristics which make man "better and more divine."[18] A good example of the view of woman as privation of man is seen in Aristotle's discussion of woman as a deformed male:

> Just as it sometimes happens that deformed offspring are produced by deformed parents, and sometimes not, so the offspring produced by the female are sometimes female, sometimes not, but male. The reason is that the female is as it were a deformed male;

and the menstrual discharge is semen, though in an impure condition; i.e., it lacks one constituent, and one only, the principle of [the sentient] soul.[19]

Although the passage above is focused on woman's deformity with regard to reproduction, woman is not simply deformed in this sense but also throughout life. The assertion that woman is deformed throughout life assists Aristotle in his proof that biological and psychological differences justify social biases:

> [I]n women, for still within the mother, the female takes longer to develop than the male does; though once birth has taken place everything reaches its perfection sooner in females than in males—e.g., puberty, maturity, old age—because females are weaker and colder in their nature; and we should look upon the female state as being as it were a deformity, though on which occurs in the ordinary course of nature.[20]

Here, Aristotle discusses deformity of male fetuses as, birth defects. It is not clear that when he moved from the discussion of the deformity of male to female fetuses that he was using the word "deformity" in the same manner. Deformity in males is the result of their activeness in the womb, whereas deformity in females is almost seen as normal. However, at least what one can interpret from this and Aristotle's other discussions on this topic is that the deformity of woman is seen in the sense that woman is privation of the man.

When Aristotle, then, uses 'opposites' in the argument in *Politics,* 1260a his use should be understood in light of what he said in *Metaphysics.* To him woman and man are more than mere opposites, specifically woman is privation of man, and that which she lacks is important and vital to being treated as an equal on the sociological level. Thus not only does the view of woman as privation of the male prove that they are opposites, but it also lends itself towards providing evidence to prove the superiority and inferiority of man and woman, respectively.

Woman's Rational Soul as Akuron

I think that the third premise of the argument in *Politics* 1260a which states that by nature man has a fully rational soul and woman has a rational soul "without authority" or *akuron* needs a more thorough explanation. The idea of a deliberative faculty as *akuron* can be interpreted in two different ways. The first is that the woman has the rational soul but instead of the rational soul ruling the irrational soul the rational soul is overruled by the irrational soul. A second interpretation is that woman has a rational soul but it is overruled in society. In other words, woman has the same powers of rationality as man, but it is a mere sociological power relationship between woman and man that makes her inferior.

One theorist who believes that Aristotle's view of the woman's soul is of a natural deterministic point of view is W. W. Fortenbaugh. Fortenbaugh claims that when Aristotle makes a reference to the deliberative faculty of the woman's soul, he is not drawing a conclusion from the role of women in society, but rather he is explaining why women have the role that they do. "[I]n the case of women a reference to their psychological make-up combined with their bodily condition explains their role in the household . . ."[21] Fortenbaugh believes that Aristotle argues that their bodily condition is weaker than that of the male, and he concludes that the deliberative faculty is *akuron* because it too is weak and is easily overruled by her emotions.

However, Fortenbaugh is quick to point out that just because a woman's deliberative faculty is *akuron,* Aristotle does not mean to say that women cannot think about things and give a well-reasoned answer. "His [Aristotle's] point is not that women deliberate only in some vague and illogical way, but that their deliberations and reflections are likely not to control their emotions."[22]

Fortenbaugh uses an example for Euripides' *Medea* to illustrate his point. Medea's anger (resulting from her husband leaving her for another woman), which tells her to kill their children, overrules her rational thought which concludes that murdering the children is an excessive action and is not in her own best interest. The result is that she acts from her emotions, but there has been some calculation within that scheme also for she knew that the killing of her children in the manner she was planning in fact would hurt Jason.

In the example above, Medea understands that she is going to act in a terrible manner, but this does not deter her from acting according to her emotions. Her reasoning is fine but it is either ignored or overpowered in light of her emotions. The conflict in Medea is intrapersonal. Fortenbaugh believes the rational soul's lack of authority functions in a similar manner in Aristotle theories; it can be contributed to an intrapersonal relationship within the soul of woman. Clearly women have reasoning powers, but the irrational and mainly appetitive part of the soul is that which rules.

The other manner in which "without authority" can be interpreted is shown by F. Sparshott. Rather than taking Aristotle to mean that the rational soul is *akuron* intrapersonally, he believes that Aristotle is referring to the soul as without authority in interpersonal or social relationships. Sparshott attempts to show that no Aristotelian texts support the view that women are ruled by their emotions, thus clearing the ground for his own argument. However, one passage in the *History of Animals* clearly shows that any attempt Sparshott does make to dismiss the idea that women are ruled by their emotions will be countered:

> [W]oman is more compassionate than man, more easily moved to tears, . . . more jealous, more querulous, more apt to scold and to strike. The female is also more despondent and despairing than the male, more shameless and more given to falsehood, more easily deceived and of more retentive memory. She is also more wakeful and more shrinking. And in general the female is less quick to take action and needs less food.[23]

Sparshott does address this passage in his paper, but the interpretation of it there seems somewhat confused. Sparshott believes that this passage supports his statement that Aristotle does not find females "to be flightier or more emotional than males."[24] In fact Sparshott states that the rendition of Aristotle as saying that woman is more emotional than man is an illusion of style. "In not one case is the contradictory or the contrary of a trait that is said to characterize women any less emotional, or any more intellectual or rational than its converse."[25] What is of interest here stylistically is not the passage of Aristotle, but the passage of Sparshott. Sparshott is quite correct in stating that Aristotle does not characterize **man as less emotional** than woman. However, this passage from Aristotle clearly states that **woman is more emotional** than man. And Sparshott also is quite right in stating that Aristotle is not putting forth the thesis that **man is more rational** than woman. What is at issue here is whether or not **woman is less rational** than man. Sparshott has turned the problem around backwards, in a certain sense. Instead of proving that females are not flightier and less rational than males interpersonally, Sparshott has proven something that is not being questioned, that man is not less emotional and more rational than woman, if he has proven anything at all.

What else might be said against this interpretation of a woman's rational soul as *akuron?* Looking at the context of the *Politics* passage, it is obvious that what Aristotle has set forth is that between man and woman there is naturally a ruler, but what is a "natural ruler?" Aristotle defines the word "nature" in the following way in the part of the *Metaphysics* known as his philosophical lexicon:

> 'Nature' means (1) the genesis of growing things. . . . (2) That immanent part of a growing thing, from which its first growth proceeds. (3) The source from which the primary movement in each natural object is present in it in virtue of its own essence. . . . (4) 'Nature' means the primary material of which any natural object consists or out of which it is made. . . . (5) 'Nature' means the *essence* of natural objects. . . . (6) By an extension of meaning from this sense of 'nature' [definition 5] every essence in general has come to be called a 'nature.'[26]

What is shown by his definitions of "nature" is that it connotes things of a scientific basis, physical characteristics about the essence of organisms. Thus "nature" for Aristotle begins with view of what the organism is in and of itself, not what a society is or even what an organism's function in society is. Therefore, the lack of authority within a woman's rational soul is a conflict within the woman and not within society.

The View From a Different Perspective

So far two things have been accomplished here. The first thing is that an Aristotelian argument for the social inferiority of women has been presented. The second is that a deeper understanding of aspects of that theory has been acquired through the exploration of some concepts particular to Aristotelians. It seems that the two accomplishments are related in a manner not discussed as of yet.

Not only do the discussions of woman as privation of man and the woman's rational soul as *akuron* strengthen the argument Aristotle provides for women's socially inferior status, but they show us that perhaps the theories Aristotle develops on women are not intentionally biased. This argument seems to be well founded given his scientific findings.

It is fair to speculate that Aristotle, as a scientist, attempted to be as objective as is humanly possible. A good deal of his biology for the animal and plant kingdoms is still in use today. There is probably little chance that he would have advanced science so rapidly if he had set out on a course to create data for that which he wanted to prove correct. Also he would not have been so close to what many currently believe are correct views and objectives of science.

However, current scientific practices do have the problem mentioned at the beginning of this paper. They lack the acknowledgment of an unriddable point of view, the fact that observations are the perceptions of an individual who is also a social creature. Not only does individual experience have an effect on the objectivity of science, but also societal experiences limit the scientist's objective point of perception.

Just as scientists today are not immune from societal forces, neither was Aristotle. In the *Generation of Animals,* there is one gross mistake that Aristotle makes that exhibits the influence that outside forces had on his "objective" scientific research. During a discussion explaining the life of bees, he dismisses a (what we now know as) correct conclusion about bees because it does not fit with the conceptions he has about nature:

> The generation of bees is a great puzzle. . . . [It is not] reasonable to hold that "bees" are female and drones male; because Nature does not assign defensive weapons to any female creature; yet while drones are without a sting, all "bees" have one. Nor is the converse view reasonable, that "bees" are male and drones female, because no male creatures make a habit of taking trouble over their young whereas in fact "bees" do. . . . [I]t is impossible that some of the "bees themselves" should be male and some female, since in all kinds of animals the male and female are different.[27]

The Bee Puzzle for Aristotle is this: what appears to be scientifically correct about bees contradicts his knowledge gained through research of animals as biological and social beings. Aristotle is perhaps unintentionally biasing his research on bees based on previous scientific discoveries. Abstracting this from the particular context, Aristotle's scientific theories are built upon each other. Perhaps this does not seem so wrong at first, but think of the implication of one mistake in this chain reaction approach to science. If it is made at the beginning and considered a scientific truth, ever subsequent research project which relies on it carries that flaw.

For Aristotle's Bee Puzzle, he starts with the truths of his past biological research. From the passage it is obvious that these were at the least: 1) Nature does not give the female creatures any defense weapons and 2) Male creatures do not care intensively for their offspring. So because Aristotle did not deny either one of these truths or state that they did not apply to the case of bees, his conclusion on the generation of bees reflects these biases which are falsehoods.[28]

What can be learned from the Bee Puzzle? Take Aristotle's approach which was abstracted above and apply it to the issue of this chapter. Aristotle uses what he already has proven to further his research or philosophical theories. In the case of women, once he has developed his physical or natural theories about woman based on scientific evidence, there are social and philosophical views of women which follow by necessity. However, because they do follow by necessity, they will perpetuate any flaws present from that which they are derived.

In the case of women's social inferiority, it is based on the "truths" of Aristotle's physical findings on women which showed women to be naturally inferior beings. Maybe these "truths" were merely incorrect data due to the unadvanced state of scientific discovery, or maybe the culture in which Aristotle lived influenced the manner in which he completed his scientific research on women. However, this is not evidence that Aristotle hated women. Neither one of these possible occurrences permits the interpretation of Aristotle as the "classic misogynist" as is found in some feminist interpretations of his works.

What Aristotle said in *De Anima* is true; knowledge of the woman's soul did assist in the understanding of his theories on women. For it is not only her "principle of life," her essence and her nature, but it is also that factor that determines the world in which she lives. However, the light shed on Aristotelian views of woman through the knowledge of the soul leaves darkened corners where perceptions are incomplete. A different perspective, one of investigating and understanding the culture in which Aristotle worked, might help to perceive despite that darkness. Our light source is limited; we cannot illuminate the corners of the picture. But the darkness does not mean that we must resort to ignorance. The way of seeing can be changed. Through this alteration more of the picture can be seen and understood.

Notes

1. The "anatomy is destiny" approach to living organisms is a deterministic theory which defends the belief that physical configuration including advantages and limitations decide the way an organism is going to live.

2. Ruth Hubbard, "Science, Fact and Feminism," *Hypatia*, spring 1988, pp. 5–18. Also see Thomas Kuhn's *The Structure of Scientific Revolutions*, Chicago University Press, 1970, for a fairly advanced view of this. And for a very brief and anecdotal presentation of the philosophical question at issue here, see Harold J. Morowitz's *Mayonnaise and the Origin of Life*, Charles Scribner's Sons, 1985; the essay "The Paradox of Paradoxes" addresses scientific objectivity specifically, and some of the other essays indirectly pose this question.

3. Aristotle, *De Anima* (402a 5–8).

4. *De Anima* (415b 9) & Aristotle, *Generation of Animals* (738b 26).

5. Aristotle, *Nicomachean Ethics* (1102a 29).

6. *De anima* (414a 29–418a 6).

7. Aristotle, *Generation of Animals* (736b 25–28). This statement is somewhat dubious. Aristotle mentioned the concept of immortality in his works, but he offered no well-developed proof of it.

8. I am uncertain about the divisions of the soul as I have listed them here. Aristotle creates a bipartite division in some works and in others he develops a variety of other divisions. What I have presented here is my attempt to create a coherent view of Aristotle's parts and faculties of the soul.

9. *Generation of Animals* (741b 7).

10. *Nicomachean Ethics* (1102a 33).

11. *Generation of Animals* (736a 25–736).

12. *Nicomachean Ethics* (1102b 30).

13. Aristotle, *Politics* (1260a 4–16).

14. *Politics* (1260b 19).

15. Premises 1,2 & 3 and conclusion 1 & 2 *Politics* (1260a); Premise 4 *Politics* (1102b 14–21); conclusion 2, see also *Politics* (1254b 9–20).

16. Aristotle, *Metaphysics* (1022b 23) & (1046a 32–36).

17. This point has been derived here from Prudence Allen, *The Concept of Woman: The Aristotelian Revolution* 750 BC–1250 AD, Eden Press, 1985. However, it is considered common knowledge among many feminist philosophers.

18. *Generation of Animals* (732a 5–10).

19. Ibid., (787a 26–30).

20. Ibid., (775a 12–16).

21. W. W. Fortenbaugh, "Aristotle on Slaves and Women," in *Articles on Aristotle*, vol. 2, p.138.

22. Fortenbaugh, p. 139.

23. *History of Animals* (608b 8–15).

24. F. Sparshott, "Aristotle on Women," *Philosophical Inquiry*, vol. vii, no. 3–4, 1985, p. 183.

25. Sparshott, p. 183–84

26. *Metaphysics*, (1014b 16–1015a 12)

27. *Generation of Animals* (759a 8–759b 17).

28. Among his conclusions are that there are King bees rather than Queen bees, that "bees" are hermaphroditic and generate other drones, that King bees generate other King bees and "bees," and that drones are not capable of any reproduction.

Suggestions for Further Reading

Books

Bluestone, Natalie Harris. *Women and the Ideal Society: Plato's "Republic and Modern Myths of Gender."* Amherst: University of Massachusetts, 1987.

Brown, Wendy. *Manhood and Politics: A Feminist Reading in Political Theory.* Totowa, NJ: Rowman and Littlefield, 1988.

Cameron, Averil and Kuhrt, Amélie (eds.). *Images of Women in Antiquity.* Detroit: Wayne State, 1983.

Cantarella, Eva. *Pandora's Daughters: The Role and Status of Women in Greek and Roman Antiquity.* Baltimore: Johns Hopkins University, 1987.

Clark, Lorenne M. G. and Lange, Lynda (eds.). *The Sexism of Social and Political Theory: Women and Reproduction from Plato to Nietzsche.* University of Toronto, 1979.

Coole, Diana H. *Women in Political Theory: From Ancient Mysoginy to Contemporary Feminism.* Brighton, England: Wheatsheaf Books, 1988.

Du Bois, Page. *Sowing the Body: Psychoanalyis and Ancient Representations of Women.* Chicago: University of Chicago, 1988.

Elshtain, Jean Bethke. *Public Man, Private Woman: Women in Social and Political Thought.* Princeton: Princeton University, 1981.

Elshtain, Jean Bethke (ed.). *The Family in Political Thought.* Amherst: University of Massachussetts, 1982.

Foley, Helen (ed.). *Reflections of Women in Antiquity.* London: Gordon and Breach, 1981.

Irigaray, Luce. *Speculum of the Other Woman* (French, 1974). Ithaca: Cornell University, 1985.

Keuls, Eva. *The Reign of the Phallus: Sexual Politics in Ancient Athens.* NY: Harper and Row, 1985.

Lefkowitz, Mary R. and Fant, Maureen B. *Women's Life in Greece and Rome. A Source Book in Translations.* Baltimore: Johns Hopkins University, 1982.

237

Lloyd, Genevive. *The Man of Reason: "Male" and "Female" in Western Philosophy.* Minneapolis: University of Minnesota, 1984.

Nye Andrea. *Words of Power: A Feminist Reading of the History of Logic.* NY: Routledge, 1990.

O'Faolain, Julia and Martines, Lauro (eds.). *Not in Gods Image: Women in History from the Greeks to the Victorians.* NY: Harper and Row, 1973.

Okin, Susan Moller. *Women in Western Political Thought.* Princeton University, 1979.

Peradotto, John and Sullivan, J. P. (eds.). *Women in the Ancient World: The Arthusa Papers.* Albany: State University of New York, 1984.

Pomeroy, Sara B. *Godesses, Wives, Whores and Slaves: Women in Classical Antiquity.* NY: Schocken, 1975.

Saxenhouse, Arlene W. *Women in the History of Political Thought: Ancient Greece to Machiavelli.* NY: Praeger, 1985.

Tuana, Nancy. *Woman and the History of Philosophy.* NY: Paragon House, 1992.

Zinserling, Verena. *Women in Greece and Rome.* NY: Abner Schram, 1972.

Essays

1. Plato

Allen, Christine Garside. "Plato on Women" *Feminist Studies* 2 (1975): 131–138.

Annas, Julia. "Plato's *Republic* and Feminism," *Philosophy* 51 (1976): 307–321.

Bluestone, Natalie Harris. "Why Women Cannot Rule: Sexism in Plato's Scholarship," *Philosophy of the Social Science* 18 (1988): 41–60.

Brown, Wendy. "Supposing Truth Were A Woman": Plato's Subversion of Masculine Discourse," *Political Theory* 16 (1988): 594–616.

Canto, Monique. "The Politics of Women's Bodies: Reflections on Plato" in Suleiman, Susan Rubin (ed.). *The Female Body in Western Culture, Contemporary Perspectives.* Harvard University, 1986, pp. 339–353.

Dikason, Anne. "Anatomy and Destiny: The Role of Biology in Plato's Views of Women," *The Philosophical Forum* 5 (1973–74): 45–53.

Freeman, Barbara. "(Re)Writing Patriarchal Texts: *The Symposium*" in Silverman, Hugh J. (ed.). *Postmodernism and Continental Philosophy.* Albany: State University of New York Press, 1988, pp. 165–177.

Irigaray, Luce. "Sorcerer Love: A Reading of Plato's *Symposium,* Diotima's Speech," *Hypatia* 3 (1989): 32–44.

Keller, Evelyn Fox. "Love and Sex in Plato's Epistemology" in *Reflections on Gender and Science.* Yale University, 1985, ch. 1, pp. 21–32.

Martin Jane Roland. "Sex Equality and Education in Plaro's Just State" in Vetterling-Braggin, Mary (ed.). *"Femininity", "Masculinity" and "Androgyny": A Modern Philosophical Discussion.* Totowa, NJ: Littlefield Adams, 1982, pp. 279–300.

Nye, Andrea. "The Hidden Host" Irigaray and Diotima at Plato's *Symposium," Hypatia* 3 (1989): 45–61.

Okin, Susan Moller. "Philosophers Queens and Private Wives: Plato on Women and the Family," *Philosophy and Public Affairs* 6 (1977): 345–369.

Pierce, Christine. "Equality: *Republic* V" *The Monist* 57 (1973): 1–11.

Pomeroy, Sarah B. "Feminism in Book V of Plato's *Republic," Apeiron* 8 (1974): 32–34.

Saxonhouse, Arlene W. "The Philosopher and the Female in the Political Thought of Plato," *Political Theory* 4 (1976): 195–212.

Saxonhause, Arlene. "Eros and the Female in Greek Political Thought: An Interpretation of Plato's *Symposium," Political Theory* 12 (1984): 5–27.

Spelman, Elizabeth V. "Woman as Body: Amcient and Contemporary Views," *Feminist Studies* 8 (1982): 109–131.

Spelman, Elizabeth V. "Plato on Women," *Newsletter on Feminism and Philosophy* (June 1989): 18–21.

2. Aristotle

Allen, Prudence. "Aristotelian and Cartesian Revolution in the Philosophy of Man and Woman," *Dialogue* 26 (1987): 263–270.

Clark, Stephen R. "Aristotle's Woman," *History of Political Thought* 3 (1982): 177–192.

Garside, Christin. "Can A Woman Be Good in the Same Way as A Man?" *Dialogue* 10 (1971): 534–544.

Green, Judith. "Aristotle on Necessary Verticality, Body-Heat, and Gendered Proper Places in the Polis: A Feminist Critique," *Hypatia* 7 (1992): 70–96.

Horowitz, Maryanne Cline. "Aristotle and Woman," *Journal of the History of Biology* 9 (1976): 183–213.

Kotzin, Rhoda H. "Aristotle's View on Women," *Newsletter on Feminism and Philosophy* (June 1989): 21–25.

Lange, Lynda. "Woman is Not a Rational Animal: On Aristotle's Biology of Reproduction" in Harding, Sandra and Hintikka, Merrill B. (eds.). *Discovering Reality: Feminist Perspectives on Epistemology, Metaphysics, Methodology, and Philosophy of Science*. Dordrecht, Holland: D. Reidel, 1983, pp. 1–16.

Mathews, Gareth. "Gender and Essence in Aristotle," *Australasian Journal of Philosophy*, supplement to volume 64 (1986): 16–25.

Smith, Nicholas D. "Plato and Aristotle on the Nature of Women," *Journal of the History of Philosophy* 21 (1983): 467–478.

Spelman, Elizabeth V. "Aristotle and the Politization of the Soul" in Harding, Sandra and Hintikka, Merrill B. (eds.). *Discovering Reality: Feminist Perspectives on Epistemology, Metaphysics, Methodology, and Philosophy of Science*. Dordrecht, Holland: D. Reidel, 1983, pp. 17–30.

Thom, Paul. "Stiff Cheese for Women," *The Philosophical Forum* 8 (1976): 94–107.

Contributors

Bat-Ami Bar On is associate professor of philosophy and Director of Women's Studies at the State University of New York at Binghamton. Her detour into canonical commentary is motivated by a need to configure a relation between feminist philosophy and philosophy. Her primary focus is socio-political and ethical issues and theory, especially as these arise in relation to everyday kinds of violence and abuse. She is working on a book about these issues.

Eve Browning Cole is associate professor of philosophy and women's studies at the University of Minnesota, Duluth. Her main research interests include ancient Greek philosophy and culture, and feminist ethics. She is presently at work on a book entitled *The Soul of the Beast in Greek Moral Philosophy.*

Cynthia Freeland is associate professor of philosophy at the University of Houston. She has published articles on Aristotle's ethics, metaphysics, and philosophy of science, as well as on feminist philosophy, including "Woman: Revealed or Reveiled?" (on Lacan) in *Hypatia;* and "Feminism & (Philosophy & Literature)", in *Philosophy and Literature.*

Judith Genova is a professor of philosophy and director of women studies at The Colorado College. Her most recent article, "Women and the Mismeasure of Thought" appeared in *Feminism and Science,* ed. Nancy Tuana (Indiana University Press, 1989) and deals with the mind/brain sciences constructions of women's thinking.

Cynthia Hampton specializes in Ancient Greek Philosophy at Ohio University where she is an associate professor. Dr. Hampton received her Ph.D. from Northwestern University in 1984. She is the author of articles and a book on Plato, *Pleasure, Knowledge, and Being: An Analysis of Plato's "Philebus",* SUNY Press, 1990.

Susan Hawthorne has degrees in Philosophy and Ancient Greek. She has taught Philosophy, Education, Literature and Women's Studies in a number of universities in Australia and most recently at San Diego State University. Her work has been published in journals, such as *Women's Studies International Forum* (UK), *NWSA Journal* (USA), *Beiträge* (Germany), *Journal of Australian Lesbian Feminist Studies* and *Meanjin* (Australia). She is the author of a feminist quiz book, *The Spinifex Book of Women's Answers,* a novel, *The Falling Woman* and a collection of poems

241

The Language in My Tongue. She has edited four collections of fiction and poetry and lives in Melbourne, Australia.

Deborah K. W. Modrak teaches philosophy at the University of Rochester and is the author of *Aristotle The Power of Perception* (1987) and articles on Aristotle's philosophy of mind, epistemology, metaphysics and ethics and Plato's epistemology.

Christine Pierce is associate professor of philosophy at North Carolina State University. She is coeditor of *People, Penguins, and Plastic Trees: Basic Issues in Environmental Ethics* (Wadsworth, 1986) and *AIDS: Ethics and Public Policy* (Wadsworth, 1988). Her articles on ethics and feminism have appeared in *The Monist, Philosophical Studies, Analysis,* and other journals and anthologies.

Christine Senack received a Bachelor of Arts degree in philosophy from Wells College. She currently is a graduate fellow in the philosophy department at Bowling Green State University in Ohio. Her interests are in resource allocation, state welfare, utilitarianism, medical ethics and feminism.

Elizabeth V. Spelman teaches in the philosophy department at Smith College. Her writings over the past ten years have focused on the mutual construction of gender, race and class and the implications of their interconnections for feminist theory and politics.

Nancy Tuana is an associate professor of the history of ideas at the University of Texas at Dallas. She has published *Woman and the History of Philosophy* (Paragon House, 1992) and *The Misbegotten Man: Scientific, Religious, and Philosophical Images of Woman's Nature* (Indiana University Press, 1993) and is editor of *Feminism and Science* (Indiana University Press, 1989) and *Re-Reading the Canon: Feminist Interpretations of Plato.*

Index

243